PUBLISHER
DAMIAN A. WASSEL
EDITOR-IN-CHIEF
ADRIAN F. WASSEL
ART DIRECTOR
NATHAN C. GOODEN
BRANDING & DESIGN
TIM DANIEL
MANAGING EDITOR
REBECCA TAYLOR
DIRECTOR OF MARKETING
DAVID DISSANAYAKE
PRODUCTION MANAGER
IAN BALDESSARI
PRINCIPAL
DAMIAN A. WASSEL SR.

WRITER
CAVAN SCOTT

ARTIST
CORIN HOWELL

COLORIST
TRIONA FARRELL

LETTERER
ANDWORLD

VAULT COMICS PRESENTS

SHADOW SERVICE

VOL. ONE
DARK ARTS

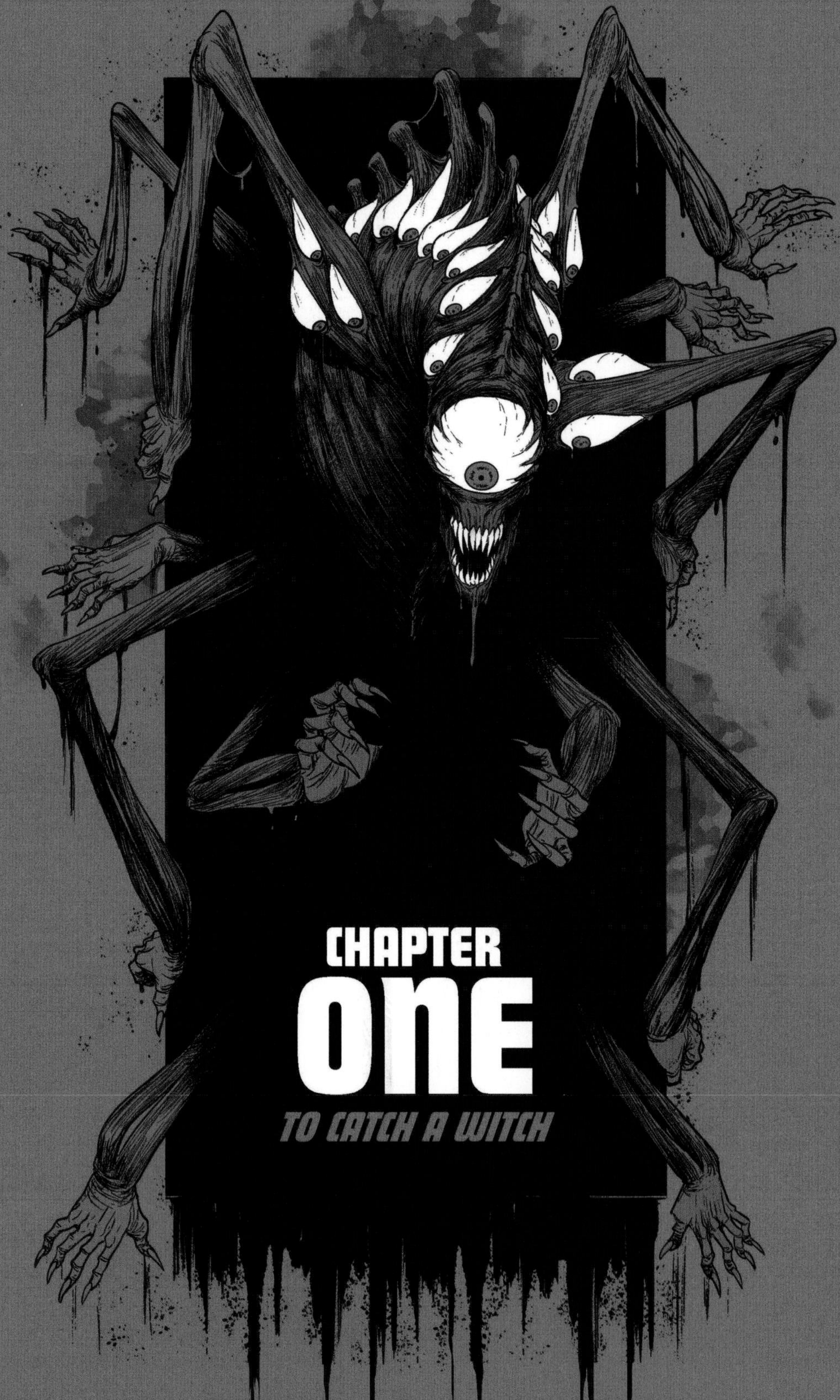
CHAPTER
ONE
TO CATCH A WITCH

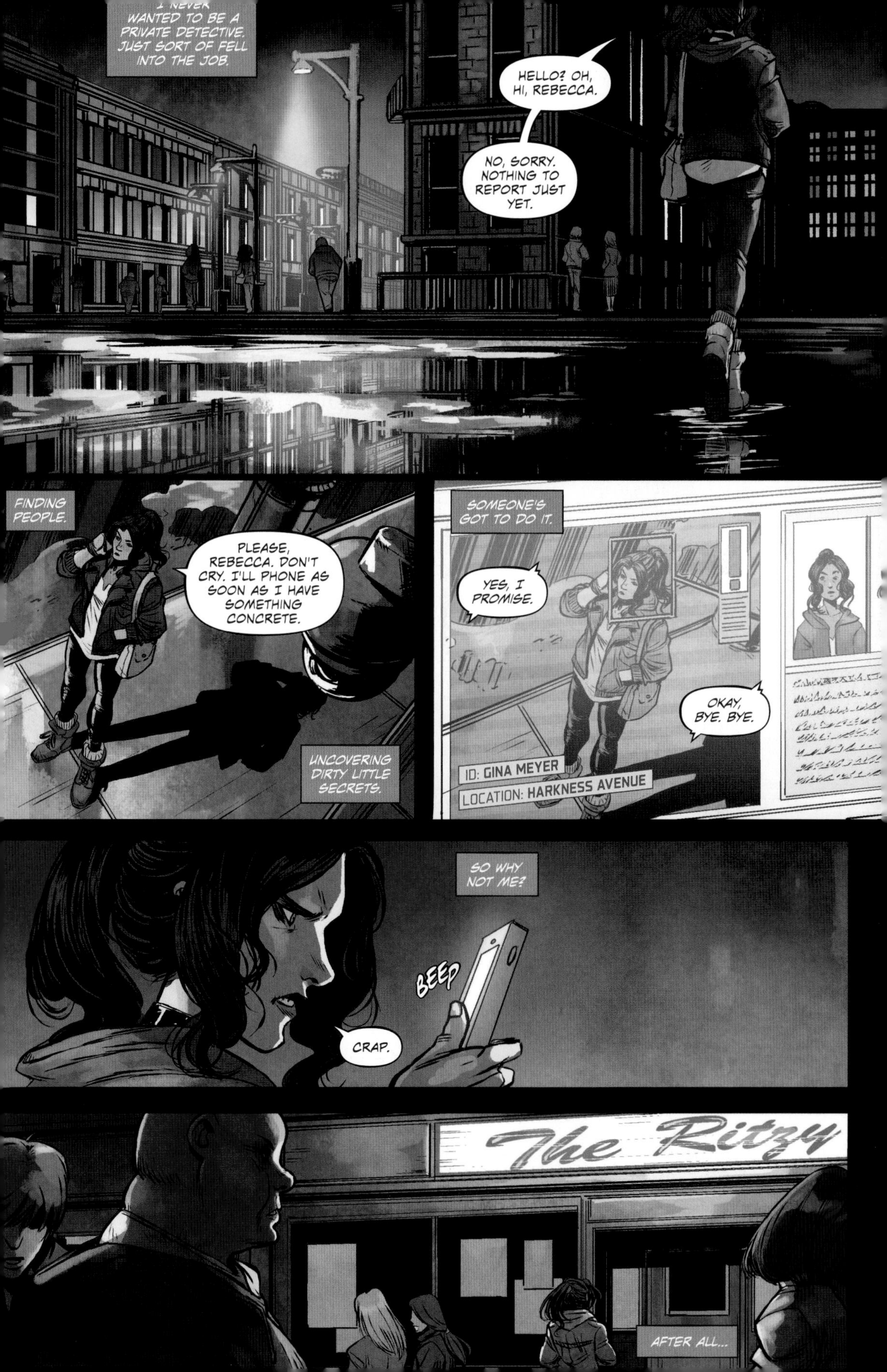
I NEVER WANTED TO BE A PRIVATE DETECTIVE. JUST SORT OF FELL INTO THE JOB.
HELLO? OH, HI, REBECCA.
NO, SORRY. NOTHING TO REPORT JUST YET.
FINDING PEOPLE.
PLEASE, REBECCA. DON'T CRY. I'LL PHONE AS SOON AS I HAVE SOMETHING CONCRETE.
UNCOVERING DIRTY LITTLE SECRETS.
SOMEONE'S GOT TO DO IT.
YES, I PROMISE.
OKAY, BYE. BYE.
ID: GINA MEYER
LOCATION: HARKNESS AVENUE
SO WHY NOT ME?
BEEP
CRAP.
The Ritzy
AFTER ALL...

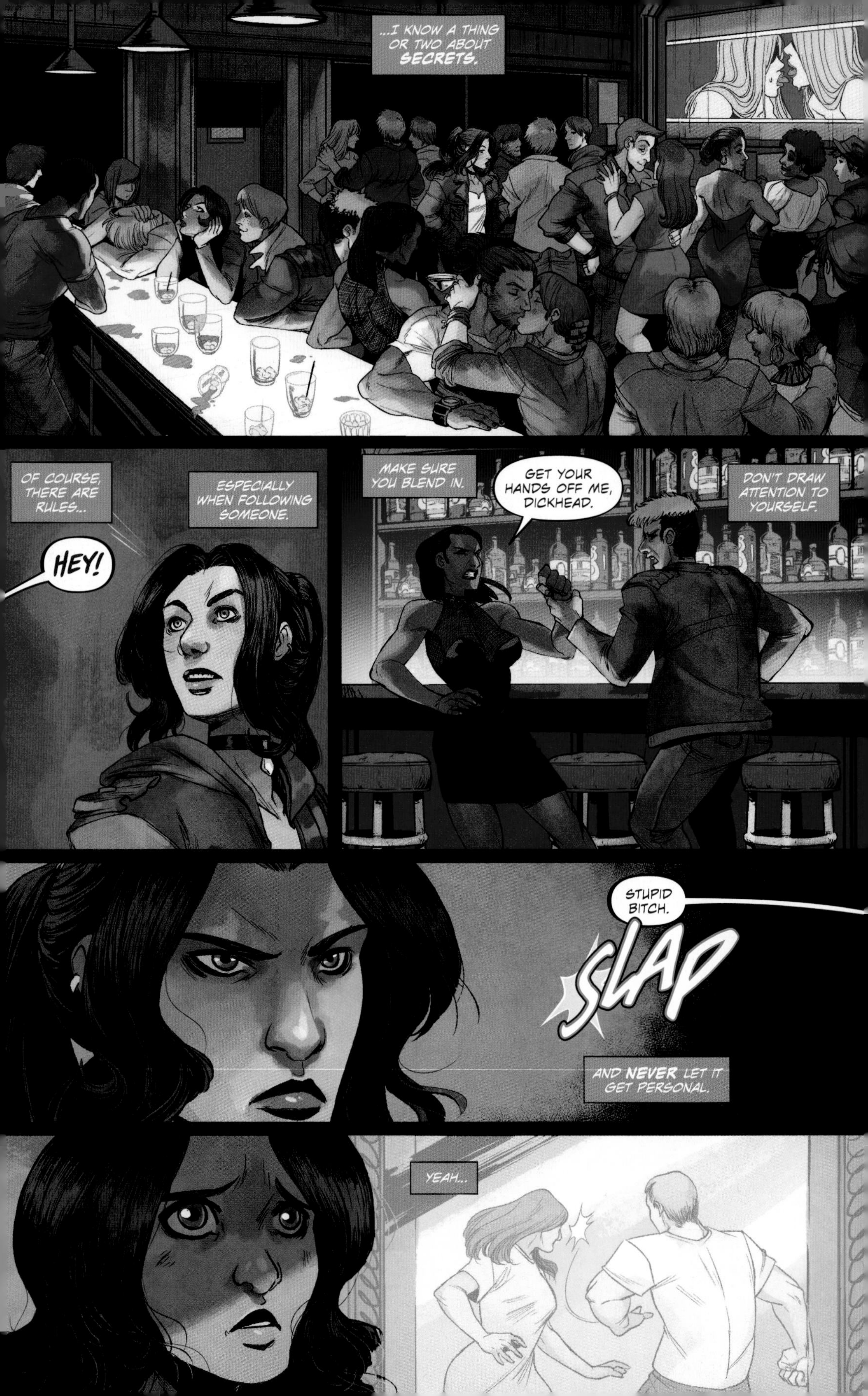
...I KNOW A THING OR TWO ABOUT SECRETS.
OF COURSE, THERE ARE RULES...
ESPECIALLY WHEN FOLLOWING SOMEONE.
HEY!
MAKE SURE YOU BLEND IN.
GET YOUR HANDS OFF ME, DICKHEAD.
DON'T DRAW ATTENTION TO YOURSELF.
STUPID BITCH.
SLAP
AND NEVER LET IT GET PERSONAL.
YEAH...

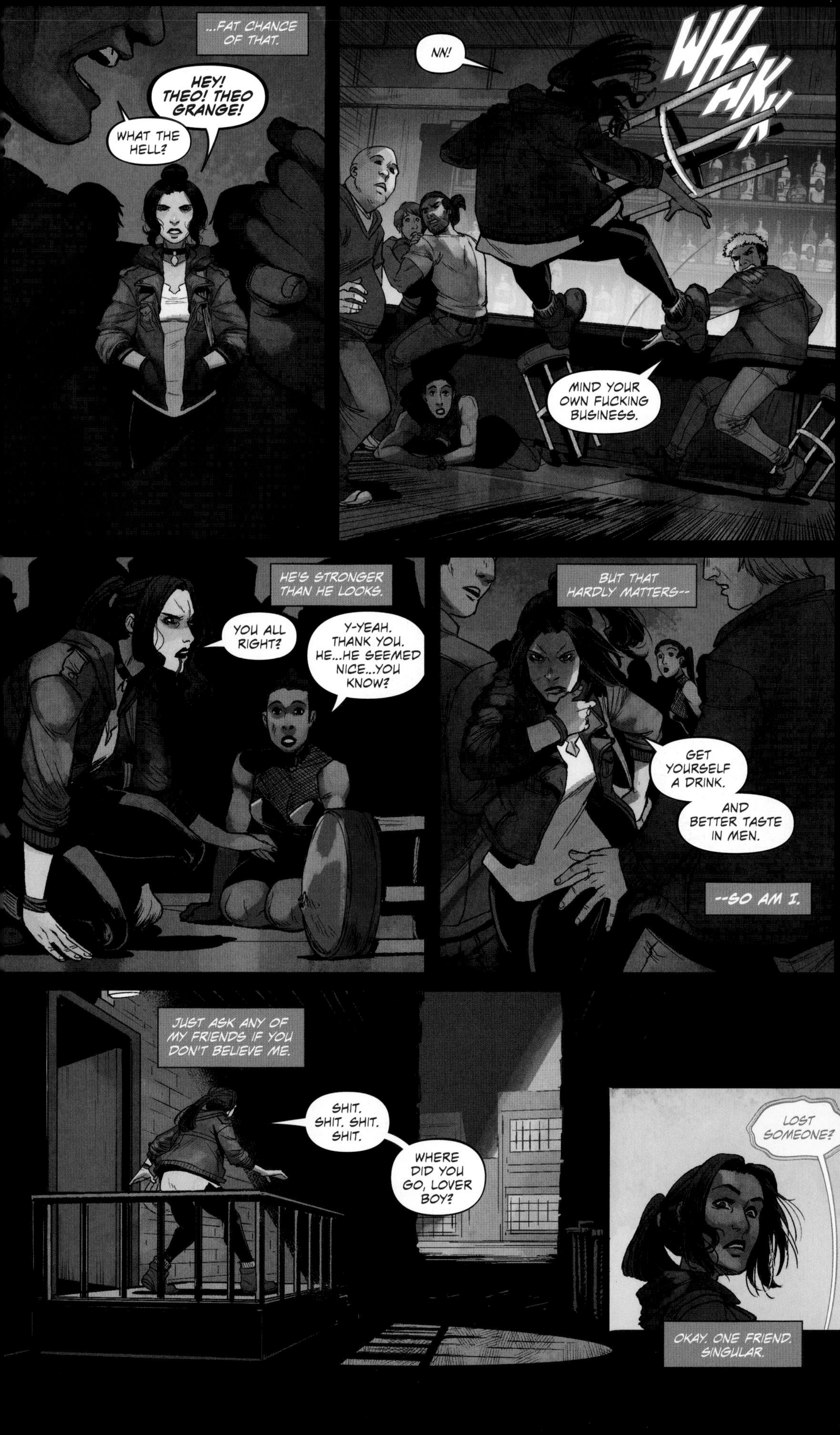

...FAT CHANCE OF THAT.
HEY! THEO! THEO GRANGE!
WHAT THE HELL?
NN!
WHHAKK!
MIND YOUR OWN FUCKING BUSINESS.
HE'S STRONGER THAN HE LOOKS.
YOU ALL RIGHT?
Y-YEAH. THANK YOU. HE...HE SEEMED NICE...YOU KNOW?
BUT THAT HARDLY MATTERS--
GET YOURSELF A DRINK.
AND BETTER TASTE IN MEN.
--SO AM I.
JUST ASK ANY OF MY FRIENDS IF YOU DON'T BELIEVE ME.
SHIT. SHIT. SHIT. SHIT.
WHERE DID YOU GO, LOVER BOY?
LOST SOMEONE?
OKAY. ONE FRIEND. SINGULAR.

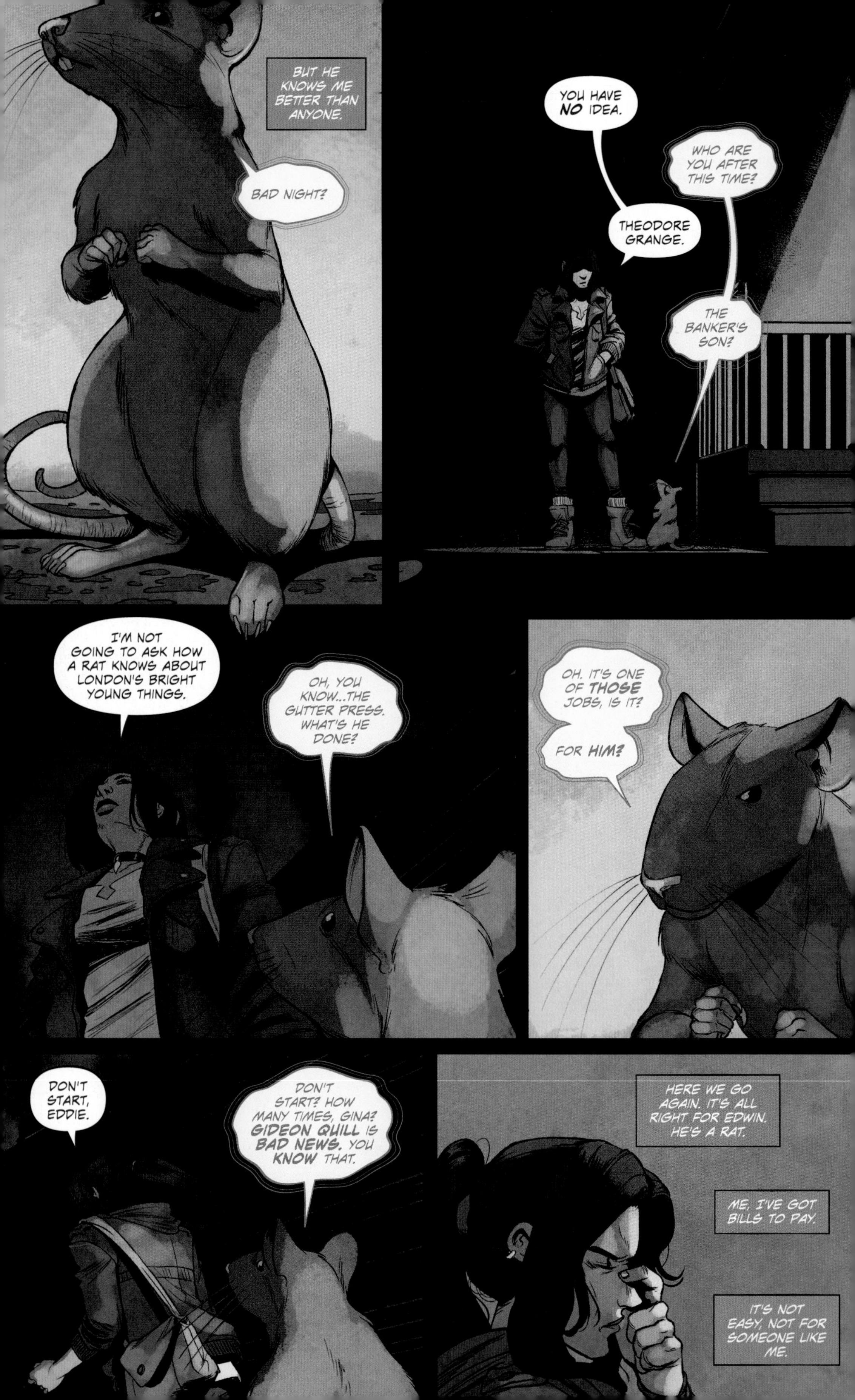
BUT HE KNOWS ME BETTER THAN ANYONE.
BAD NIGHT?
YOU HAVE NO IDEA.
WHO ARE YOU AFTER THIS TIME?
THEODORE GRANGE.
THE BANKER'S SON?
I'M NOT GOING TO ASK HOW A RAT KNOWS ABOUT LONDON'S BRIGHT YOUNG THINGS.
OH, YOU KNOW...THE GUTTER PRESS. WHAT'S HE DONE?
OH. IT'S ONE OF THOSE JOBS, IS IT?
FOR HIM?
DON'T START, EDDIE.
DON'T START? HOW MANY TIMES, GINA? GIDEON QUILL IS BAD NEWS. YOU KNOW THAT.
HERE WE GO AGAIN. IT'S ALL RIGHT FOR EDWIN. HE'S A RAT.
ME, I'VE GOT BILLS TO PAY.
IT'S NOT EASY, NOT FOR SOMEONE LIKE ME.

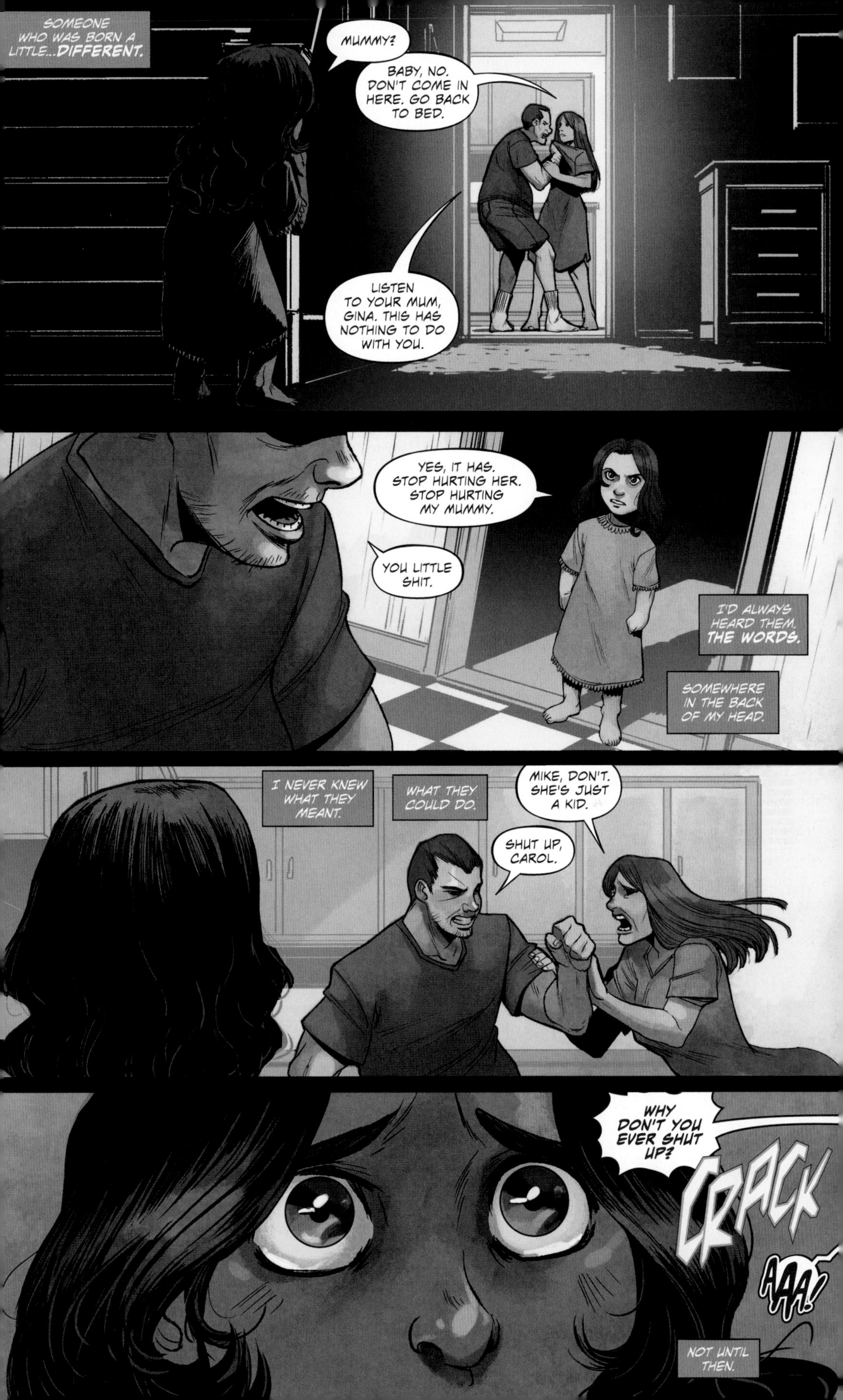
SOMEONE WHO WAS BORN A LITTLE...DIFFERENT.
MUMMY?
BABY, NO. DON'T COME IN HERE. GO BACK TO BED.
LISTEN TO YOUR MUM, GINA. THIS HAS NOTHING TO DO WITH YOU.
YES, IT HAS. STOP HURTING HER. STOP HURTING MY MUMMY.
YOU LITTLE SHIT.
I'D ALWAYS HEARD THEM, THE WORDS.
SOMEWHERE IN THE BACK OF MY HEAD.
I NEVER KNEW WHAT THEY MEANT.
WHAT THEY COULD DO.
MIKE, DON'T. SHE'S JUST A KID.
SHUT UP, CAROL.
WHY DON'T YOU EVER SHUT UP?
CRACK
AAA!
NOT UNTIL THEN.

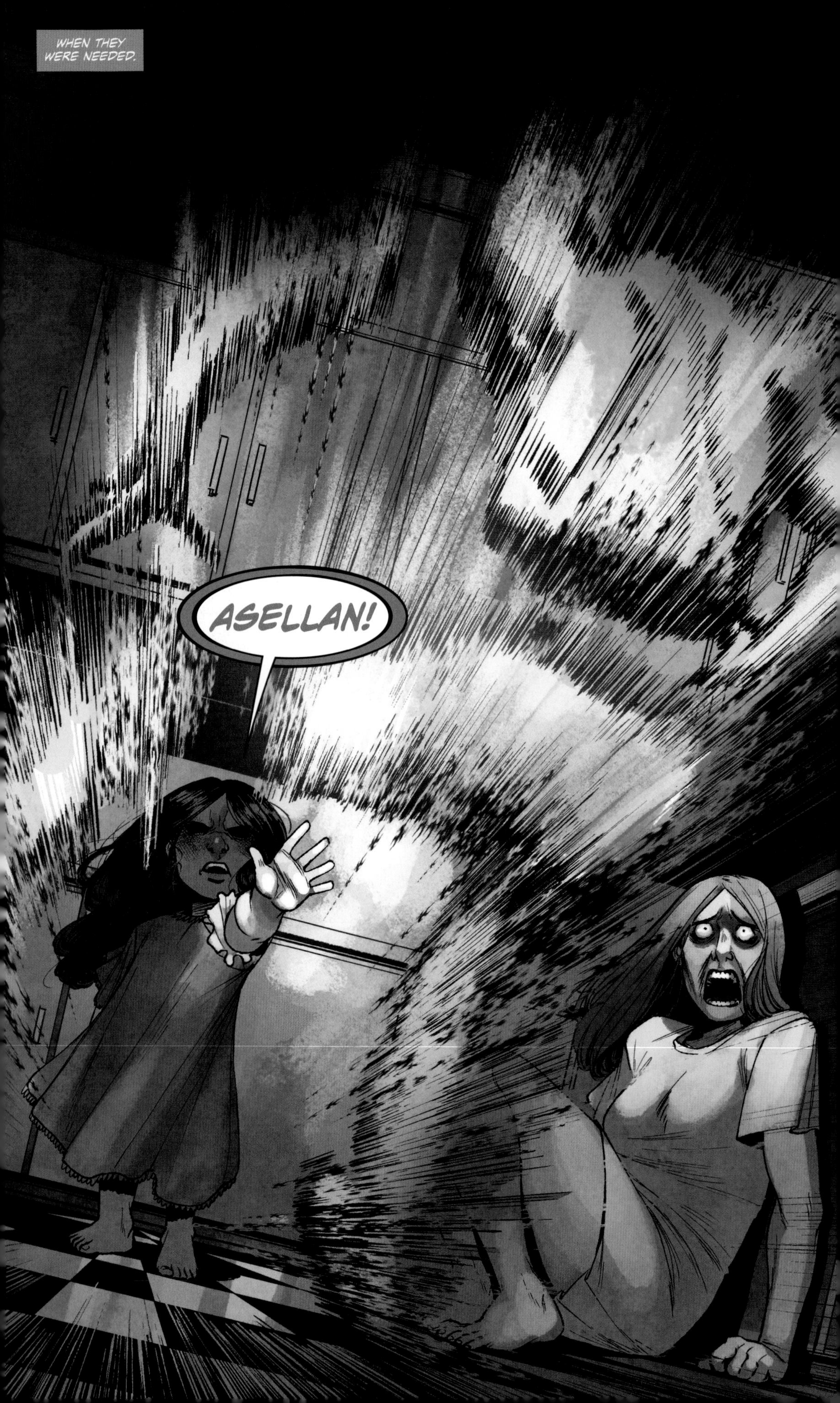
WHEN THEY WERE NEEDED.
ASELLAN!

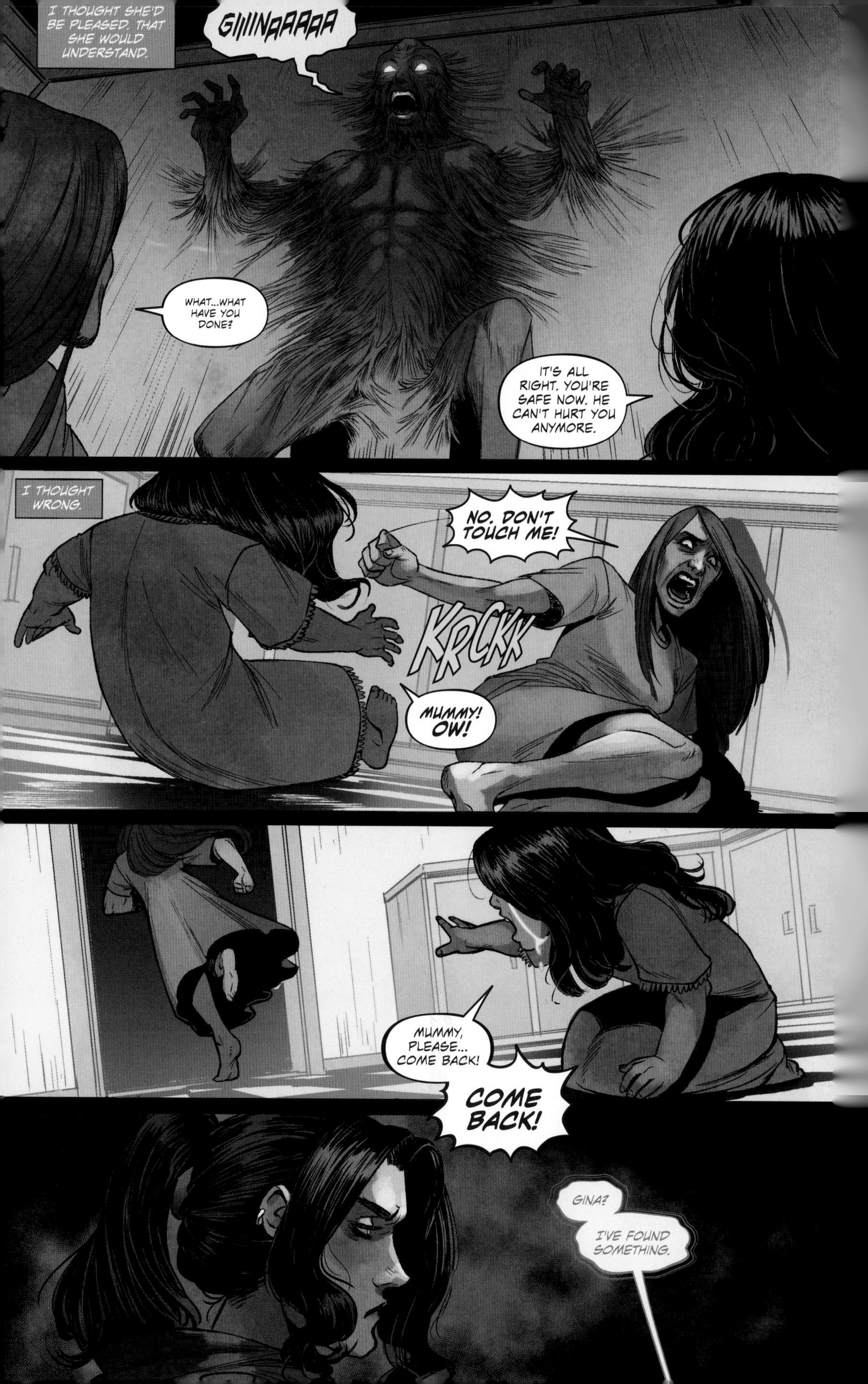
I THOUGHT SHE'D BE PLEASED. THAT SHE WOULD UNDERSTAND.
GIIIINAAAAA
WHAT...WHAT HAVE YOU DONE?
IT'S ALL RIGHT. YOU'RE SAFE NOW. HE CAN'T HURT YOU ANYMORE.
I THOUGHT WRONG.
NO. DON'T TOUCH ME!
KRCKK
MUMMY! OW!
MUMMY, PLEASE... COME BACK!
COME BACK!
GINA?
I'VE FOUND SOMETHING.

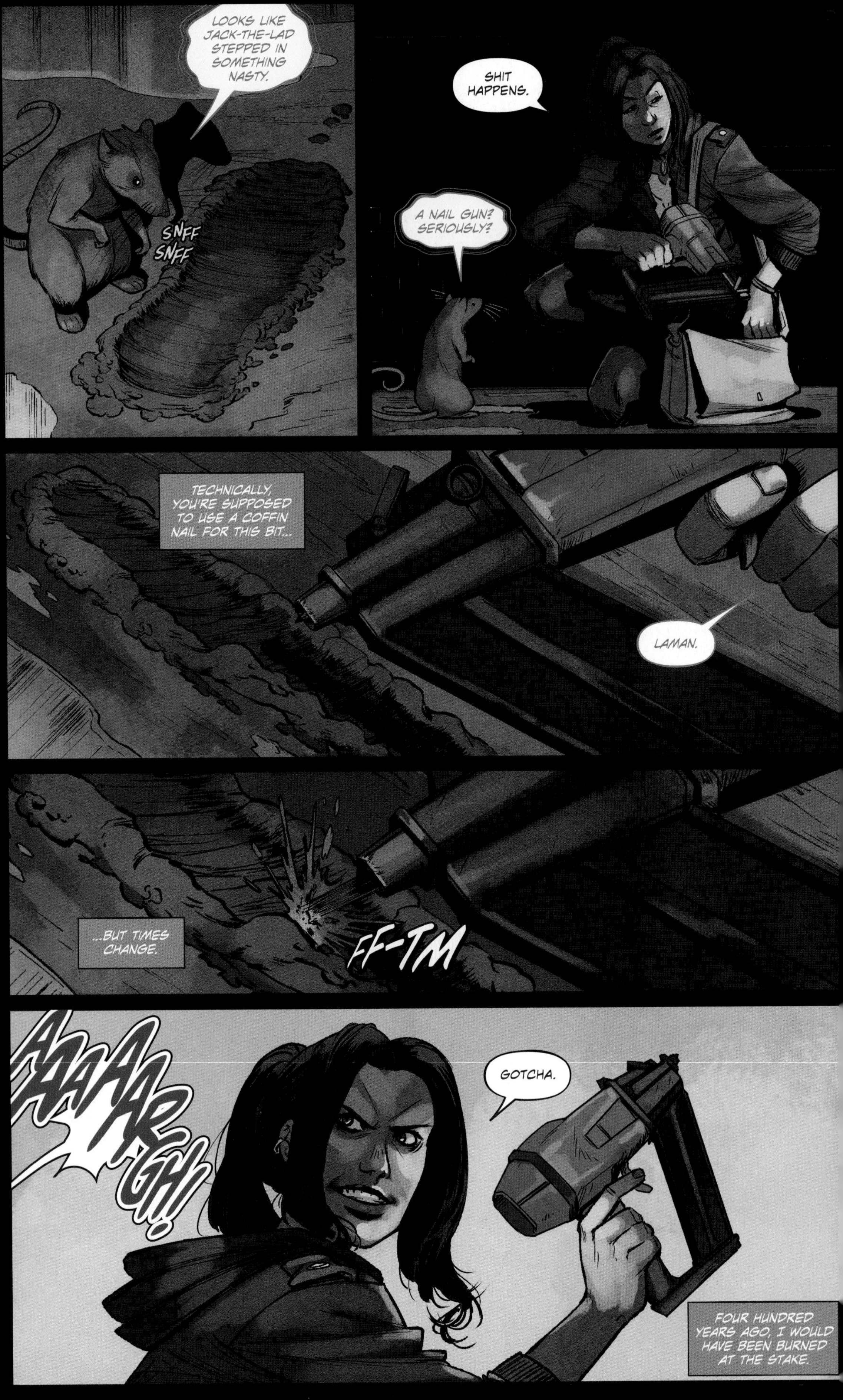
LOOKS LIKE JACK-THE-LAD STEPPED IN SOMETHING NASTY.
SNFF SNFF
SHIT HAPPENS.
A NAIL GUN? SERIOUSLY?
TECHNICALLY, YOU'RE SUPPOSED TO USE A COFFIN NAIL FOR THIS BIT...
LAMAN.
...BUT TIMES CHANGE.
FF-TM
AAAAARGH!
GOTCHA.
FOUR HUNDRED YEARS AGO, I WOULD HAVE BEEN BURNED AT THE STAKE.

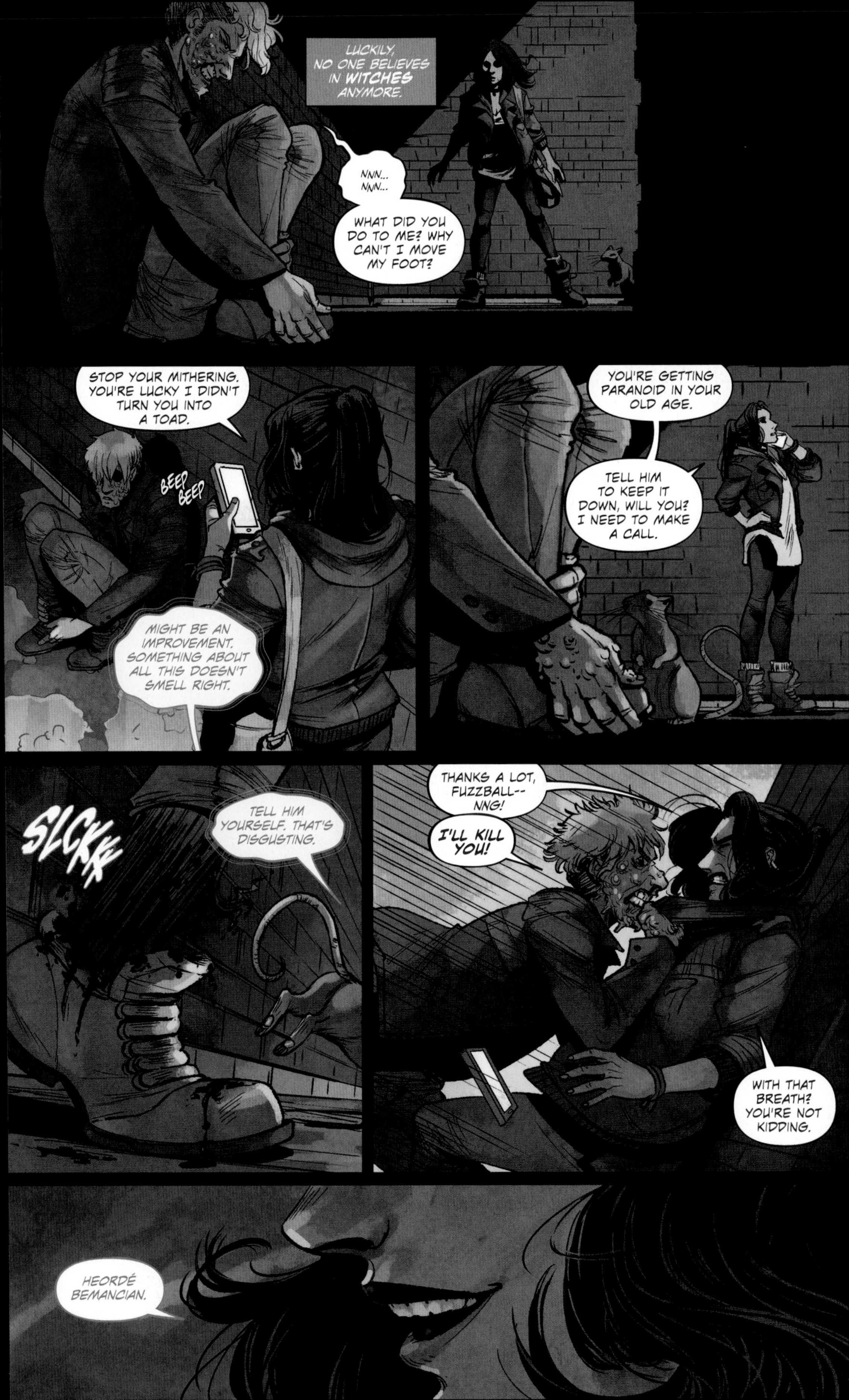
LUCKILY, NO ONE BELIEVES IN WITCHES ANYMORE.
NNN... NNN...
WHAT DID YOU DO TO ME? WHY CAN'T I MOVE MY FOOT?
STOP YOUR MITHERING. YOU'RE LUCKY I DIDN'T TURN YOU INTO A TOAD.
BEEP BEEP
MIGHT BE AN IMPROVEMENT. SOMETHING ABOUT ALL THIS DOESN'T SMELL RIGHT.
YOU'RE GETTING PARANOID IN YOUR OLD AGE.
TELL HIM TO KEEP IT DOWN, WILL YOU? I NEED TO MAKE A CALL.
SLCKK
TELL HIM YOURSELF. THAT'S DISGUSTING.
THANKS A LOT, FUZZBALL-- NNG!
I'LL KILL YOU!
WITH THAT BREATH? YOU'RE NOT KIDDING.
HEORDÉ BEMANCIAN.

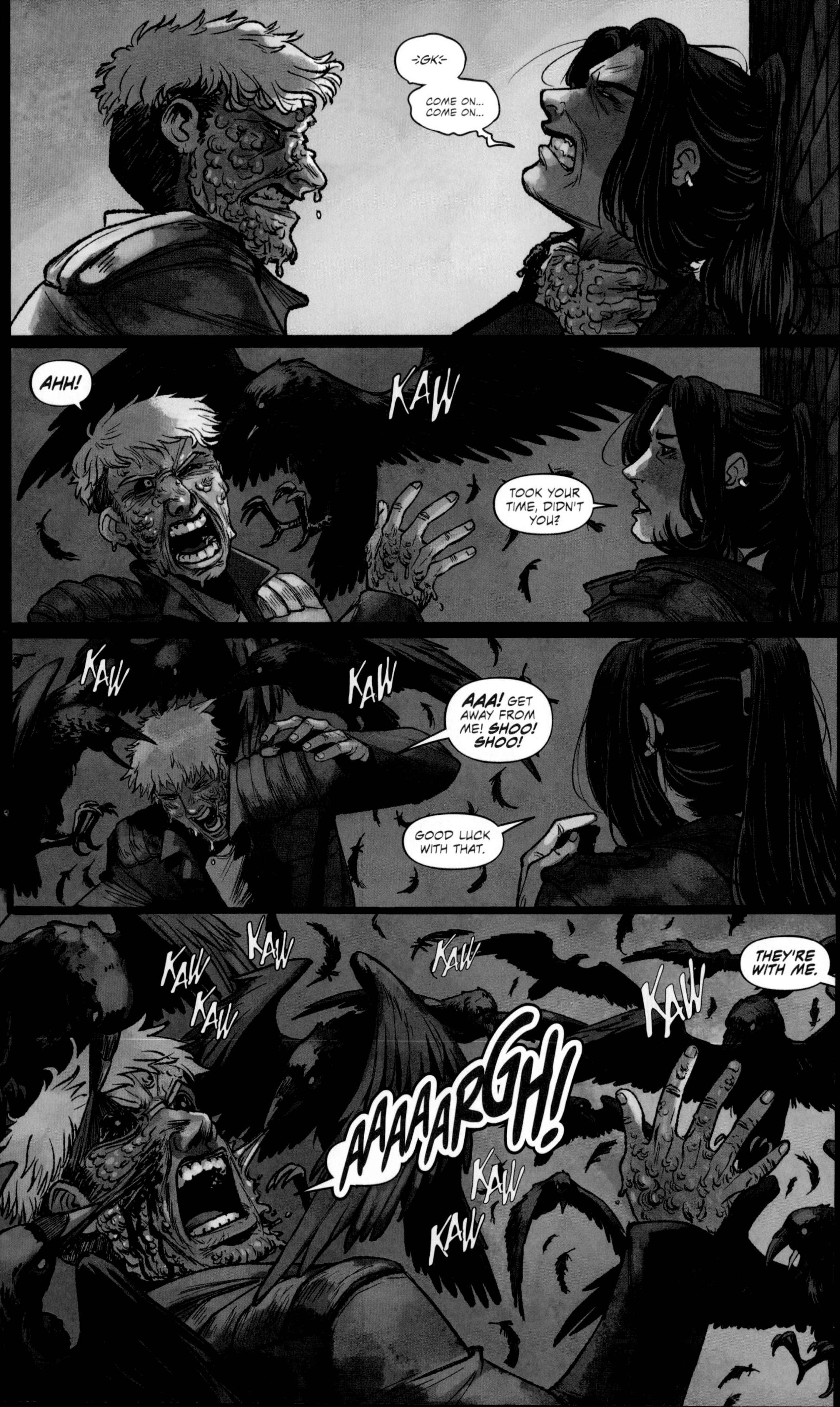
-GK-
COME ON... COME ON...
AHH!
KAW
TOOK YOUR TIME, DIDN'T YOU?
KAW
KAW
AAA! GET AWAY FROM ME! SHOO! SHOO!
GOOD LUCK WITH THAT.
KAW
KAW
KAW
KAW
THEY'RE WITH ME.
KAW
AAAAARGH!
KAW
KAW

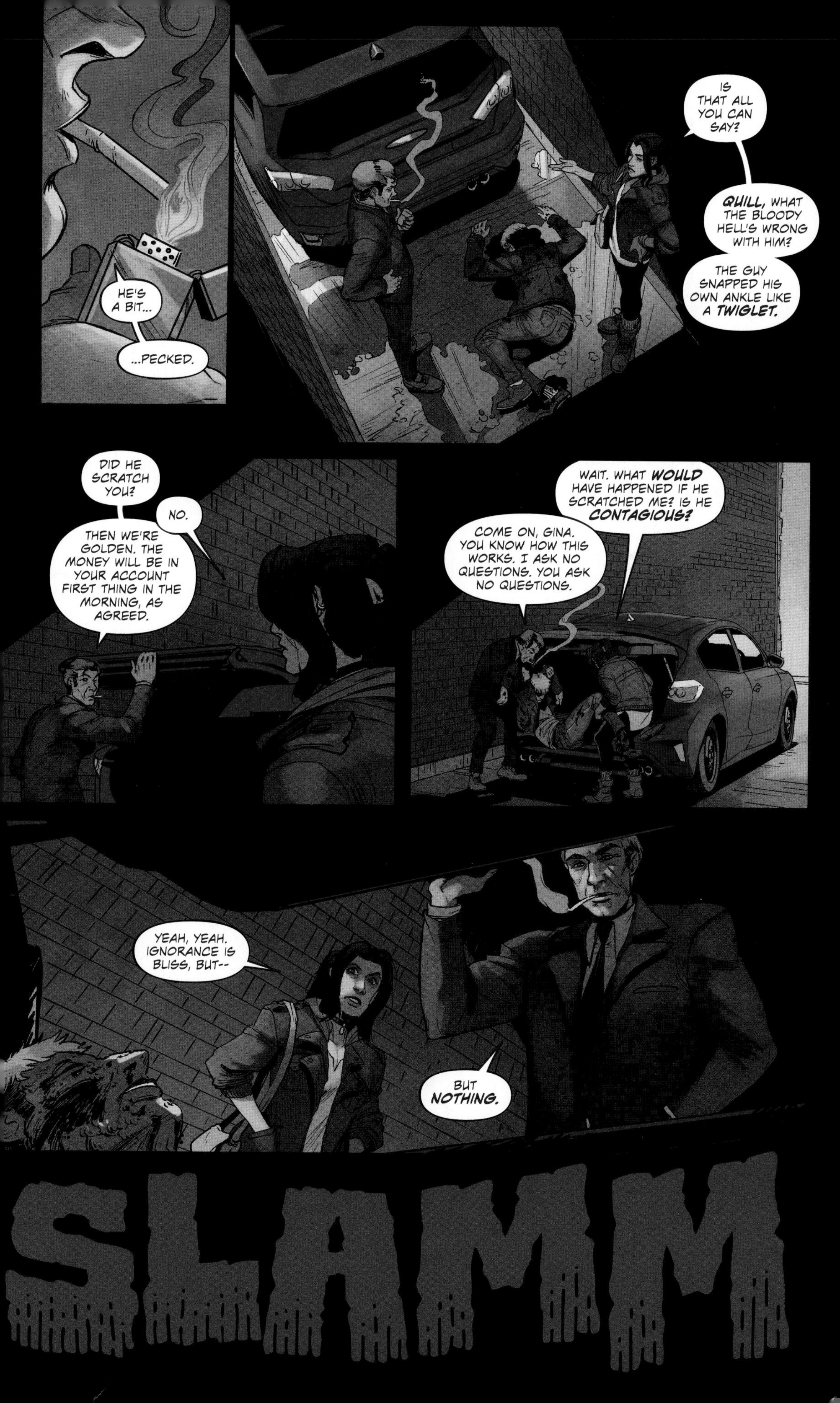
HE'S A BIT...
...PECKED.
IS THAT ALL YOU CAN SAY?
QUILL, WHAT THE BLOODY HELL'S WRONG WITH HIM?
THE GUY SNAPPED HIS OWN ANKLE LIKE A TWIGLET.
DID HE SCRATCH YOU?
NO.
THEN WE'RE GOLDEN. THE MONEY WILL BE IN YOUR ACCOUNT FIRST THING IN THE MORNING, AS AGREED.
WAIT. WHAT WOULD HAVE HAPPENED IF HE SCRATCHED ME? IS HE CONTAGIOUS?
COME ON, GINA. YOU KNOW HOW THIS WORKS. I ASK NO QUESTIONS. YOU ASK NO QUESTIONS.
YEAH, YEAH. IGNORANCE IS BLISS, BUT--
BUT NOTHING.
SLAMM

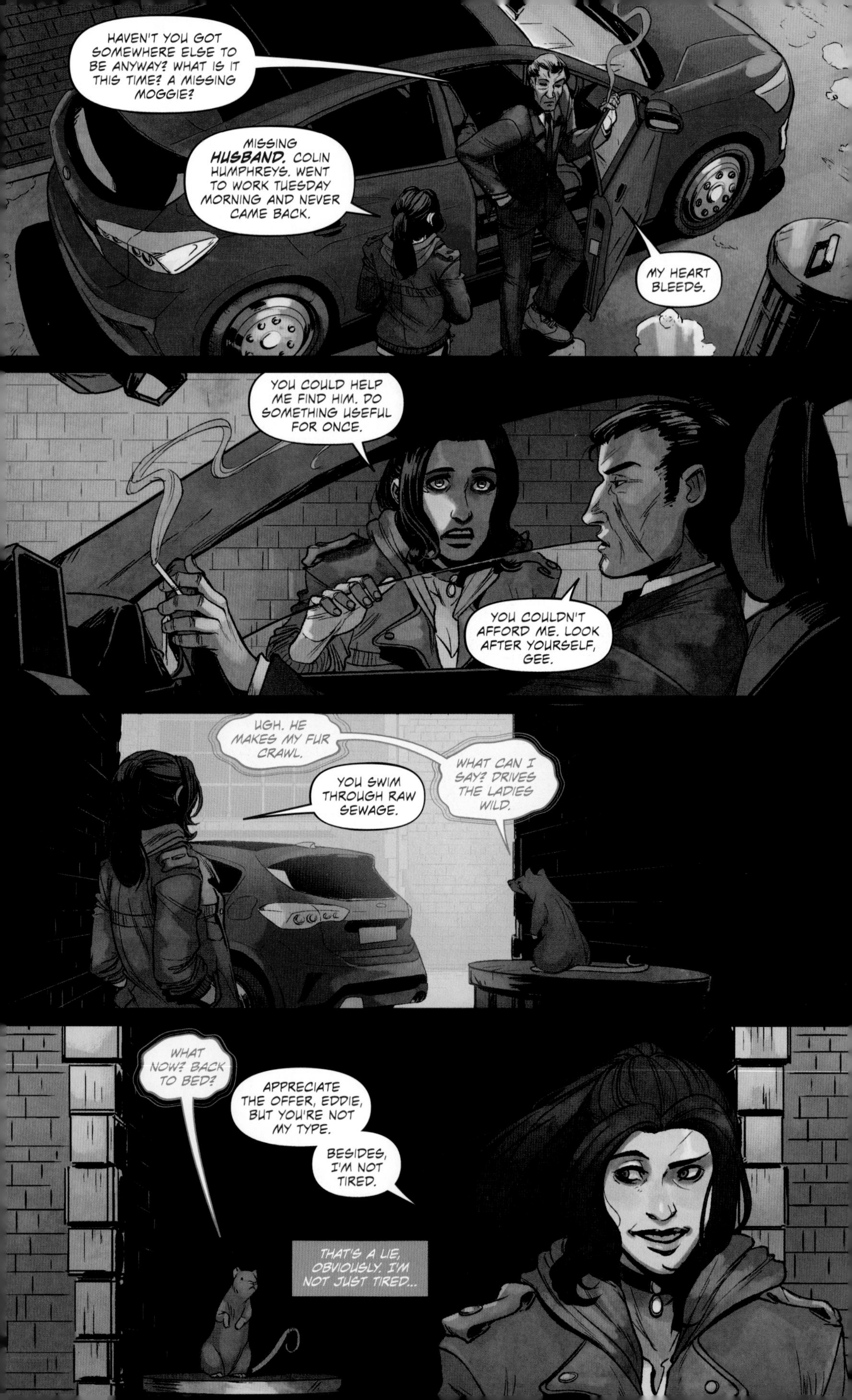
HAVEN'T YOU GOT SOMEWHERE ELSE TO BE ANYWAY? WHAT IS IT THIS TIME? A MISSING MOGGIE?
MISSING HUSBAND. COLIN HUMPHREYS. WENT TO WORK TUESDAY MORNING AND NEVER CAME BACK.
MY HEART BLEEDS.
YOU COULD HELP ME FIND HIM. DO SOMETHING USEFUL FOR ONCE.
YOU COULDN'T AFFORD ME. LOOK AFTER YOURSELF, GEE.
UGH. HE MAKES MY FUR CRAWL.
YOU SWIM THROUGH RAW SEWAGE.
WHAT CAN I SAY? DRIVES THE LADIES WILD.
WHAT NOW? BACK TO BED?
APPRECIATE THE OFFER, EDDIE, BUT YOU'RE NOT MY TYPE.
BESIDES, I'M NOT TIRED.
THAT'S A LIE, OBVIOUSLY. I'M NOT JUST TIRED...

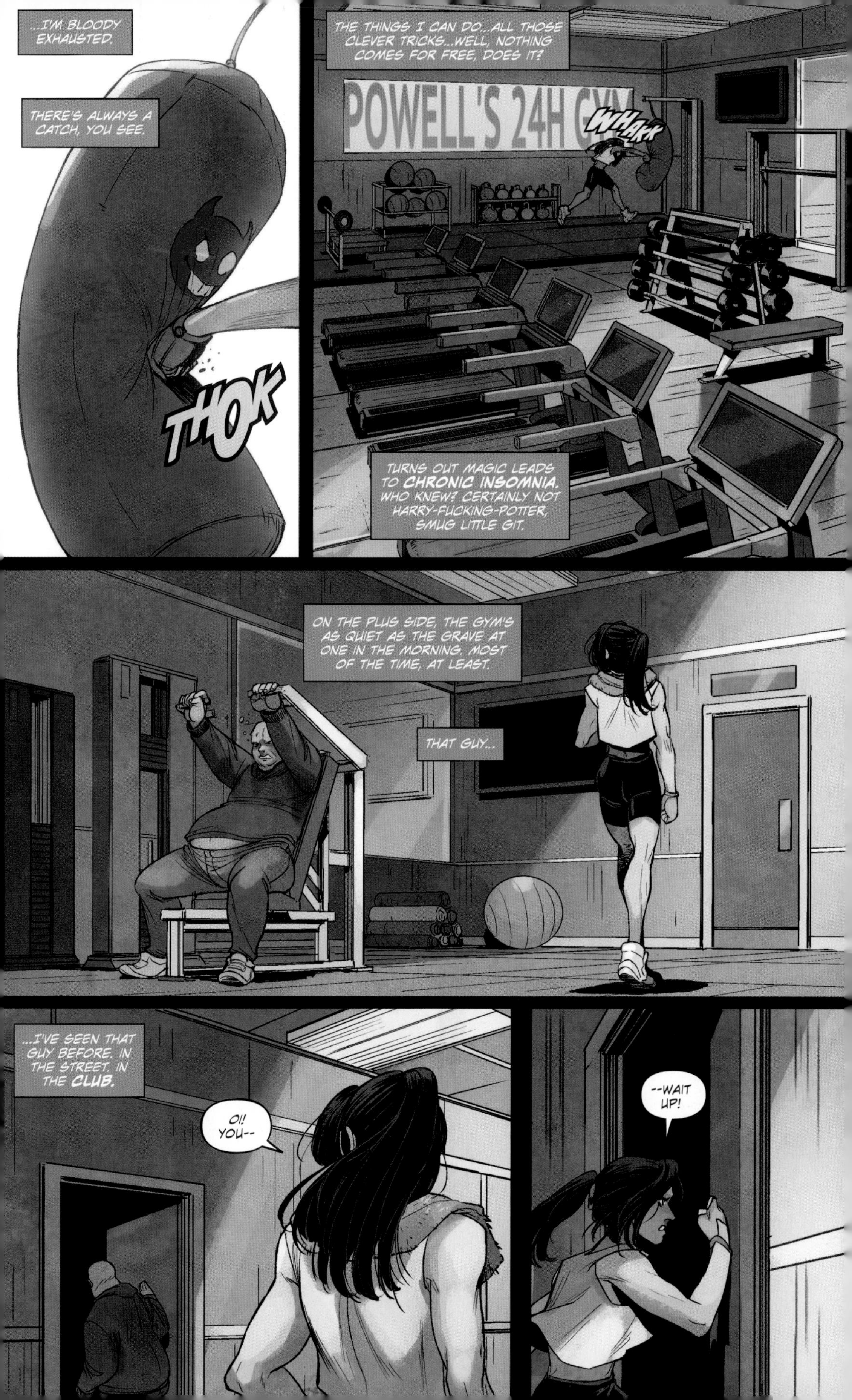
...I'M BLOODY EXHAUSTED.
THERE'S ALWAYS A CATCH, YOU SEE.
THOK
THE THINGS I CAN DO...ALL THOSE CLEVER TRICKS...WELL, NOTHING COMES FOR FREE, DOES IT?
POWELL'S 24H GYM
WHAKK
TURNS OUT MAGIC LEADS TO CHRONIC INSOMNIA. WHO KNEW? CERTAINLY NOT HARRY-FUCKING-POTTER, SMUG LITTLE GIT.
ON THE PLUS SIDE, THE GYM'S AS QUIET AS THE GRAVE AT ONE IN THE MORNING. MOST OF THE TIME, AT LEAST.
THAT GUY...
...I'VE SEEN THAT GUY BEFORE. IN THE STREET. IN THE CLUB.
OI! YOU--
--WAIT UP!

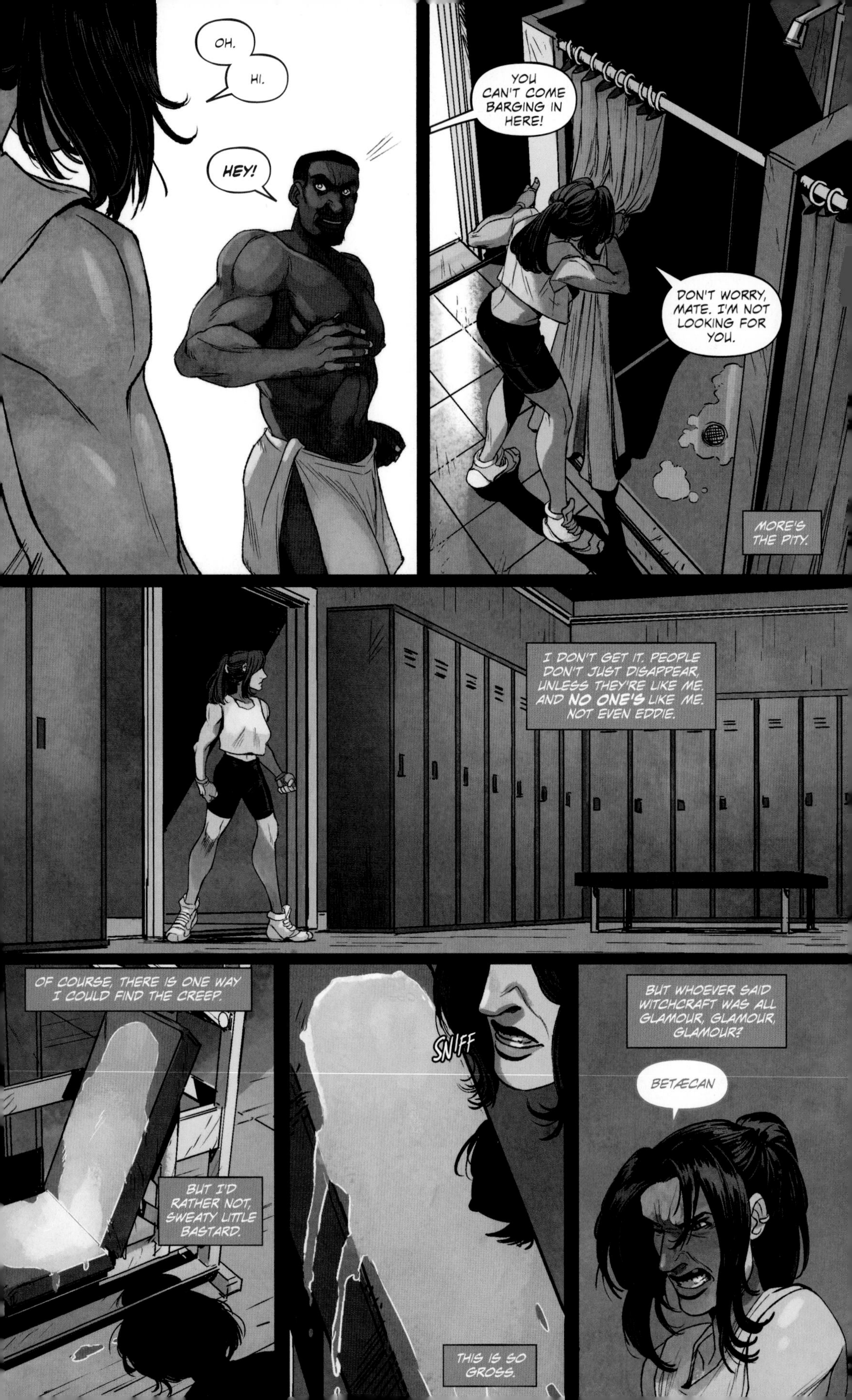
OH.
HI.
HEY!
YOU CAN'T COME BARGING IN HERE!
DON'T WORRY, MATE. I'M NOT LOOKING FOR YOU.
MORE'S THE PITY.
I DON'T GET IT. PEOPLE DON'T JUST DISAPPEAR, UNLESS THEY'RE LIKE ME. AND NO ONE'S LIKE ME. NOT EVEN EDDIE.
OF COURSE, THERE IS ONE WAY I COULD FIND THE CREEP.
BUT I'D RATHER NOT, SWEATY LITTLE BASTARD.
SNIFF
THIS IS SO GROSS.
BUT WHOEVER SAID WITCHCRAFT WAS ALL GLAMOUR, GLAMOUR, GLAMOUR?
BETÆCAN

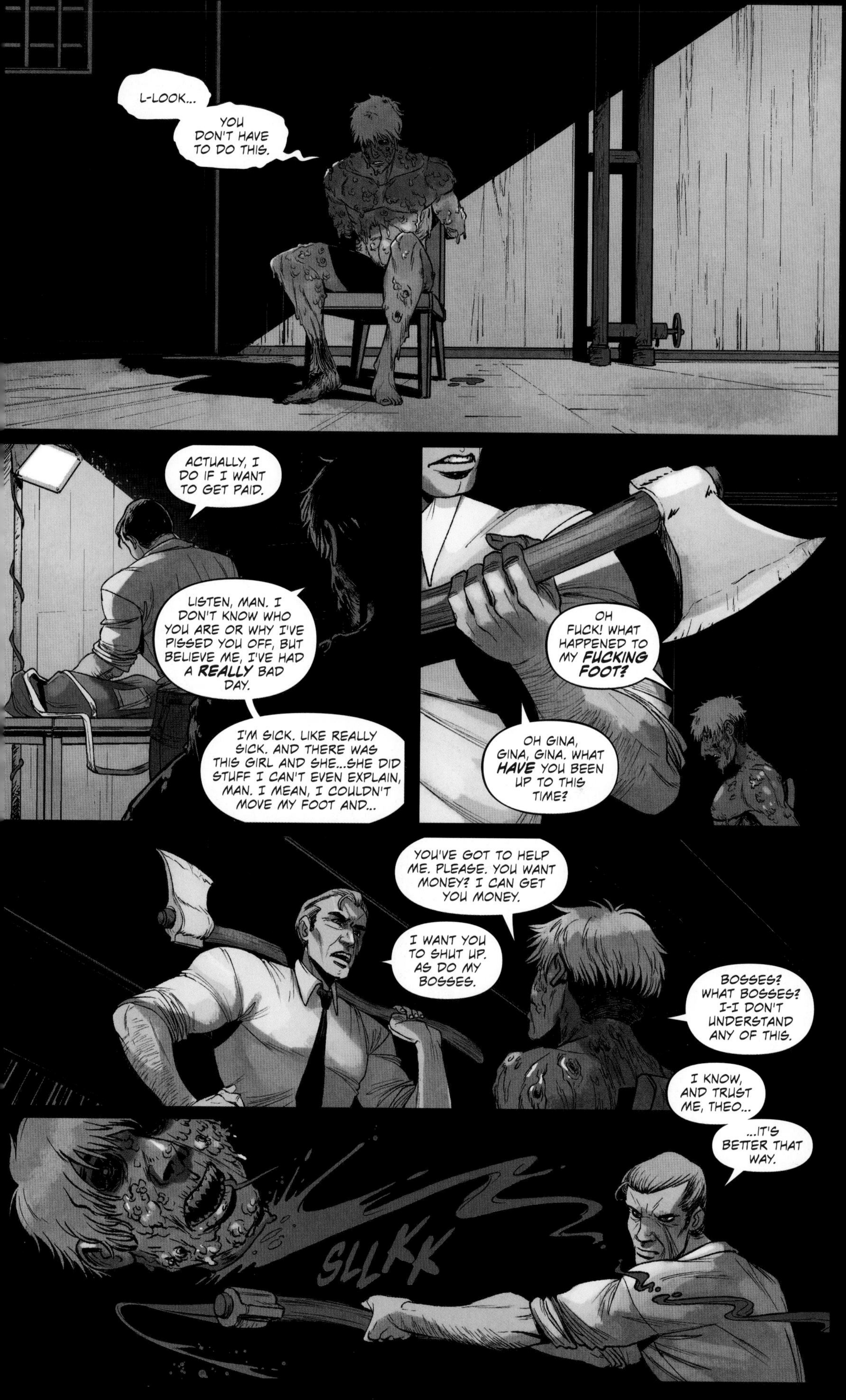
L-LOOK...
YOU DON'T HAVE TO DO THIS.
ACTUALLY, I DO IF I WANT TO GET PAID.
LISTEN, MAN. I DON'T KNOW WHO YOU ARE OR WHY I'VE PISSED YOU OFF, BUT BELIEVE ME, I'VE HAD A **REALLY** BAD DAY.
I'M SICK. LIKE REALLY SICK. AND THERE WAS THIS GIRL AND SHE...SHE DID STUFF I CAN'T EVEN EXPLAIN, MAN. I MEAN, I COULDN'T MOVE MY FOOT AND...
OH FUCK! WHAT HAPPENED TO MY ***FUCKING FOOT?***
OH GINA, GINA, GINA. WHAT ***HAVE*** YOU BEEN UP TO THIS TIME?
YOU'VE GOT TO HELP ME. PLEASE. YOU WANT MONEY? I CAN GET YOU MONEY.
I WANT YOU TO SHUT UP. AS DO MY BOSSES.
BOSSES? WHAT BOSSES? I-I DON'T UNDERSTAND ANY OF THIS.
I KNOW, AND TRUST ME, THEO...
...IT'S BETTER THAT WAY.
SLLKK

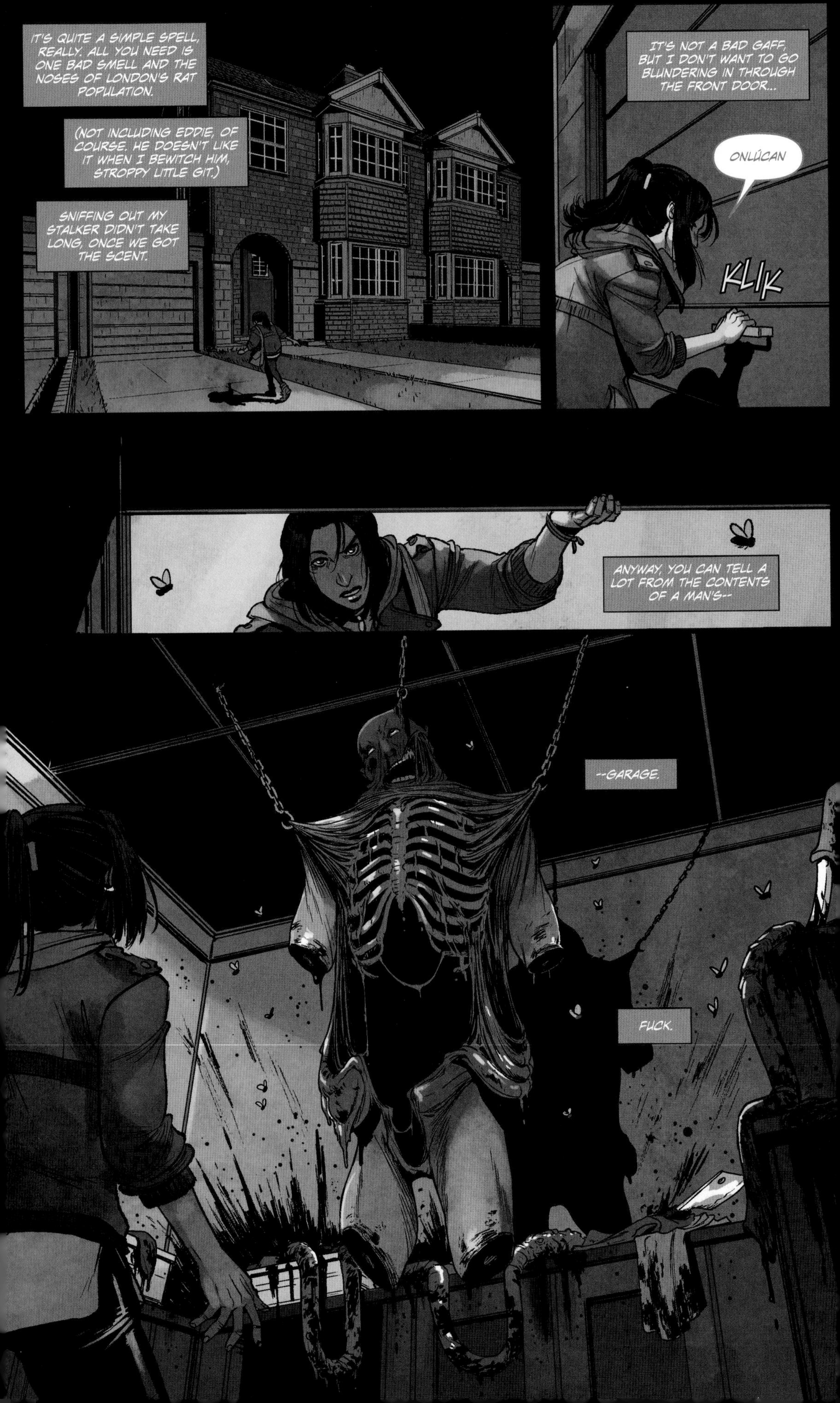
IT'S QUITE A SIMPLE SPELL, REALLY. ALL YOU NEED IS ONE BAD SMELL AND THE NOSES OF LONDON'S RAT POPULATION.
(NOT INCLUDING EDDIE, OF COURSE. HE DOESN'T LIKE IT WHEN I BEWITCH HIM, STROPPY LITTLE GIT.)
SNIFFING OUT MY STALKER DIDN'T TAKE LONG, ONCE WE GOT THE SCENT.
IT'S NOT A BAD GAFF, BUT I DON'T WANT TO GO BLUNDERING IN THROUGH THE FRONT DOOR...
ONLÚCAN
KLIK
ANYWAY, YOU CAN TELL A LOT FROM THE CONTENTS OF A MAN'S--
--GARAGE.
FUCK.

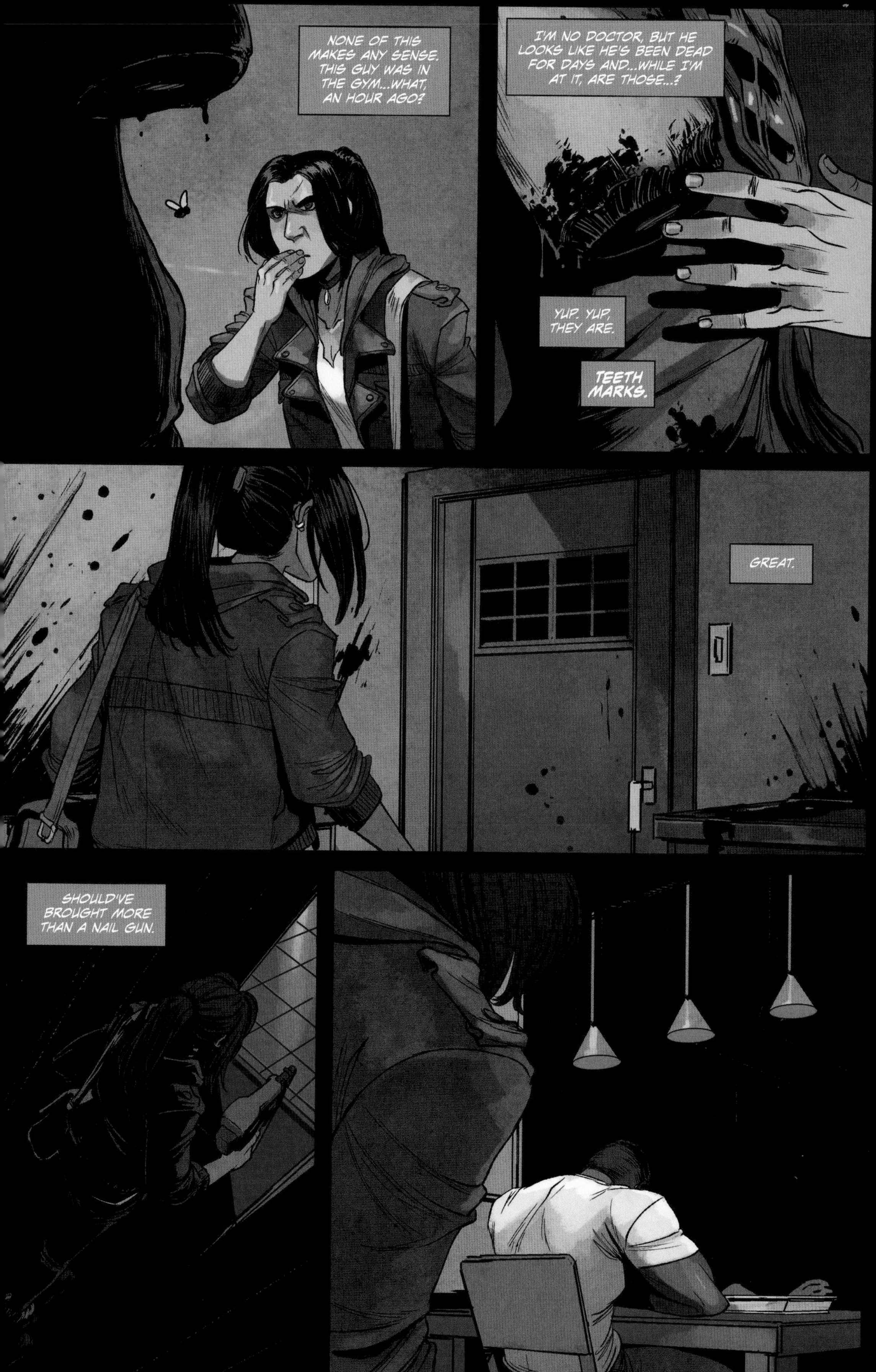
NONE OF THIS MAKES ANY SENSE. THIS GUY WAS IN THE GYM...WHAT, AN HOUR AGO?
I'M NO DOCTOR, BUT HE LOOKS LIKE HE'S BEEN DEAD FOR DAYS AND...WHILE I'M AT IT, ARE THOSE...?
YUP. YUP, THEY ARE.
TEETH MARKS.
GREAT.
SHOULD'VE BROUGHT MORE THAN A NAIL GUN.

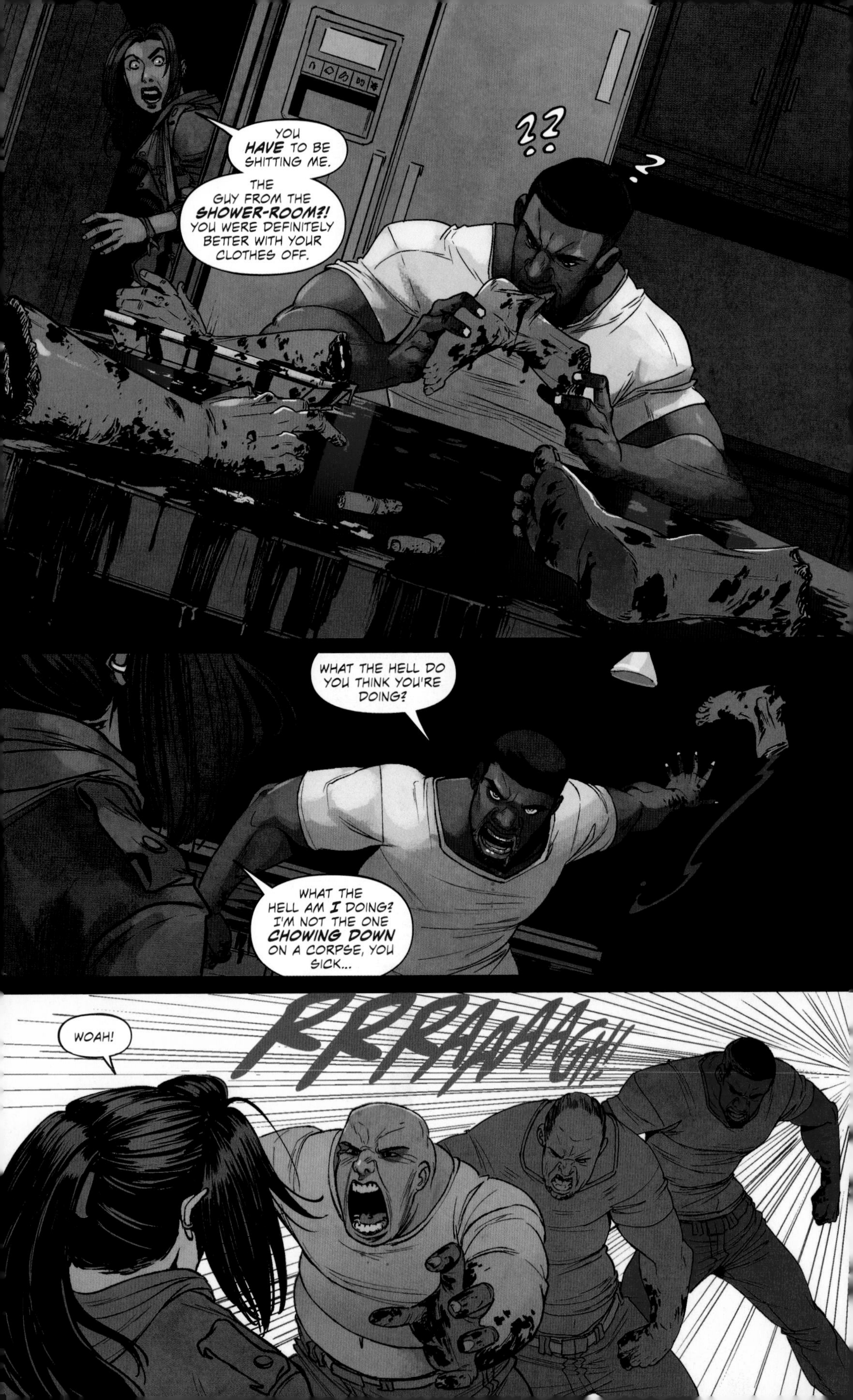

??
?
YOU HAVE TO BE SHITTING ME.
THE GUY FROM THE SHOWER-ROOM?! YOU WERE DEFINITELY BETTER WITH YOUR CLOTHES OFF.
WHAT THE HELL DO YOU THINK YOU'RE DOING?
WHAT THE HELL AM I DOING? I'M NOT THE ONE CHOWING DOWN ON A CORPSE, YOU SICK...
RRRAAAAAGH!
WOAH!

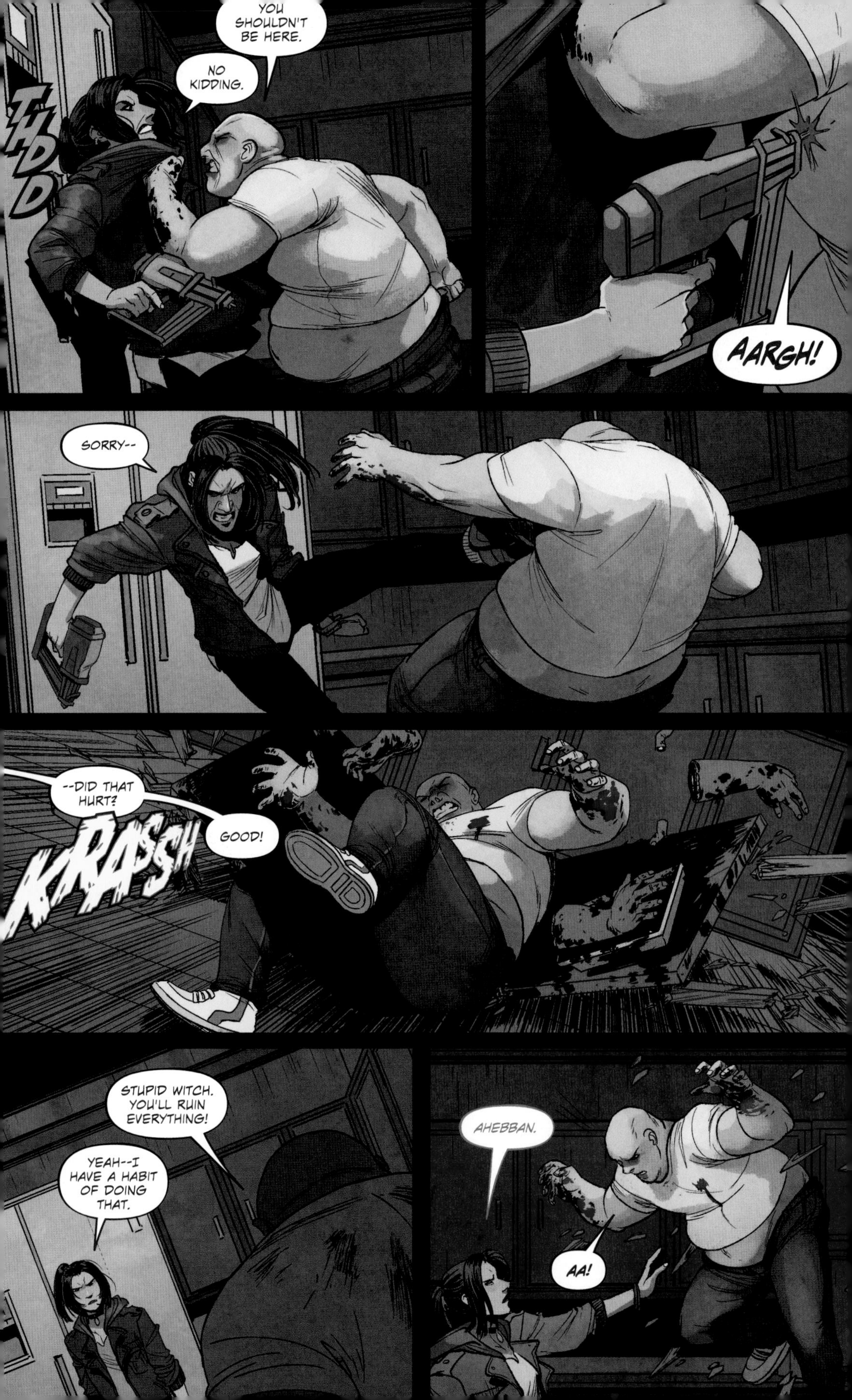
YOU SHOULDN'T BE HERE.
NO KIDDING.
THDD
AARGH!
SORRY--
--DID THAT HURT?
GOOD!
KRASH
STUPID WITCH. YOU'LL RUIN EVERYTHING!
YEAH--I HAVE A HABIT OF DOING THAT.
AHEBBAN.
AA!

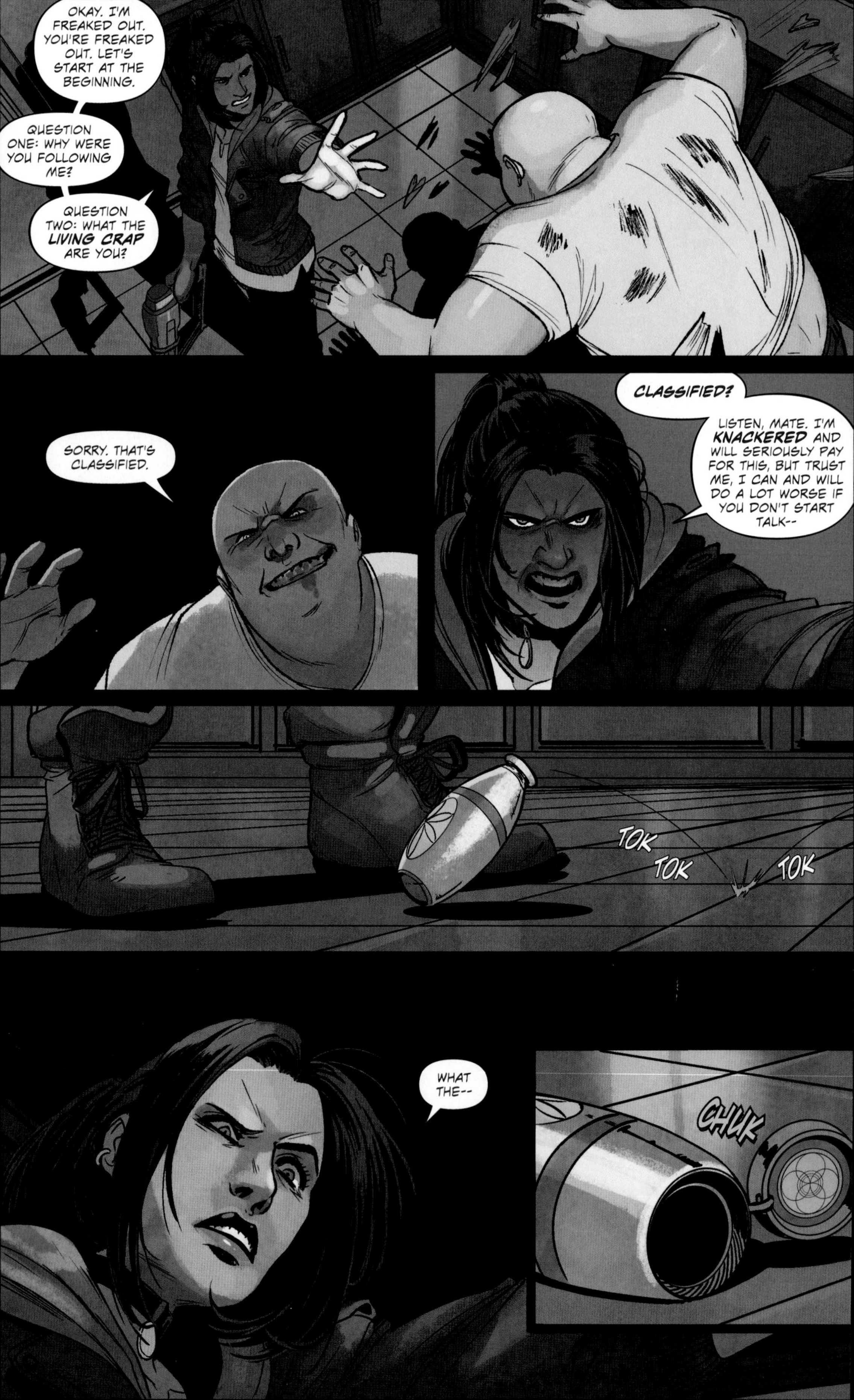
OKAY. I'M FREAKED OUT. YOU'RE FREAKED OUT. LET'S START AT THE BEGINNING.
QUESTION ONE: WHY WERE YOU FOLLOWING ME?
QUESTION TWO: WHAT THE LIVING CRAP ARE YOU?
SORRY. THAT'S CLASSIFIED.
CLASSIFIED?
LISTEN, MATE. I'M KNACKERED AND WILL SERIOUSLY PAY FOR THIS, BUT TRUST ME, I CAN AND WILL DO A LOT WORSE IF YOU DON'T START TALK--
TOK
TOK
TOK
WHAT THE--
CHUK

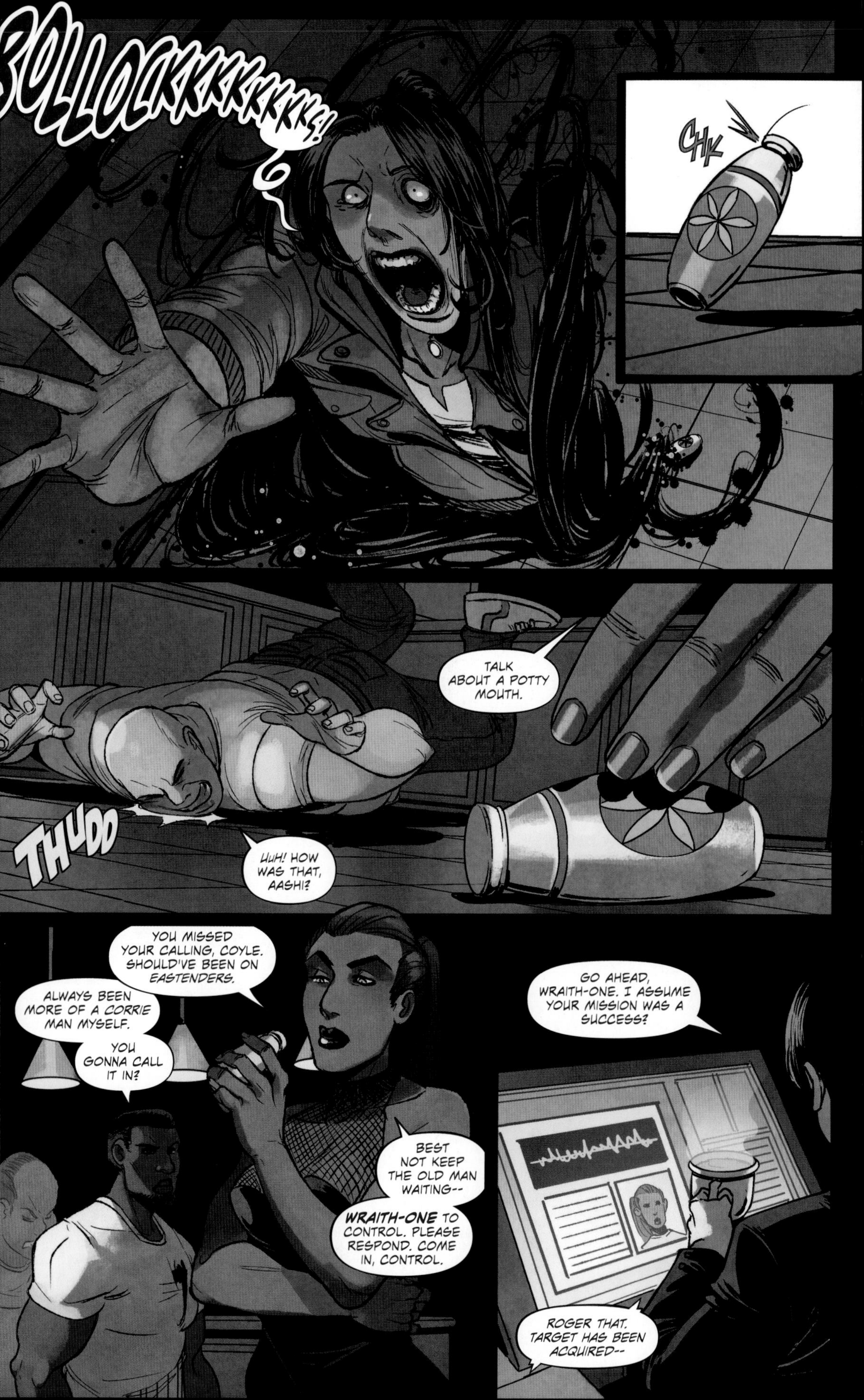
BOLLOCKKKKKKKS!
CHK
TALK ABOUT A POTTY MOUTH.
THUDD
UUH! HOW WAS THAT, AASHI?
YOU MISSED YOUR CALLING, COYLE. SHOULD'VE BEEN ON EASTENDERS.
ALWAYS BEEN MORE OF A CORRIE MAN MYSELF.
YOU GONNA CALL IT IN?
BEST NOT KEEP THE OLD MAN WAITING--
WRAITH-ONE TO CONTROL. PLEASE RESPOND. COME IN, CONTROL.
GO AHEAD, WRAITH-ONE. I ASSUME YOUR MISSION WAS A SUCCESS?
ROGER THAT. TARGET HAS BEEN ACQUIRED--

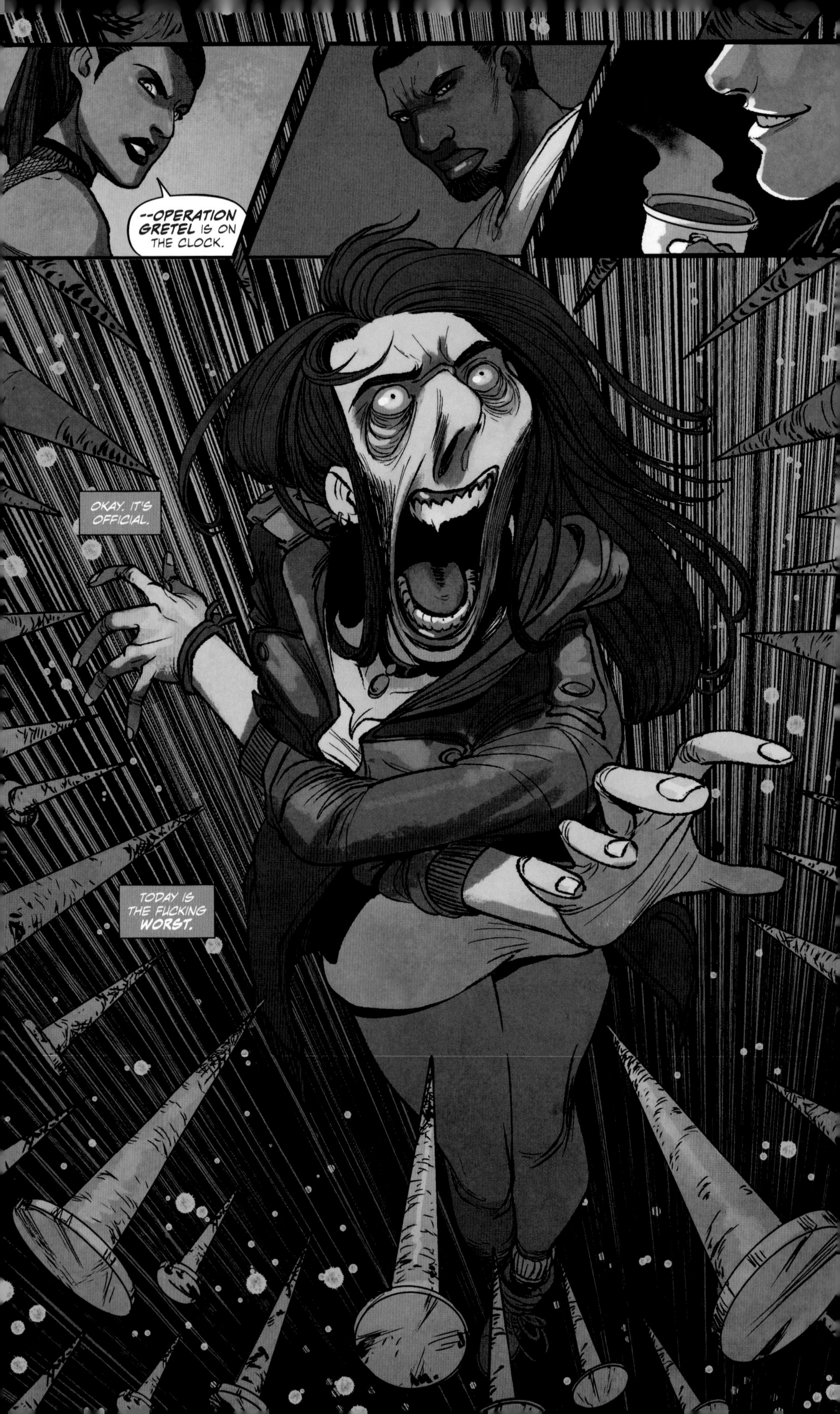
--OPERATION GRETEL IS ON THE CLOCK.
OKAY. IT'S OFFICIAL.
TODAY IS THE FUCKING WORST.

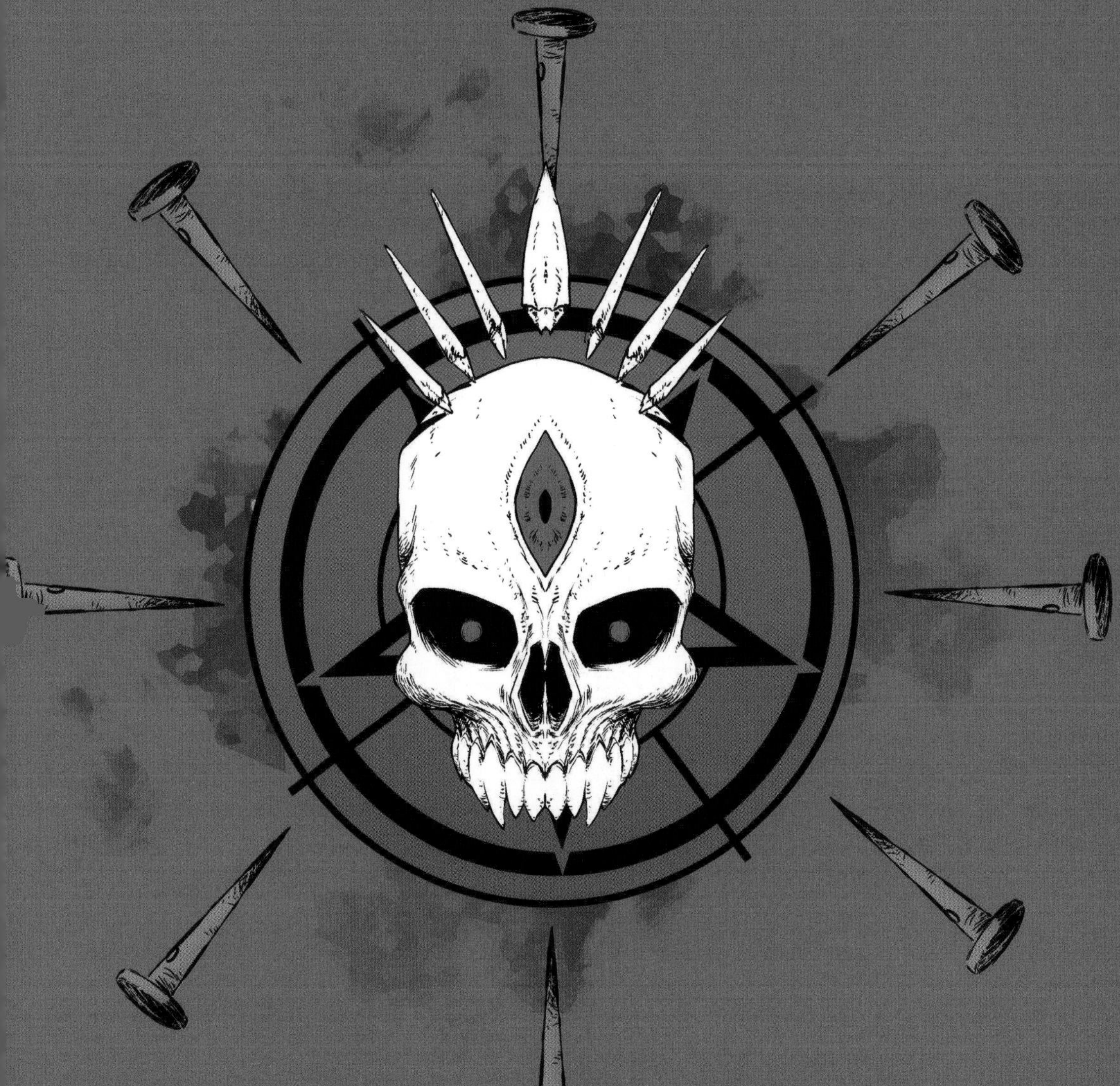

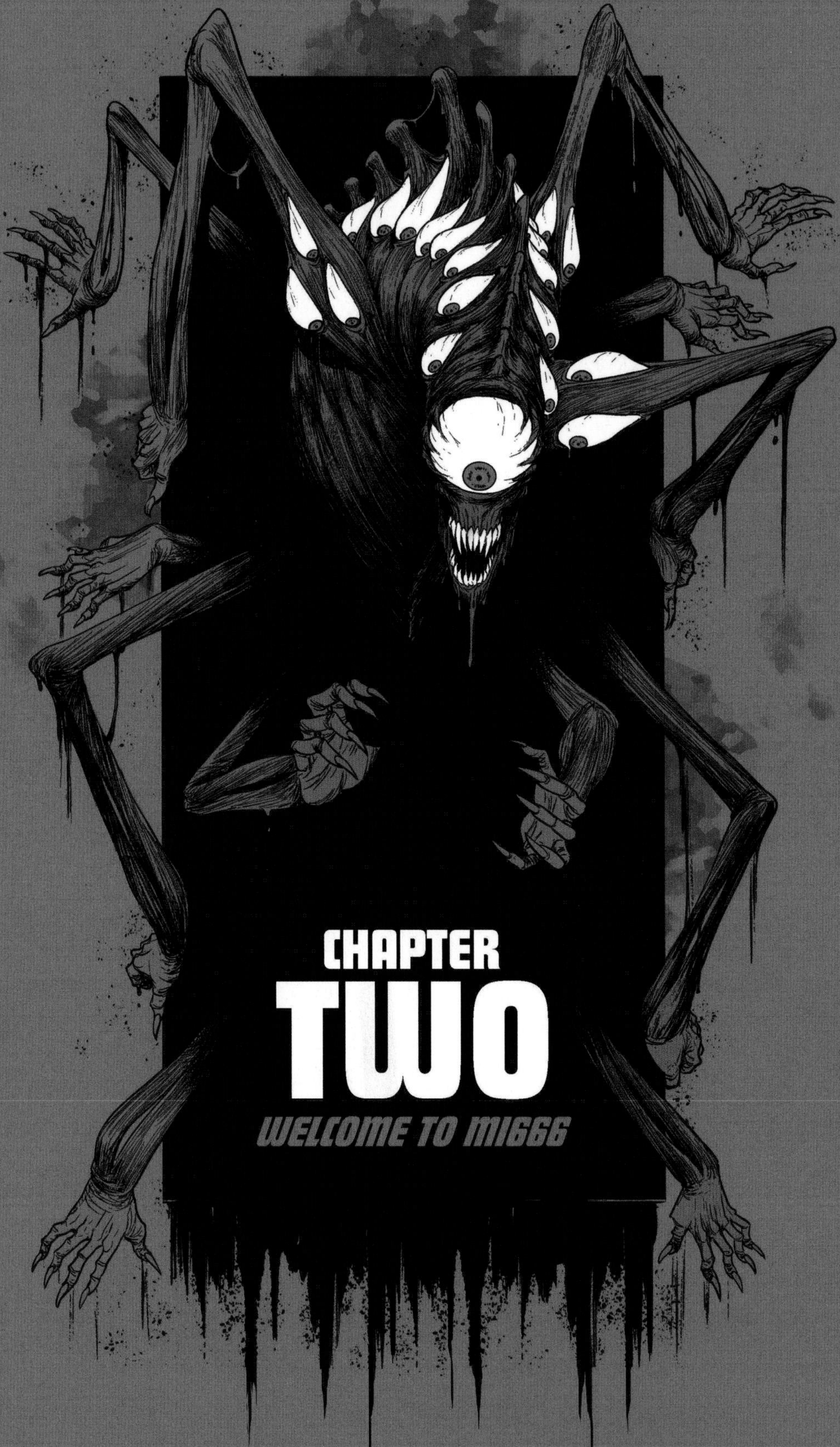
CHAPTER
TWO
WELCOME TO MI666

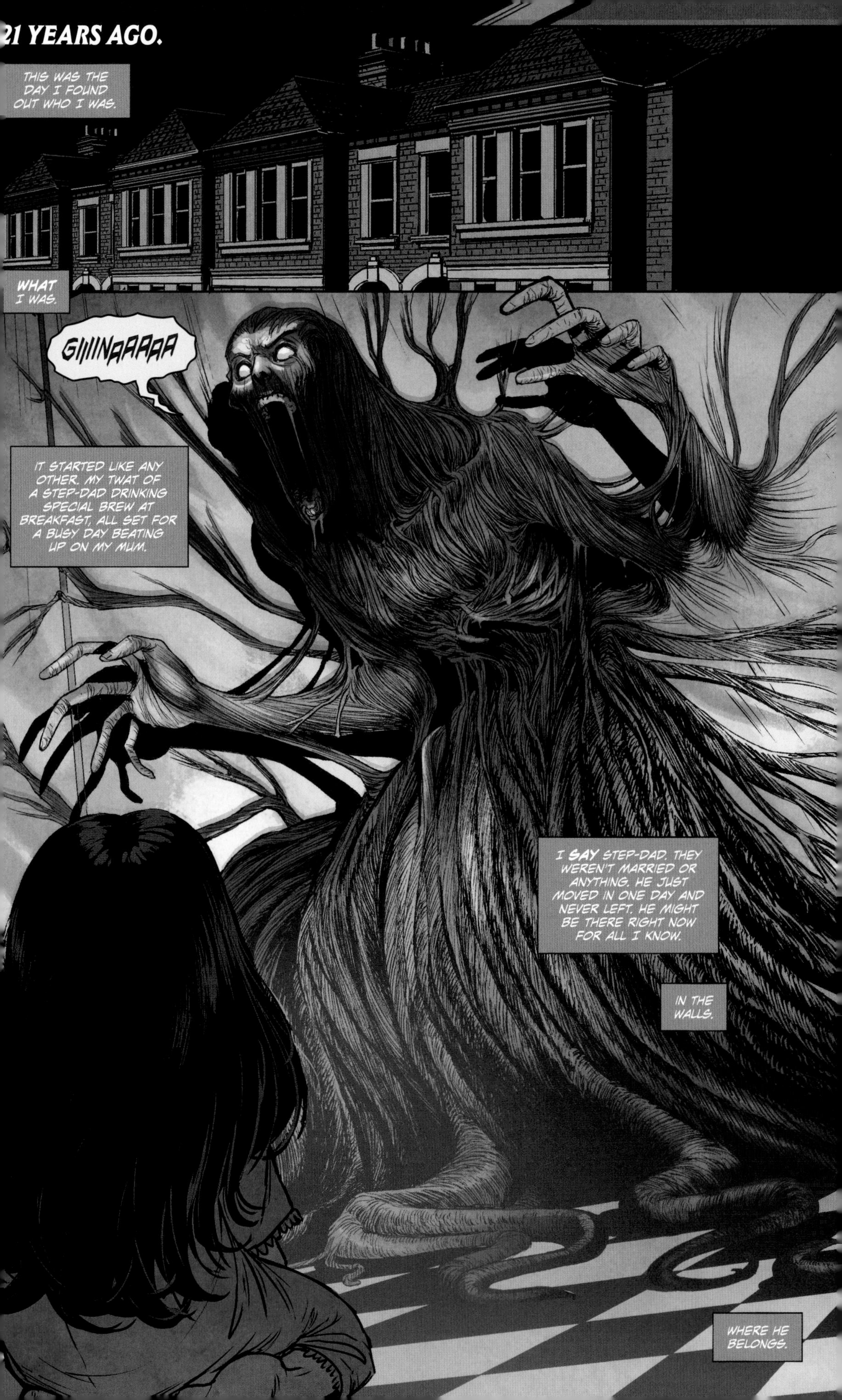

21 YEARS AGO.
THIS WAS THE DAY I FOUND OUT WHO I WAS.
WHAT I WAS.
GIIIINAAAAA
IT STARTED LIKE ANY OTHER. MY TWAT OF A STEP-DAD DRINKING SPECIAL BREW AT BREAKFAST, ALL SET FOR A BUSY DAY BEATING UP ON MY MUM.
I SAY STEP-DAD. THEY WEREN'T MARRIED OR ANYTHING. HE JUST MOVED IN ONE DAY AND NEVER LEFT. HE MIGHT BE THERE RIGHT NOW FOR ALL I KNOW.
IN THE WALLS.
WHERE HE BELONGS.

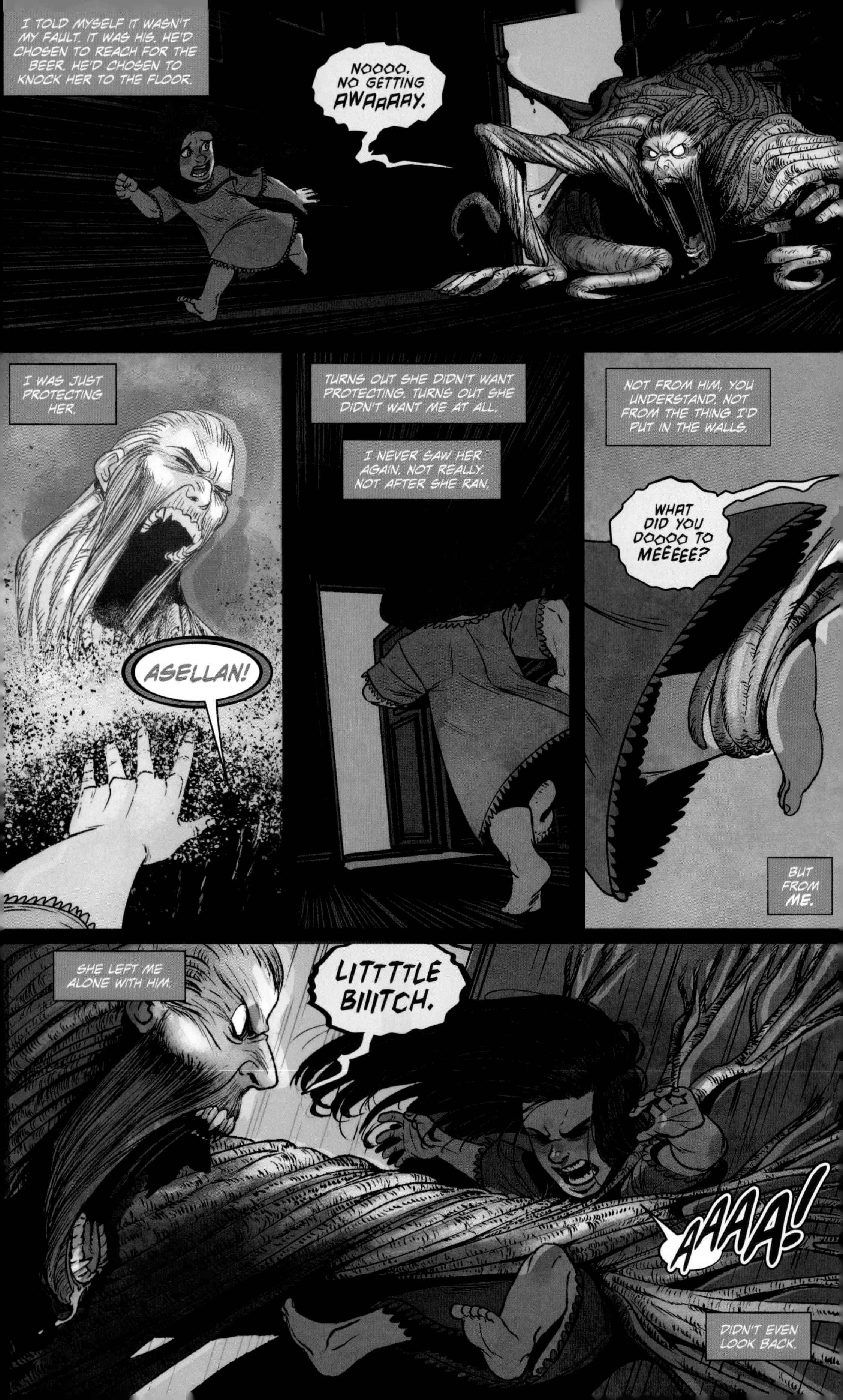
I TOLD MYSELF IT WASN'T MY FAULT. IT WAS HIS. HE'D CHOSEN TO REACH FOR THE BEER. HE'D CHOSEN TO KNOCK HER TO THE FLOOR.
NOOOO. NO GETTING AWAAAAY.
I WAS JUST PROTECTING HER.
ASELLAN!
TURNS OUT SHE DIDN'T WANT PROTECTING. TURNS OUT SHE DIDN'T WANT ME AT ALL.
I NEVER SAW HER AGAIN. NOT REALLY. NOT AFTER SHE RAN.
NOT FROM HIM, YOU UNDERSTAND. NOT FROM THE THING I'D PUT IN THE WALLS.
WHAT DID YOU DOOOO TO MEEEEE?
BUT FROM ME.
SHE LEFT ME ALONE WITH HIM.
LITTTTLE BIIITCH.
AAAA!
DIDN'T EVEN LOOK BACK.

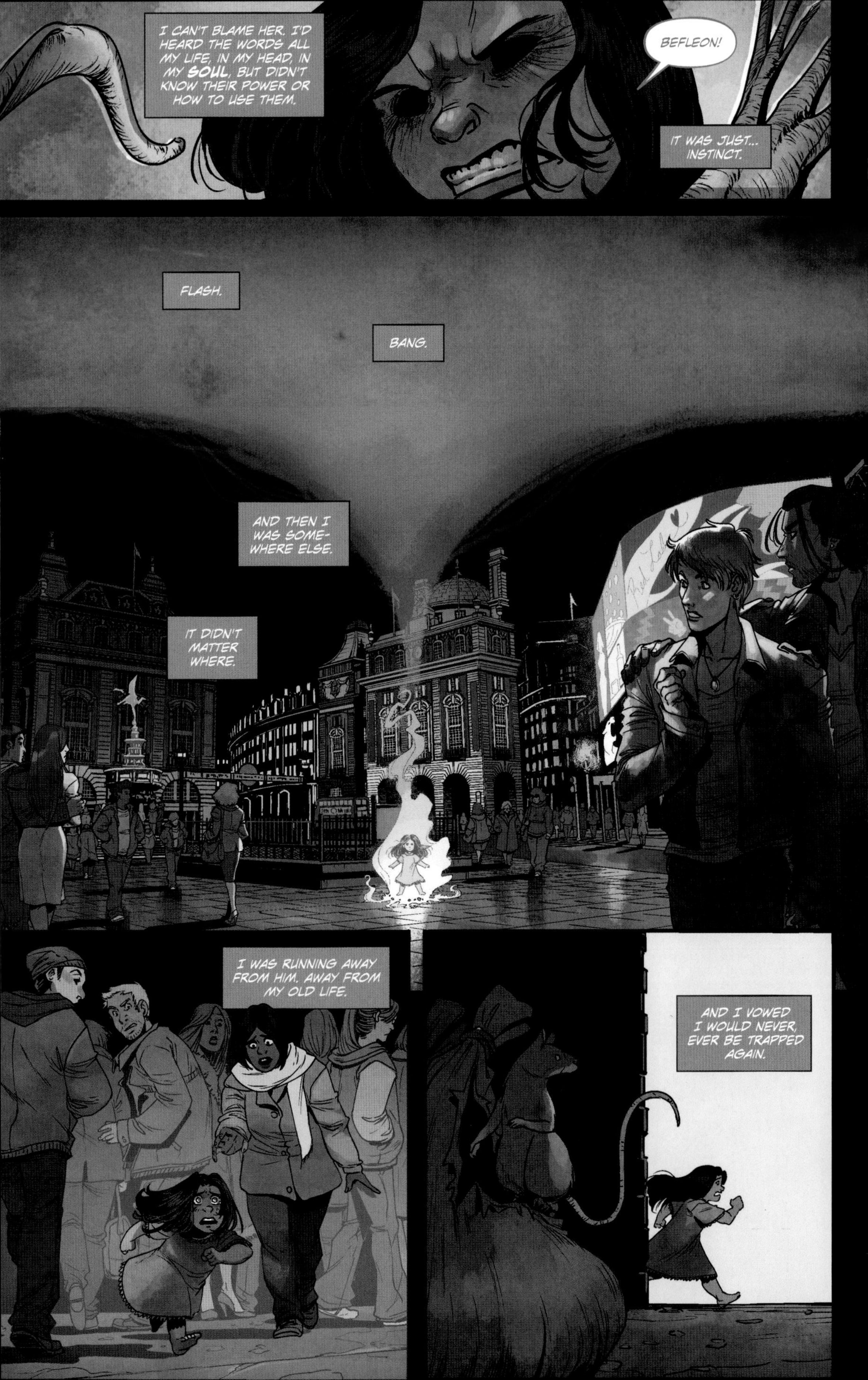
I CAN'T BLAME HER. I'D HEARD THE WORDS ALL MY LIFE, IN MY HEAD, IN MY SOUL, BUT DIDN'T KNOW THEIR POWER OR HOW TO USE THEM.
BEFLEON!
IT WAS JUST... INSTINCT.
FLASH.
BANG.
AND THEN I WAS SOME-WHERE ELSE.
IT DIDN'T MATTER WHERE.
I WAS RUNNING AWAY FROM HIM. AWAY FROM MY OLD LIFE.
AND I VOWED I WOULD NEVER, EVER BE TRAPPED AGAIN.

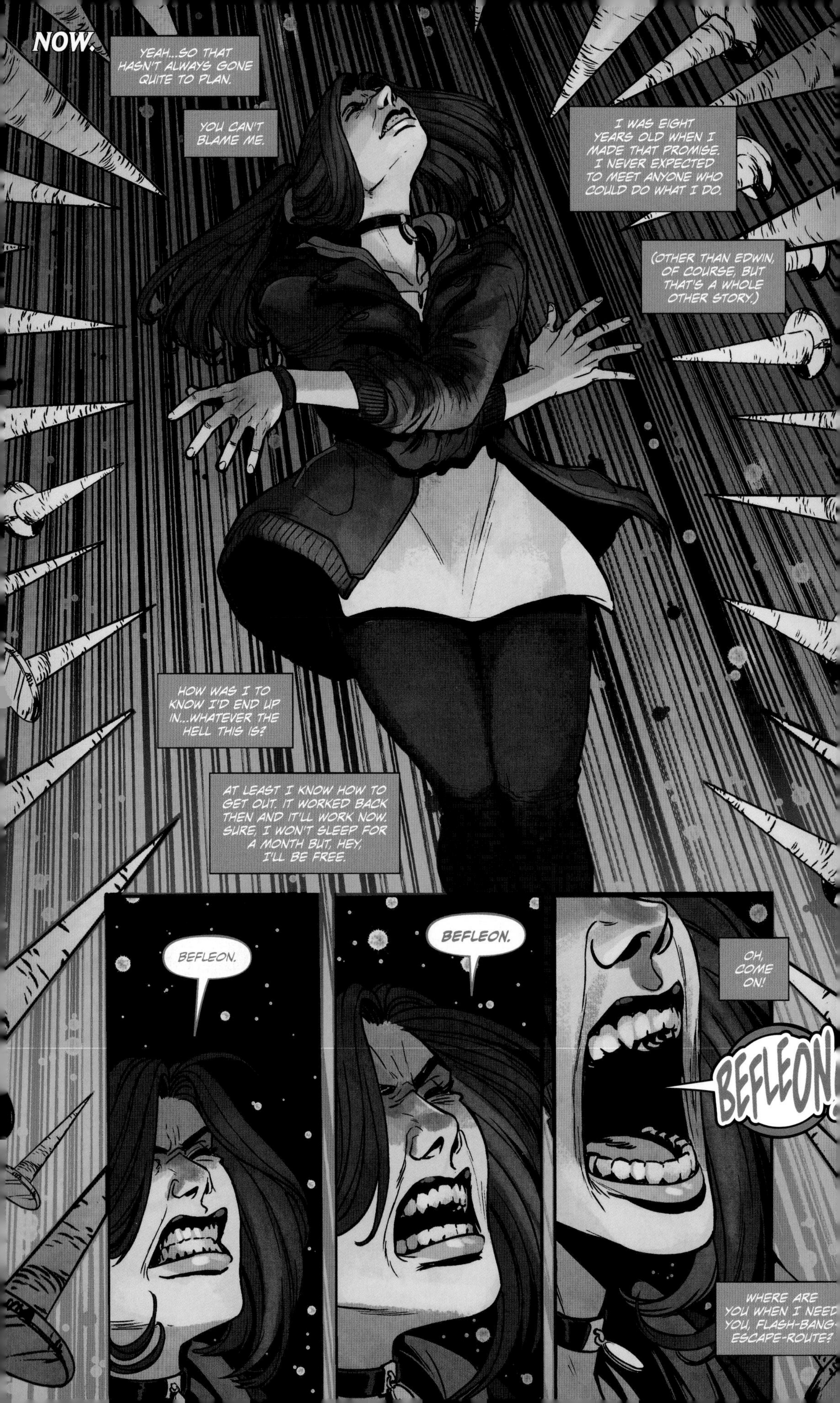
NOW.
YEAH...SO THAT HASN'T ALWAYS GONE QUITE TO PLAN.
YOU CAN'T BLAME ME.
I WAS EIGHT YEARS OLD WHEN I MADE THAT PROMISE. I NEVER EXPECTED TO MEET ANYONE WHO COULD DO WHAT I DO.
(OTHER THAN EDWIN, OF COURSE, BUT THAT'S A WHOLE OTHER STORY.)
HOW WAS I TO KNOW I'D END UP IN...WHATEVER THE HELL THIS IS?
AT LEAST I KNOW HOW TO GET OUT. IT WORKED BACK THEN AND IT'LL WORK NOW. SURE, I WON'T SLEEP FOR A MONTH BUT, HEY, I'LL BE FREE.
BEFLEON.
BEFLEON.
OH, COME ON!
BEFLEON!
WHERE ARE YOU WHEN I NEED YOU, FLASH-BANG ESCAPE-ROUTE?

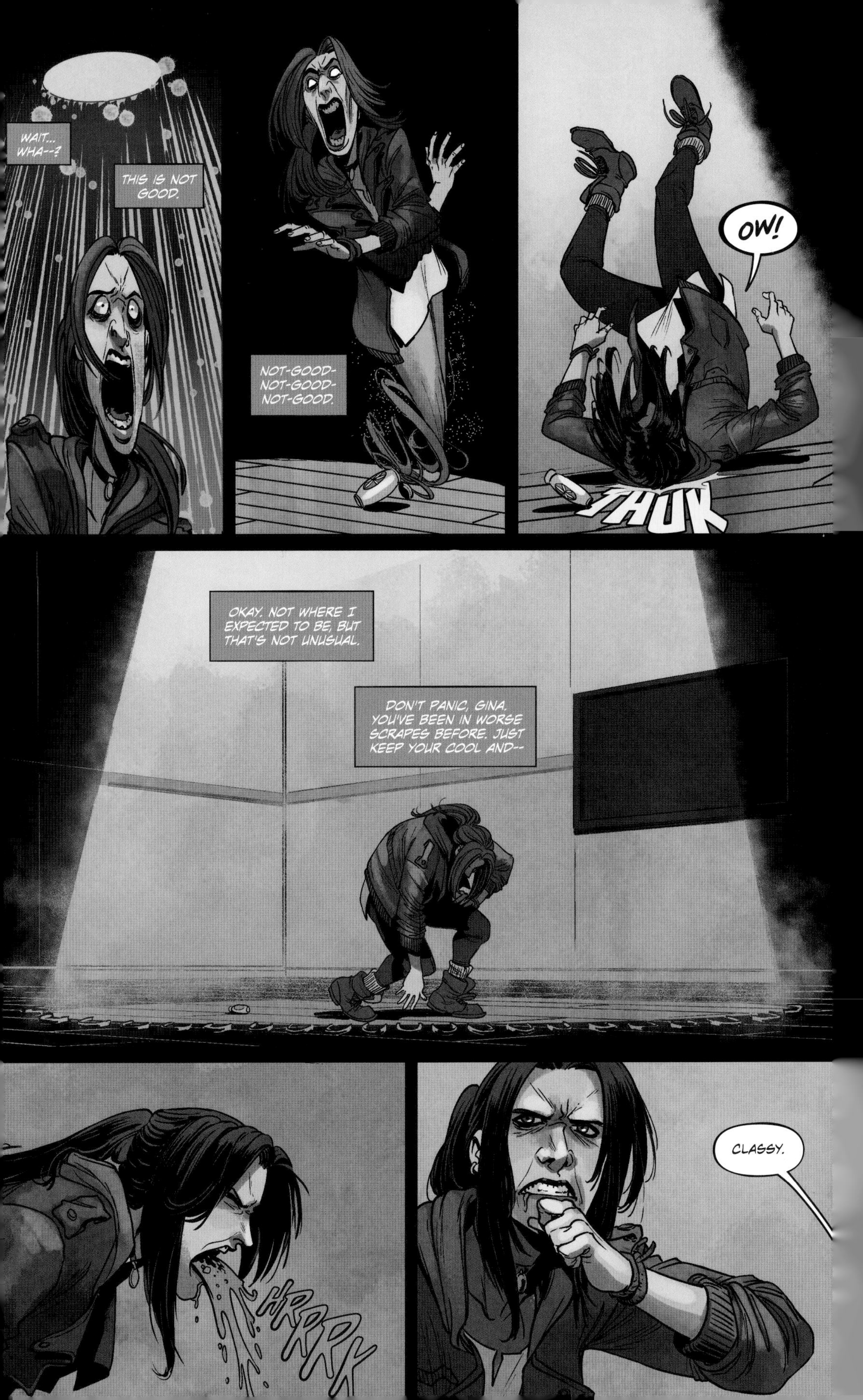
WAIT... WHA--?
THIS IS NOT GOOD.
NOT-GOOD- NOT-GOOD- NOT-GOOD.
OW!
THUK
OKAY. NOT WHERE I EXPECTED TO BE, BUT THAT'S NOT UNUSUAL.
DON'T PANIC, GINA. YOU'VE BEEN IN WORSE SCRAPES BEFORE. JUST KEEP YOUR COOL AND--
HRRRK
CLASSY.

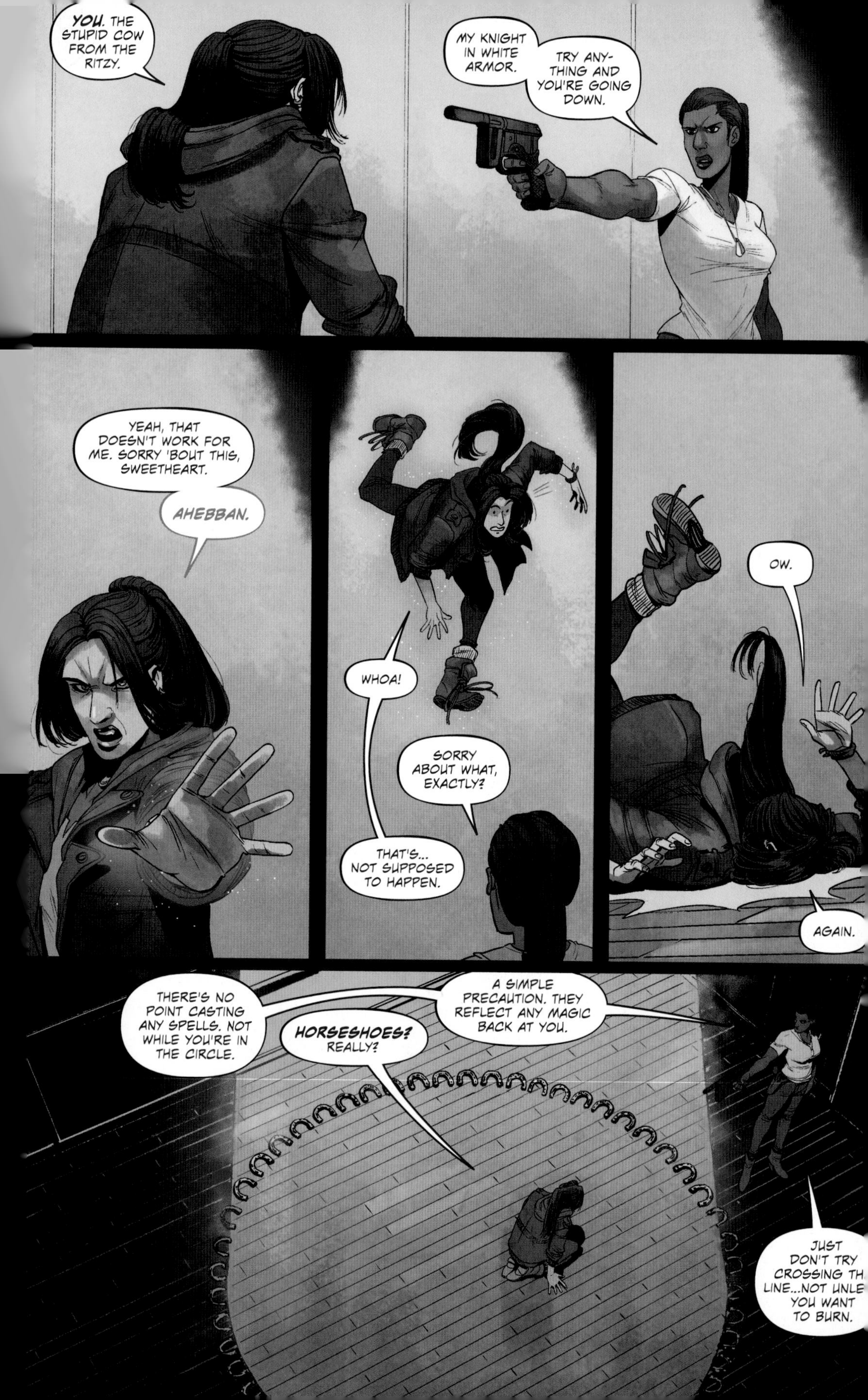

YOU. THE STUPID COW FROM THE RITZY.
MY KNIGHT IN WHITE ARMOR.
TRY ANYTHING AND YOU'RE GOING DOWN.
YEAH, THAT DOESN'T WORK FOR ME. SORRY 'BOUT THIS, SWEETHEART.
AHEBBAN.
WHOA!
SORRY ABOUT WHAT, EXACTLY?
THAT'S... NOT SUPPOSED TO HAPPEN.
OW.
AGAIN.
THERE'S NO POINT CASTING ANY SPELLS. NOT WHILE YOU'RE IN THE CIRCLE.
HORSESHOES? REALLY?
A SIMPLE PRECAUTION. THEY REFLECT ANY MAGIC BACK AT YOU.

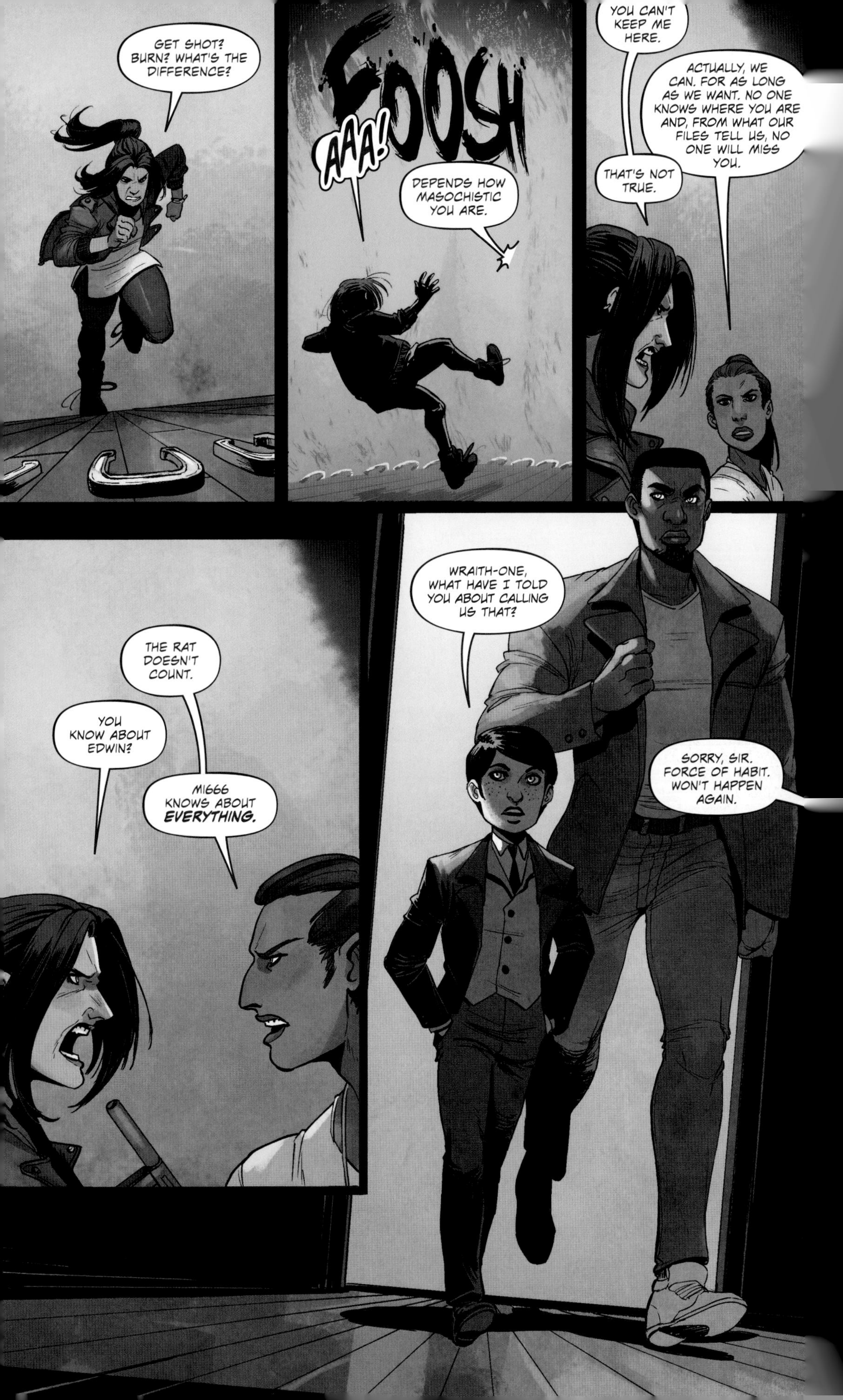
GET SHOT? BURN? WHAT'S THE DIFFERENCE?
FOOSH
AAA!
DEPENDS HOW MASOCHISTIC YOU ARE.
YOU CAN'T KEEP ME HERE.
ACTUALLY, WE CAN. FOR AS LONG AS WE WANT. NO ONE KNOWS WHERE YOU ARE AND, FROM WHAT OUR FILES TELL US, NO ONE WILL MISS YOU.
THAT'S NOT TRUE.
THE RAT DOESN'T COUNT.
YOU KNOW ABOUT EDWIN?
MI666 KNOWS ABOUT EVERYTHING.
WRAITH-ONE, WHAT HAVE I TOLD YOU ABOUT CALLING US THAT?
SORRY, SIR. FORCE OF HABIT. WON'T HAPPEN AGAIN.

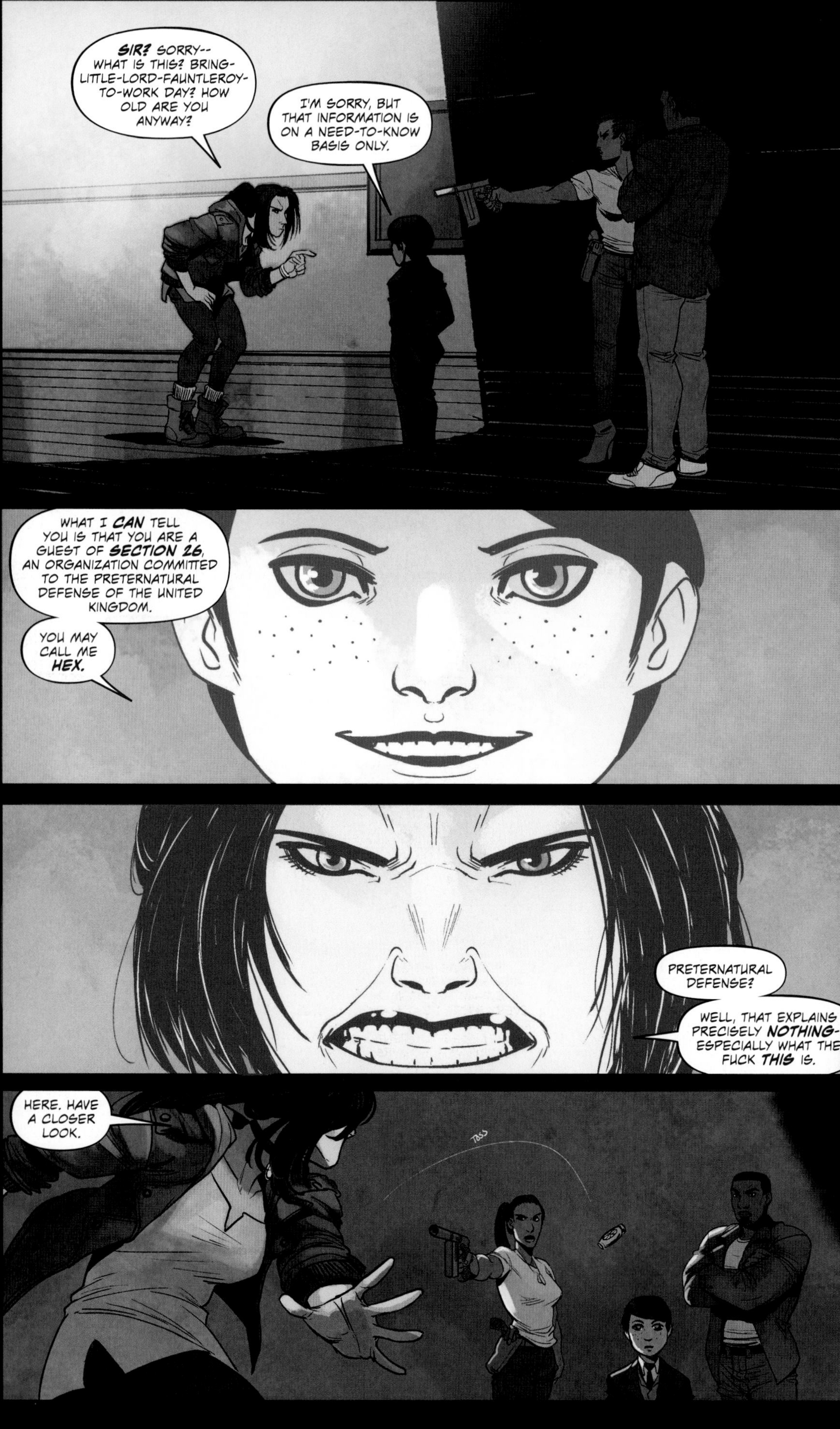
SIR? SORRY-- WHAT IS THIS? BRING-LITTLE-LORD-FAUNTLEROY-TO-WORK DAY? HOW OLD ARE YOU ANYWAY?
I'M SORRY, BUT THAT INFORMATION IS ON A NEED-TO-KNOW BASIS ONLY.
WHAT I CAN TELL YOU IS THAT YOU ARE A GUEST OF SECTION 26, AN ORGANIZATION COMMITTED TO THE PRETERNATURAL DEFENSE OF THE UNITED KINGDOM.
YOU MAY CALL ME HEX.
PRETERNATURAL DEFENSE?
WELL, THAT EXPLAINS PRECISELY NOTHING-- ESPECIALLY WHAT THE FUCK THIS IS.
HERE. HAVE A CLOSER LOOK.
TOSS

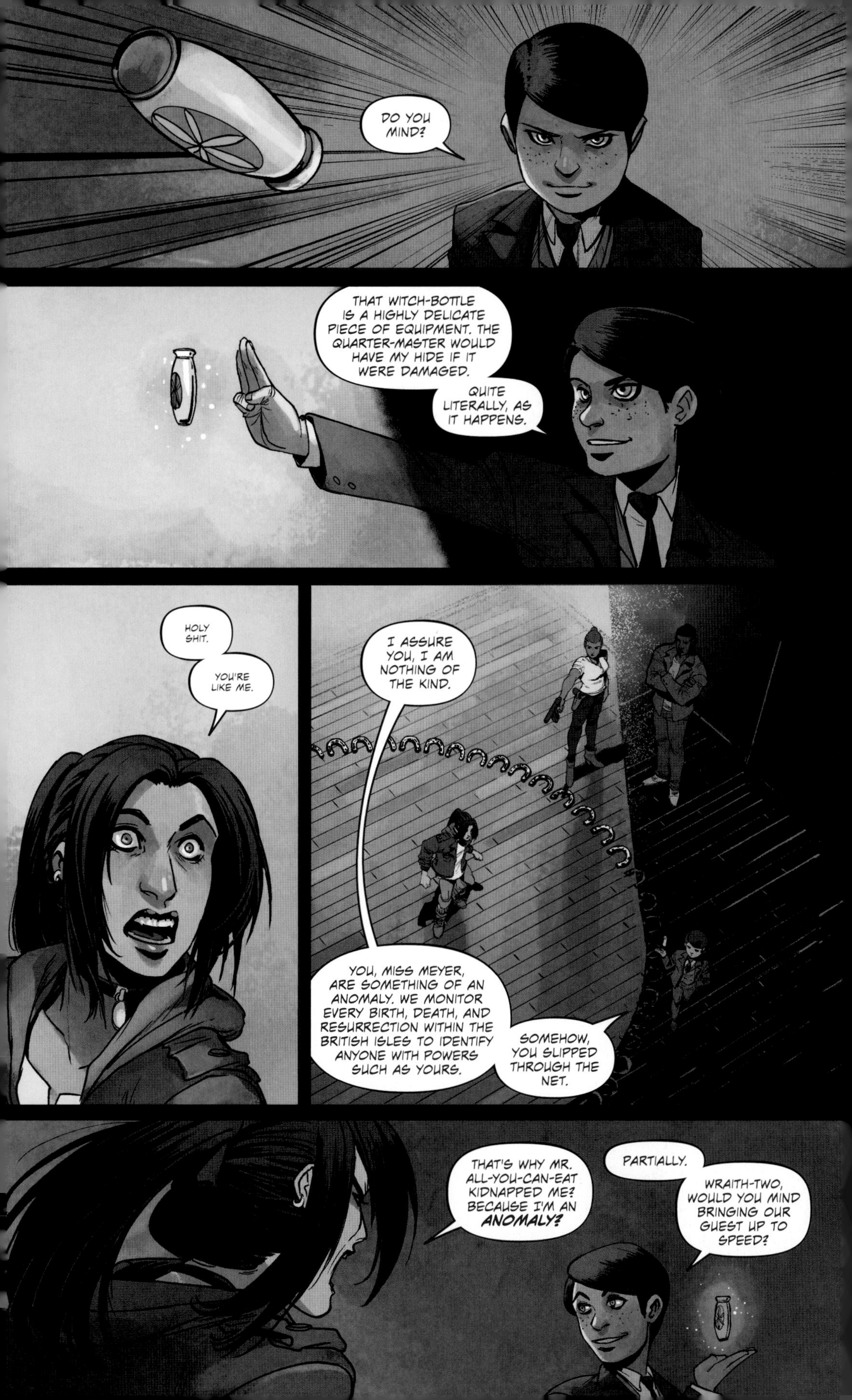
DO YOU MIND?
THAT WITCH-BOTTLE IS A HIGHLY DELICATE PIECE OF EQUIPMENT. THE QUARTER-MASTER WOULD HAVE MY HIDE IF IT WERE DAMAGED.
QUITE LITERALLY, AS IT HAPPENS.
HOLY SHIT.
YOU'RE LIKE ME.
I ASSURE YOU, I AM NOTHING OF THE KIND.
YOU, MISS MEYER, ARE SOMETHING OF AN ANOMALY. WE MONITOR EVERY BIRTH, DEATH, AND RESURRECTION WITHIN THE BRITISH ISLES TO IDENTIFY ANYONE WITH POWERS SUCH AS YOURS.
SOMEHOW, YOU SLIPPED THROUGH THE NET.
THAT'S WHY MR. ALL-YOU-CAN-EAT KIDNAPPED ME? BECAUSE I'M AN ***ANOMALY?***
PARTIALLY.
WRAITH-TWO, WOULD YOU MIND BRINGING OUR GUEST UP TO SPEED?

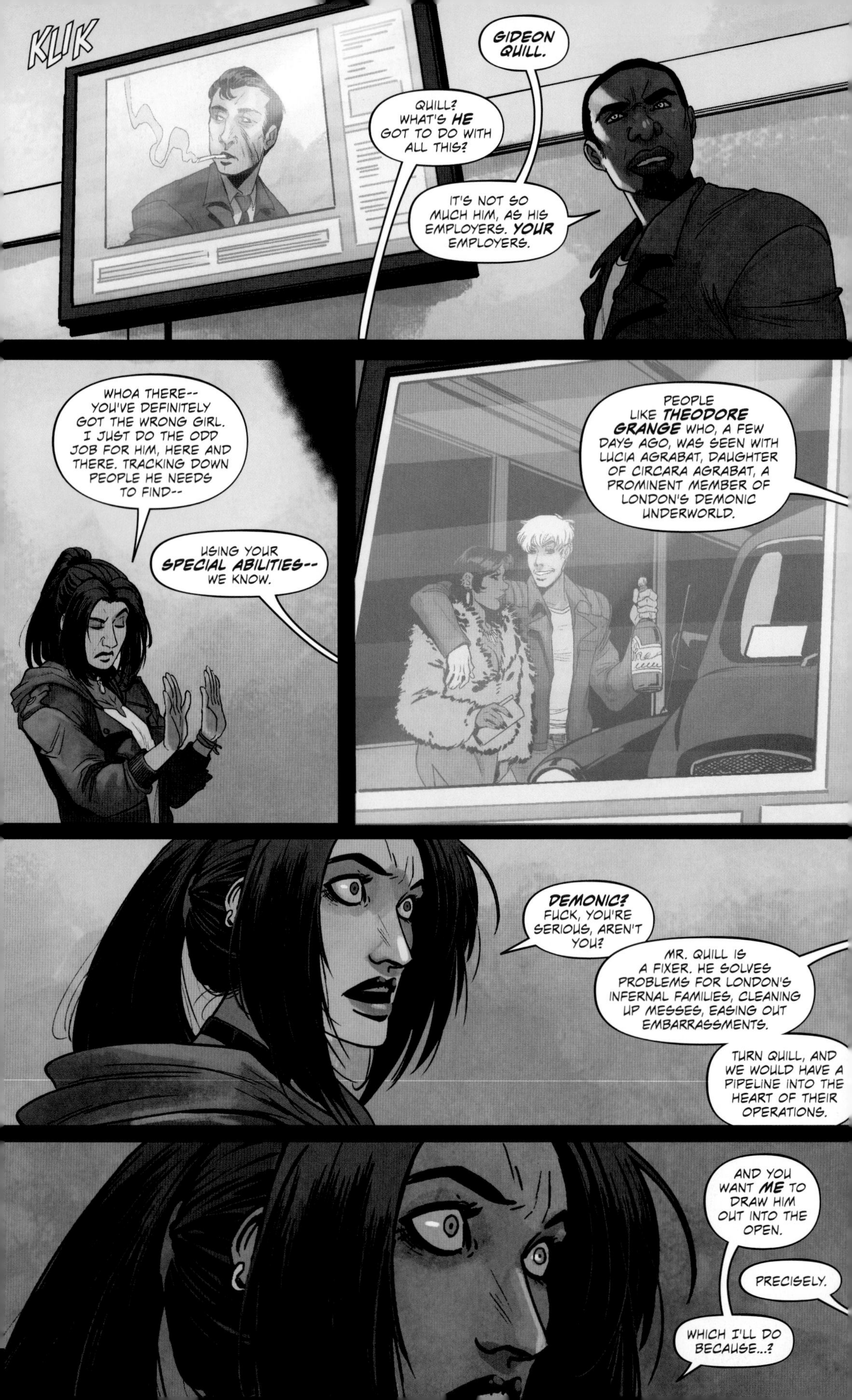
KLIK
GIDEON QUILL.
QUILL? WHAT'S HE GOT TO DO WITH ALL THIS?
IT'S NOT SO MUCH HIM, AS HIS EMPLOYERS. YOUR EMPLOYERS.
WHOA THERE-- YOU'VE DEFINITELY GOT THE WRONG GIRL. I JUST DO THE ODD JOB FOR HIM, HERE AND THERE. TRACKING DOWN PEOPLE HE NEEDS TO FIND--
USING YOUR SPECIAL ABILITIES-- WE KNOW.
PEOPLE LIKE THEODORE GRANGE WHO, A FEW DAYS AGO, WAS SEEN WITH LUCIA AGRABAT, DAUGHTER OF CIRCARA AGRABAT, A PROMINENT MEMBER OF LONDON'S DEMONIC UNDERWORLD.
DEMONIC? FUCK, YOU'RE SERIOUS, AREN'T YOU?
MR. QUILL IS A FIXER. HE SOLVES PROBLEMS FOR LONDON'S INFERNAL FAMILIES, CLEANING UP MESSES, EASING OUT EMBARRASSMENTS.
TURN QUILL, AND WE WOULD HAVE A PIPELINE INTO THE HEART OF THEIR OPERATIONS.
AND YOU WANT ME TO DRAW HIM OUT INTO THE OPEN.
PRECISELY.
WHICH I'LL DO BECAUSE...?

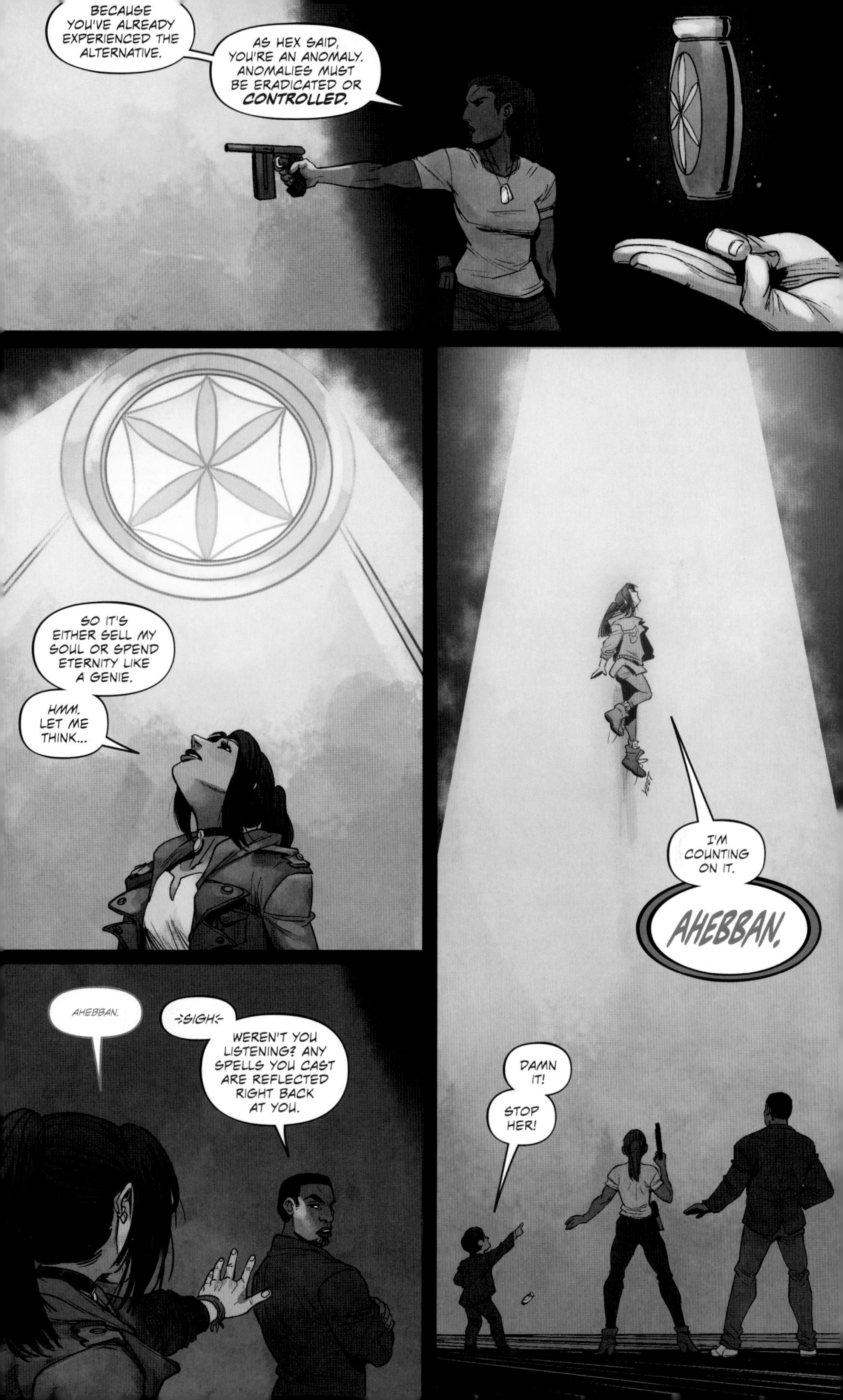

BECAUSE YOU'VE ALREADY EXPERIENCED THE ALTERNATIVE.
AS HEX SAID, YOU'RE AN ANOMALY. ANOMALIES MUST BE ERADICATED OR **CONTROLLED.**
SO IT'S EITHER SELL MY SOUL OR SPEND ETERNITY LIKE A GENIE.
HMM. LET ME THINK...
I'M COUNTING ON IT.
AHEBBAN.
AHEBBAN.
-SIGH-
WEREN'T YOU LISTENING? ANY SPELLS YOU CAST ARE REFLECTED RIGHT BACK AT YOU.
DAMN IT!
STOP HER!

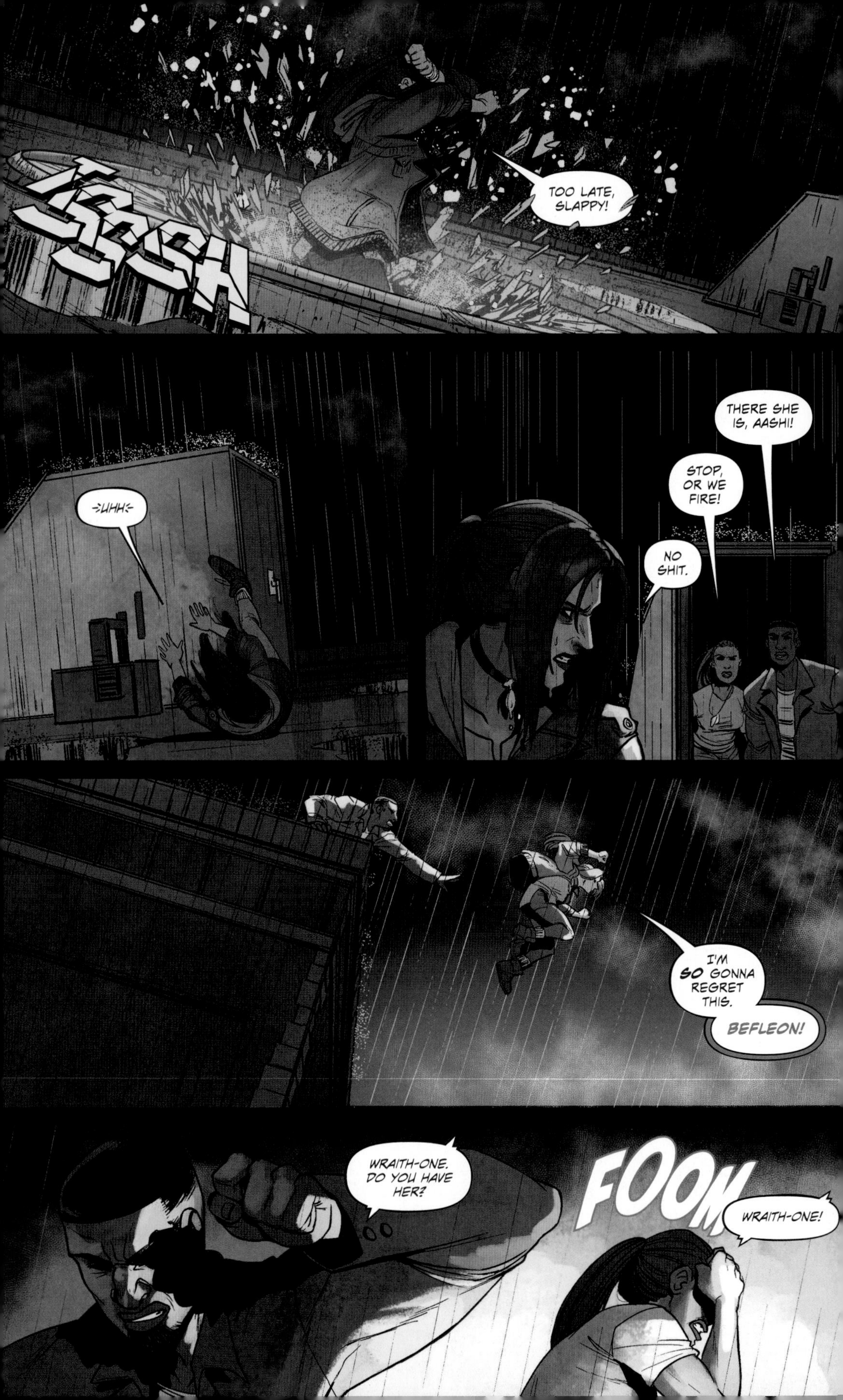
TRASH
TOO LATE, SLAPPY!
UHH
THERE SHE IS, AASHI!
STOP, OR WE FIRE!
NO SHIT.
I'M SO GONNA REGRET THIS.
BEFLEON!
WRAITH-ONE. DO YOU HAVE HER?
FOOM
WRAITH-ONE!

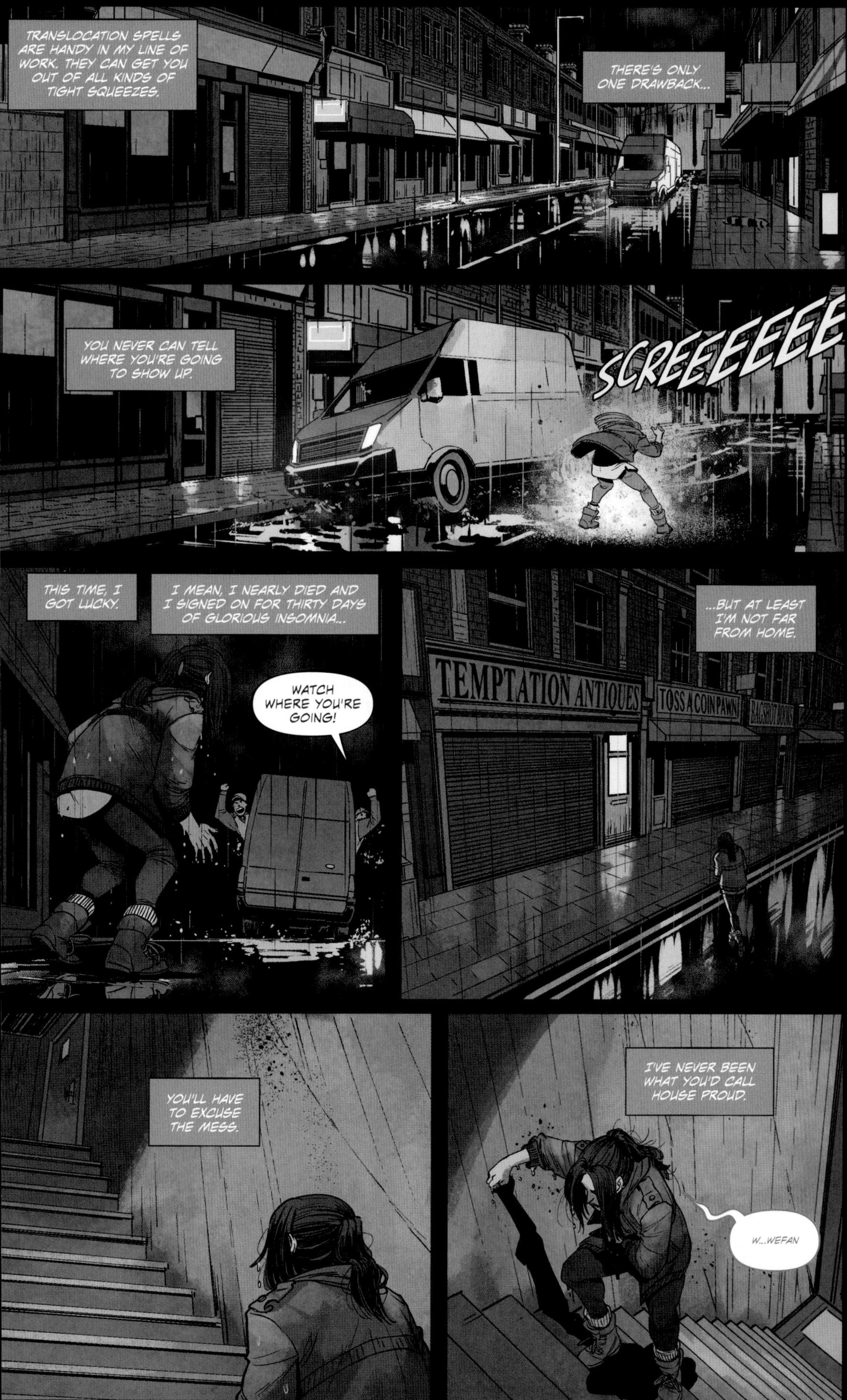
TRANSLOCATION SPELLS ARE HANDY IN MY LINE OF WORK. THEY CAN GET YOU OUT OF ALL KINDS OF TIGHT SQUEEZES.
THERE'S ONLY ONE DRAWBACK...
YOU NEVER CAN TELL WHERE YOU'RE GOING TO SHOW UP.
SCREEEEEEE
THIS TIME, I GOT LUCKY.
I MEAN, I NEARLY DIED AND I SIGNED ON FOR THIRTY DAYS OF GLORIOUS INSOMNIA...
WATCH WHERE YOU'RE GOING!
...BUT AT LEAST I'M NOT FAR FROM HOME.
TEMPTATION ANTIQUES
TOSS A COIN PAWN
BAGSHOT BOOKS
YOU'LL HAVE TO EXCUSE THE MESS.
I'VE NEVER BEEN WHAT YOU'D CALL HOUSE PROUD.
W...WEFAN

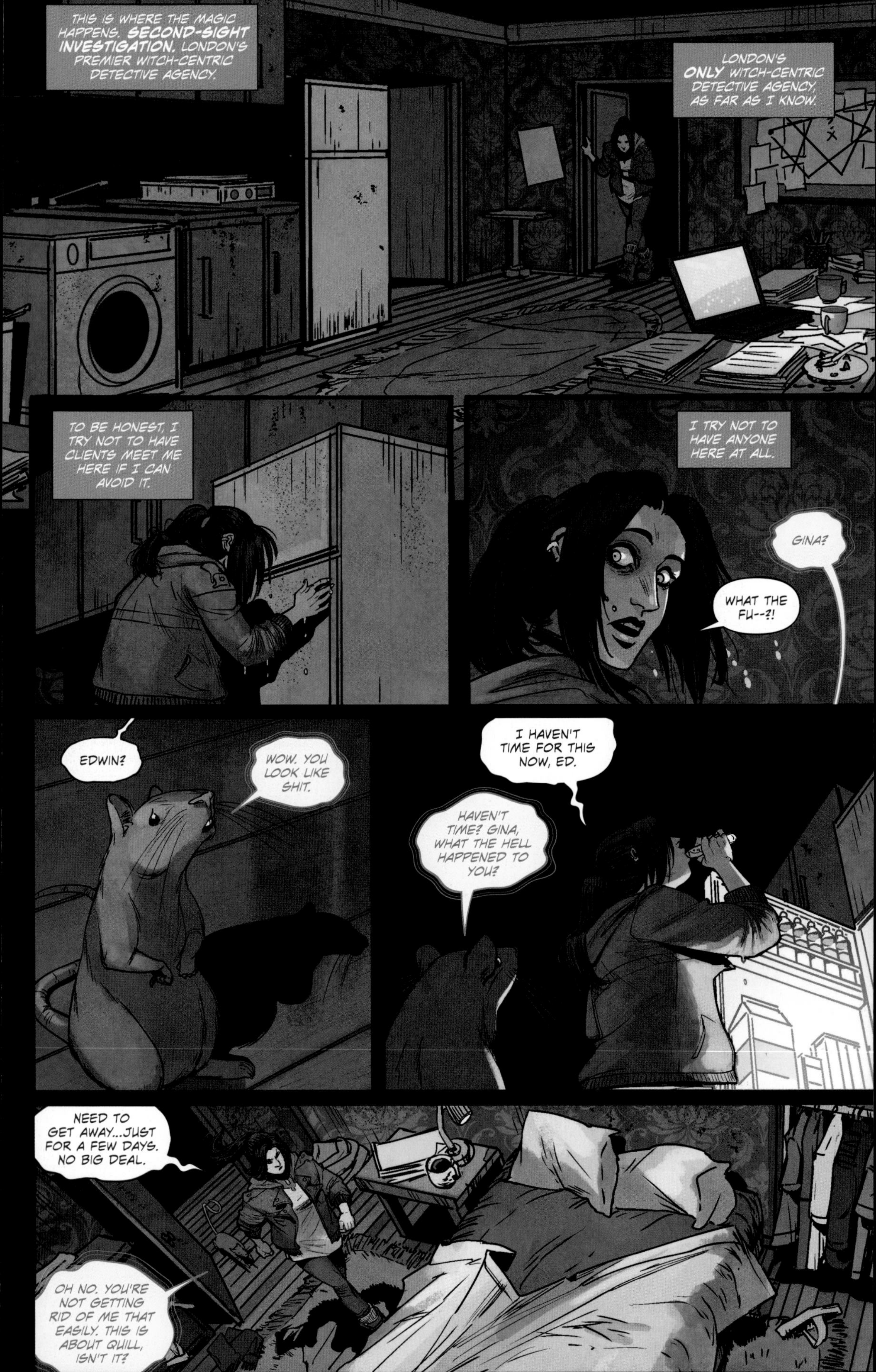
THIS IS WHERE THE MAGIC HAPPENS. SECOND-SIGHT INVESTIGATION. LONDON'S PREMIER WITCH-CENTRIC DETECTIVE AGENCY.
LONDON'S ONLY WITCH-CENTRIC DETECTIVE AGENCY, AS FAR AS I KNOW.
TO BE HONEST, I TRY NOT TO HAVE CLIENTS MEET ME HERE IF I CAN AVOID IT.
I TRY NOT TO HAVE ANYONE HERE AT ALL.
GINA?
WHAT THE FU--?!
EDWIN?
WOW. YOU LOOK LIKE SHIT.
I HAVEN'T TIME FOR THIS NOW, ED.
HAVEN'T TIME? GINA, WHAT THE HELL HAPPENED TO YOU?
NEED TO GET AWAY...JUST FOR A FEW DAYS. NO BIG DEAL.
OH NO. YOU'RE NOT GETTING RID OF ME THAT EASILY. THIS IS ABOUT QUILL, ISN'T IT?

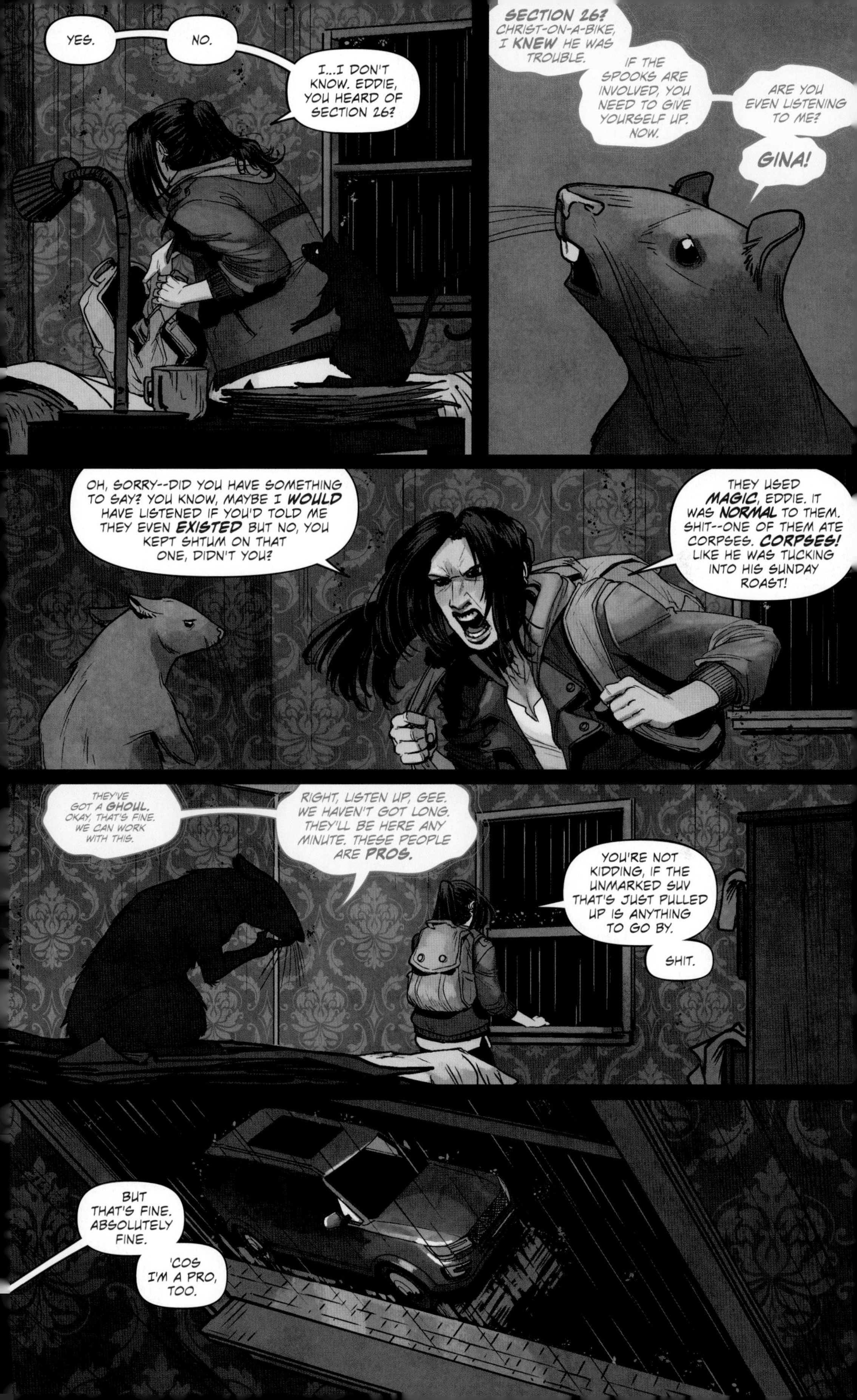
YES.
NO.
I...I DON'T KNOW. EDDIE, YOU HEARD OF SECTION 26?
SECTION 26? CHRIST-ON-A-BIKE, I KNEW HE WAS TROUBLE.
IF THE SPOOKS ARE INVOLVED, YOU NEED TO GIVE YOURSELF UP. NOW.
ARE YOU EVEN LISTENING TO ME?
GINA!
OH, SORRY--DID YOU HAVE SOMETHING TO SAY? YOU KNOW, MAYBE I WOULD HAVE LISTENED IF YOU'D TOLD ME THEY EVEN EXISTED BUT NO, YOU KEPT SHTUM ON THAT ONE, DIDN'T YOU?
THEY USED MAGIC, EDDIE. IT WAS NORMAL TO THEM. SHIT--ONE OF THEM ATE CORPSES. CORPSES! LIKE HE WAS TUCKING INTO HIS SUNDAY ROAST!
THEY'VE GOT A GHOUL. OKAY, THAT'S FINE. WE CAN WORK WITH THIS.
RIGHT, LISTEN UP, GEE. WE HAVEN'T GOT LONG. THEY'LL BE HERE ANY MINUTE. THESE PEOPLE ARE PROS.
YOU'RE NOT KIDDING, IF THE UNMARKED SUV THAT'S JUST PULLED UP IS ANYTHING TO GO BY.
SHIT.
BUT THAT'S FINE. ABSOLUTELY FINE.
'COS I'M A PRO, TOO.

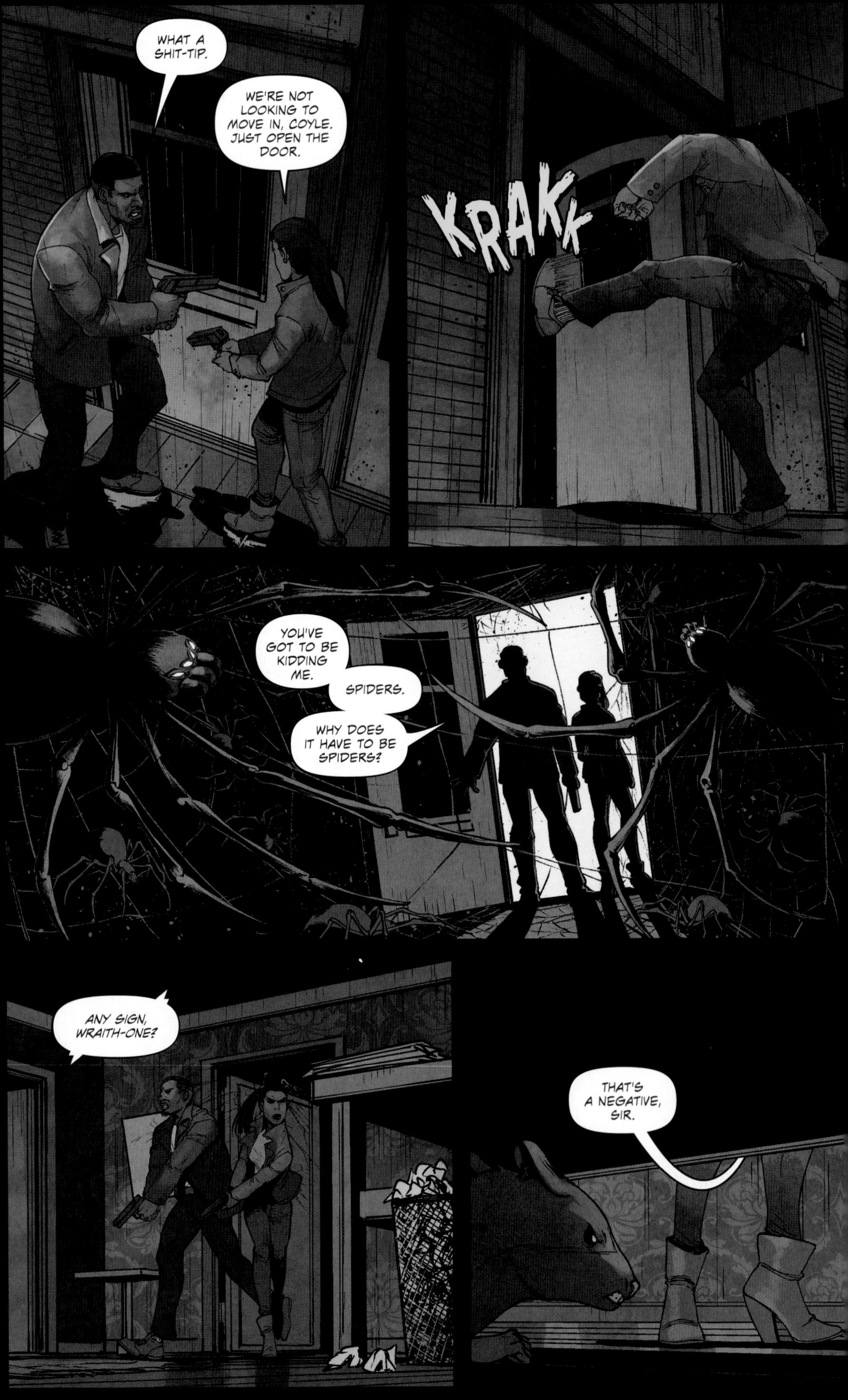

WHAT A SHIT-TIP.
WE'RE NOT LOOKING TO MOVE IN, COYLE. JUST OPEN THE DOOR.
KRAKK
YOU'VE GOT TO BE KIDDING ME.
SPIDERS.
WHY DOES IT HAVE TO BE SPIDERS?
ANY SIGN, WRAITH-ONE?
THAT'S A NEGATIVE, SIR.

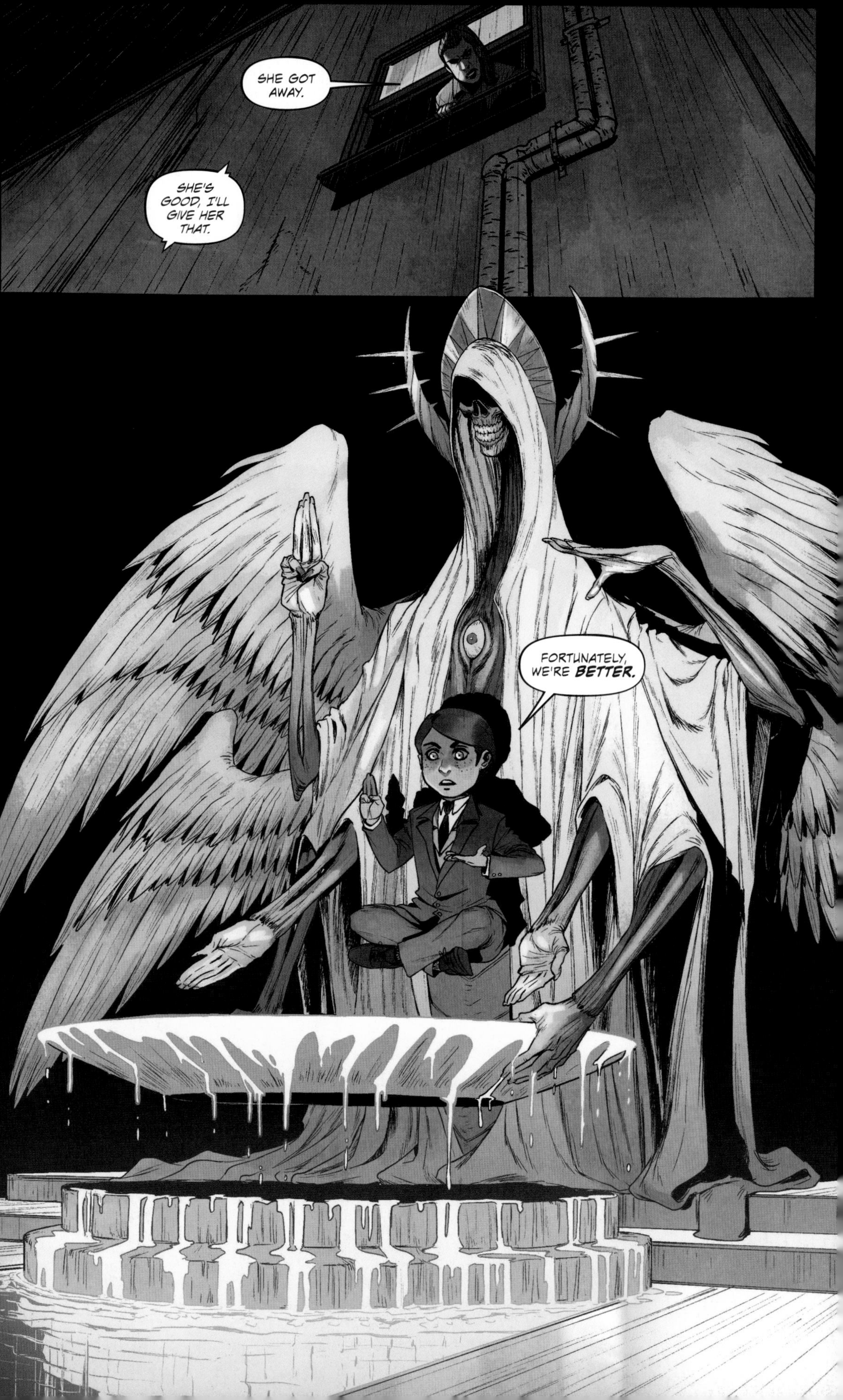
SHE GOT AWAY.
SHE'S GOOD, I'LL GIVE HER THAT.
FORTUNATELY, WE'RE BETTER.

I KNOW WHAT IT LOOKS LIKE. THAT I'M RUNNING AWAY.

BUT IT'S NOT LIKE WHEN I WAS A KID. THIS IS DIFFERENT.

THIS IS LAYING LOW. IT'S A P.I. THING. NOT THE SAME AT ALL.

MISS MEYER?

OH...H-HI, REBECCA. LOOK, THIS ISN'T A GREAT TIME--

IT'S ABOUT COLIN.

YOU'VE HEARD FROM HIM?

NO, BUT MY FRIEND SALLY... SHE SPOTTED HIM ON A NEWS REPORT ONLINE.

HANG ON. I'LL SEND IT OVER.

A NEWS REPORT?

OKAY. GOT IT. WOW.

I'M ASSUMING THIS ISN'T EXACTLY USUAL.

USUAL?

TING

IT SAYS THE POLICE WANT HIM FOR FOOTBALL HOOLIGANISM, OF ALL THINGS. I DON'T GET IT. COLIN DOESN'T EVEN LIKE FOOTBALL.

WHY MANCHESTER? DOES HE KNOW ANYONE UP THERE?

NOT THAT I KNOW.

FOOTBALL VIO OLD TRAFFE

THEN I BETTER FIND OUT.

YOU'LL GO?

'COURSE. ALL PART OF THE SERVICE.

⇋ ⊖Eust

⇋ ⊖Euston Station

SEE? IT'S NOT RUNNING AWAY IF YOU'RE WORKING, RIGHT?

BESIDES, BLACK MAGIC OPS OR NOT, I GAVE REBECCA MY WORD...

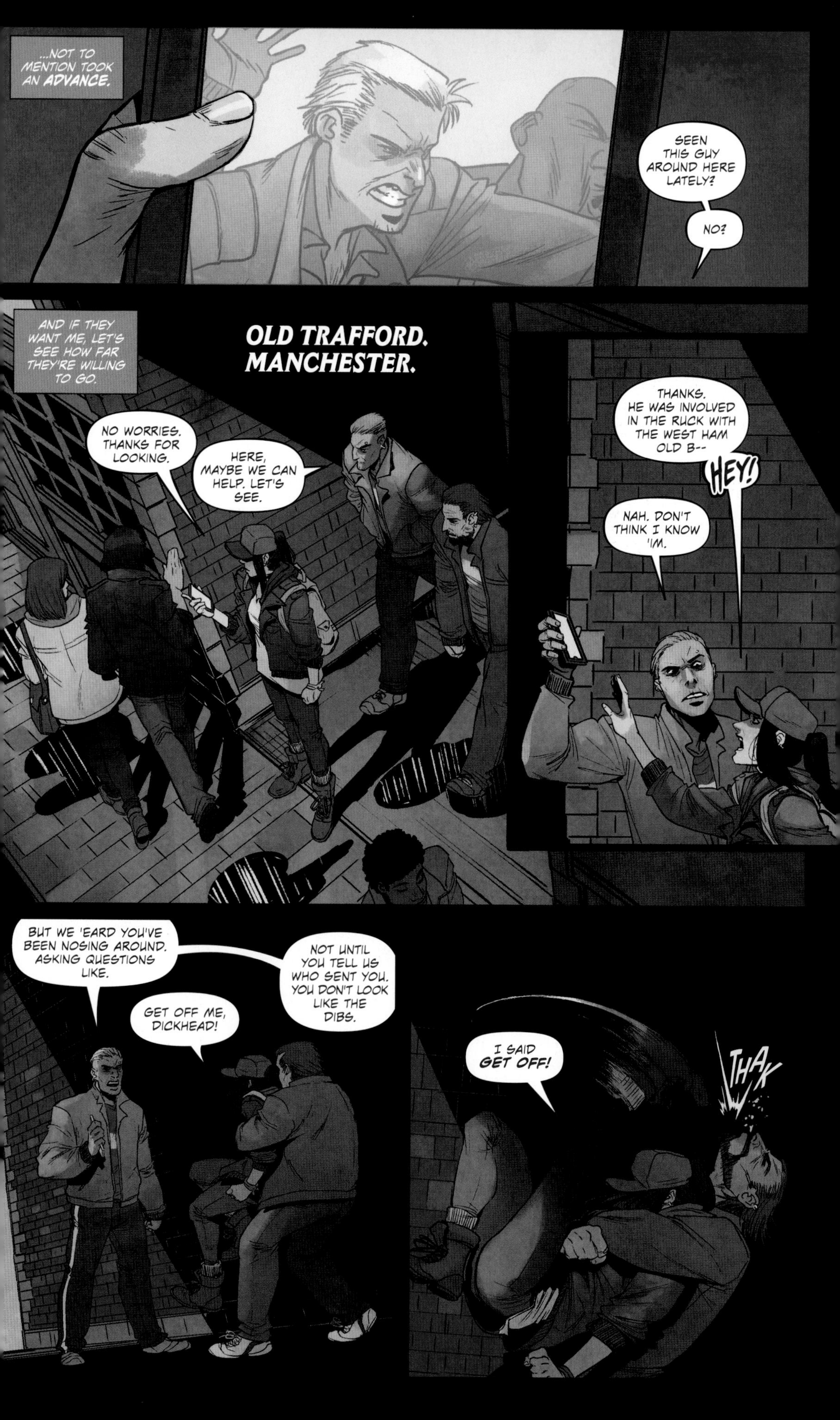
...NOT TO MENTION TOOK AN ADVANCE.
SEEN THIS GUY AROUND HERE LATELY?
NO?
AND IF THEY WANT ME, LET'S SEE HOW FAR THEY'RE WILLING TO GO.
OLD TRAFFORD. MANCHESTER.
NO WORRIES. THANKS FOR LOOKING.
HERE, MAYBE WE CAN HELP. LET'S SEE.
THANKS. HE WAS INVOLVED IN THE RUCK WITH THE WEST HAM OLD B--
HEY!
NAH. DON'T THINK I KNOW 'IM.
BUT WE 'EARD YOU'VE BEEN NOSING AROUND. ASKING QUESTIONS LIKE.
GET OFF ME, DICKHEAD!
NOT UNTIL YOU TELL US WHO SENT YOU. YOU DON'T LOOK LIKE THE DIBS.
I SAID GET OFF!
THAK

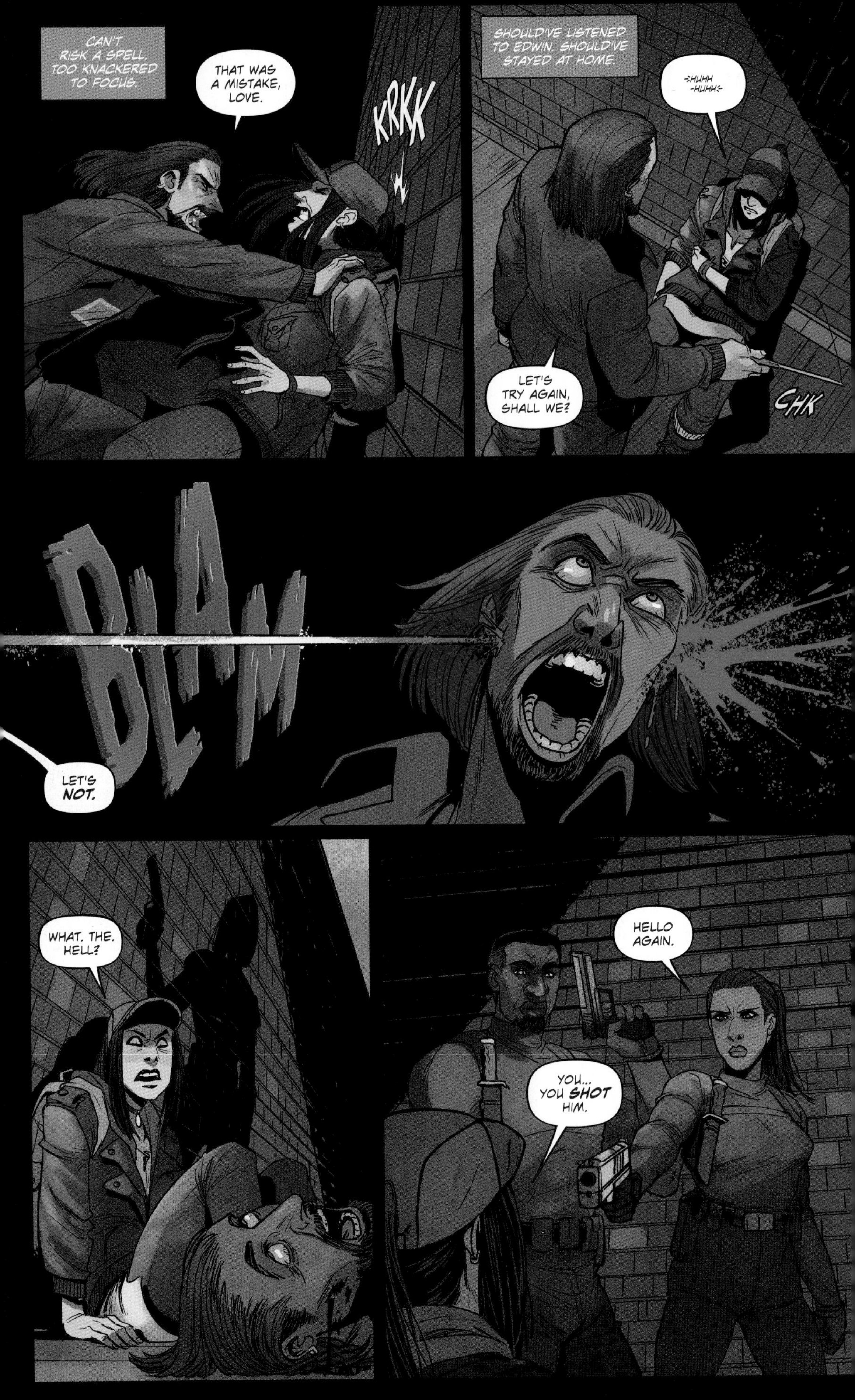
CAN'T RISK A SPELL. TOO KNACKERED TO FOCUS.
THAT WAS A MISTAKE, LOVE.
KRKK
SHOULD'VE LISTENED TO EDWIN. SHOULD'VE STAYED AT HOME.
-HUHH -HUHH-
LET'S TRY AGAIN, SHALL WE?
CHK
BLAM
LET'S NOT.
WHAT. THE. HELL?
HELLO AGAIN.
YOU... YOU SHOT HIM.

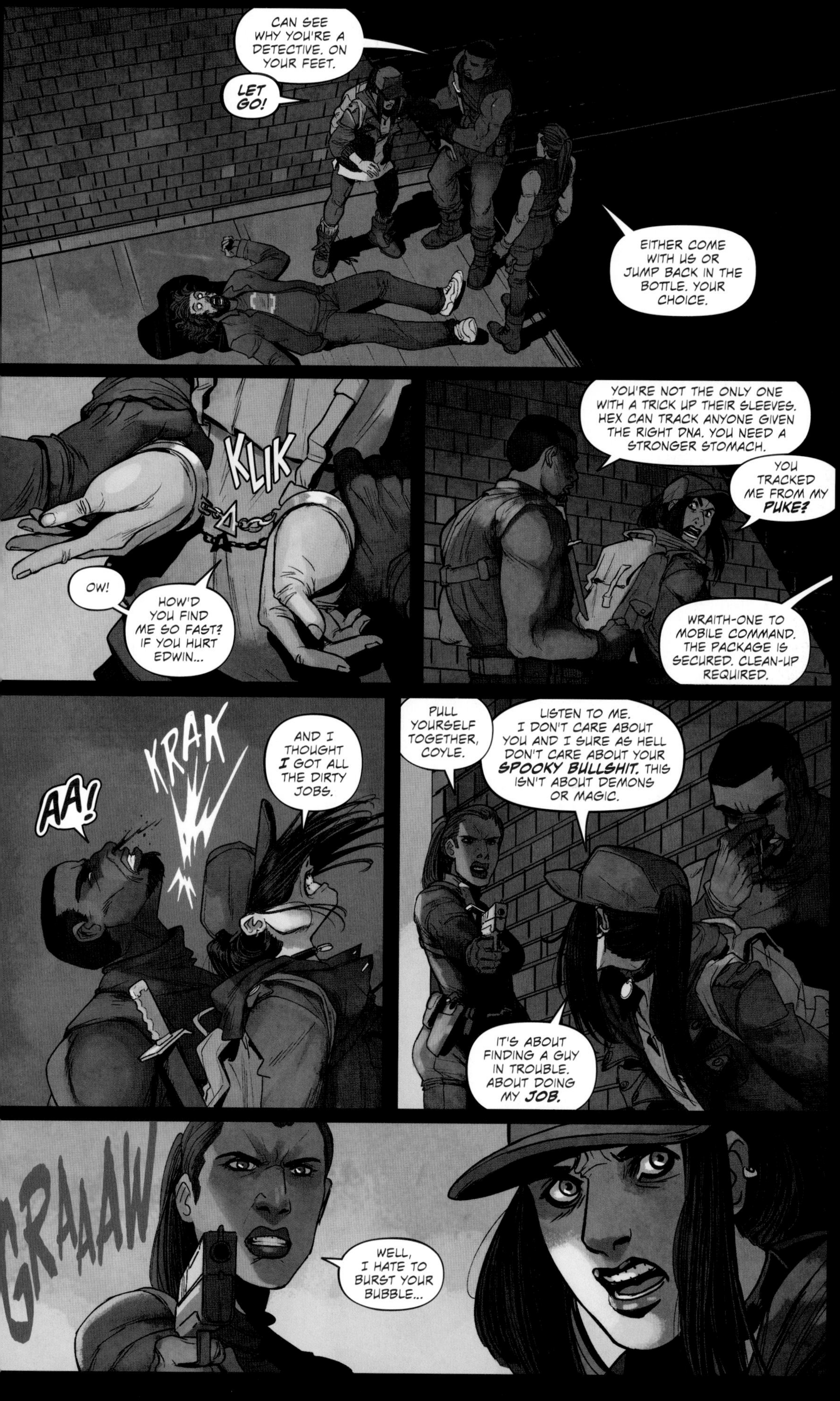
CAN SEE WHY YOU'RE A DETECTIVE. ON YOUR FEET.
LET GO!
EITHER COME WITH US OR JUMP BACK IN THE BOTTLE. YOUR CHOICE.
KLIK
OW!
HOW'D YOU FIND ME SO FAST? IF YOU HURT EDWIN...
YOU'RE NOT THE ONLY ONE WITH A TRICK UP THEIR SLEEVES. HEX CAN TRACK ANYONE GIVEN THE RIGHT DNA. YOU NEED A STRONGER STOMACH.
YOU TRACKED ME FROM MY PUKE?
WRAITH-ONE TO MOBILE COMMAND. THE PACKAGE IS SECURED. CLEAN-UP REQUIRED.
AA!
KRAK
AND I THOUGHT I GOT ALL THE DIRTY JOBS.
PULL YOURSELF TOGETHER, COYLE.
LISTEN TO ME. I DON'T CARE ABOUT YOU AND I SURE AS HELL DON'T CARE ABOUT YOUR SPOOKY BULLSHIT. THIS ISN'T ABOUT DEMONS OR MAGIC.
IT'S ABOUT FINDING A GUY IN TROUBLE. ABOUT DOING MY JOB.
GRAAAW
WELL, I HATE TO BURST YOUR BUBBLE...

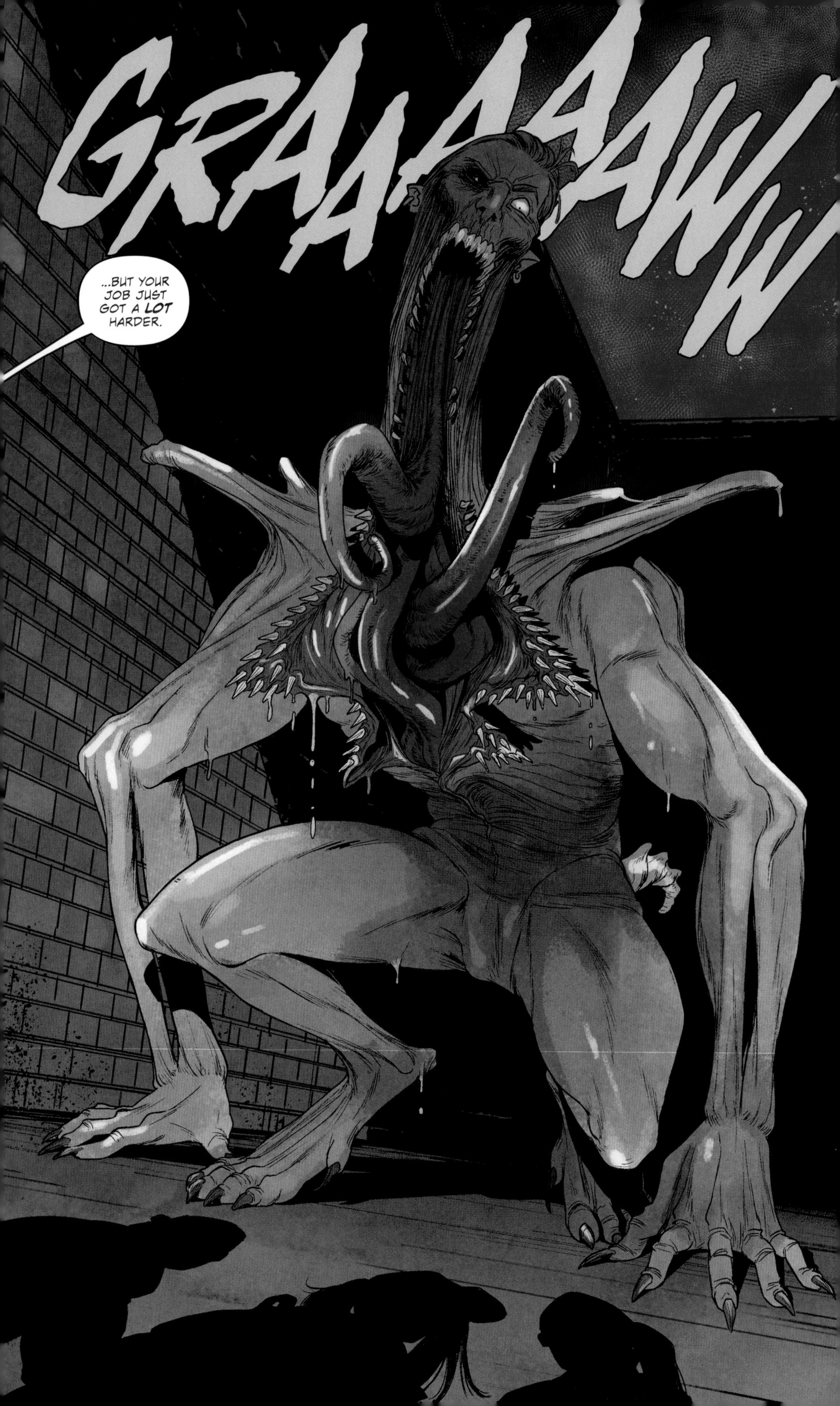
GRAAAAAWW
...BUT YOUR JOB JUST GOT A **LOT** HARDER.

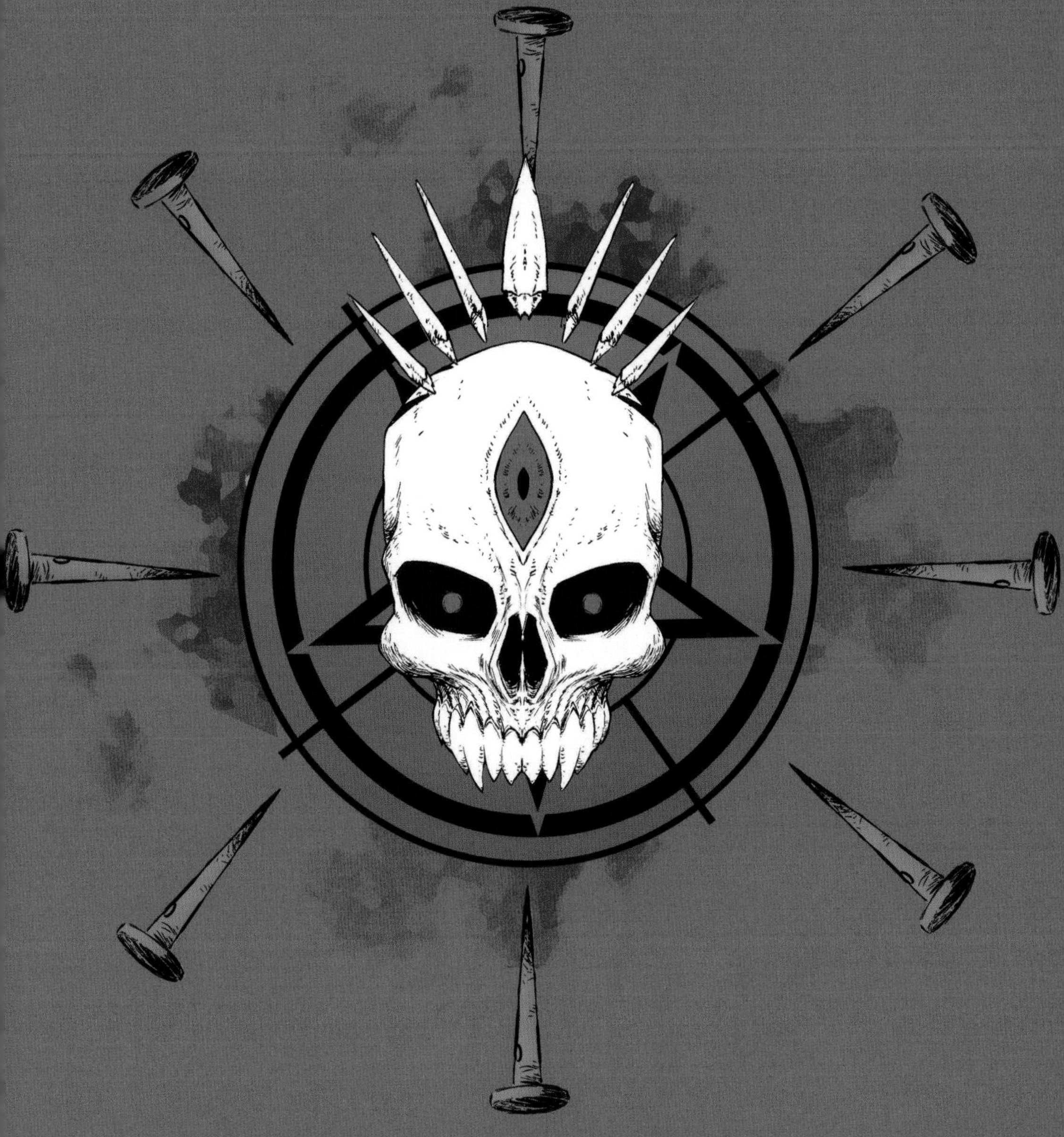

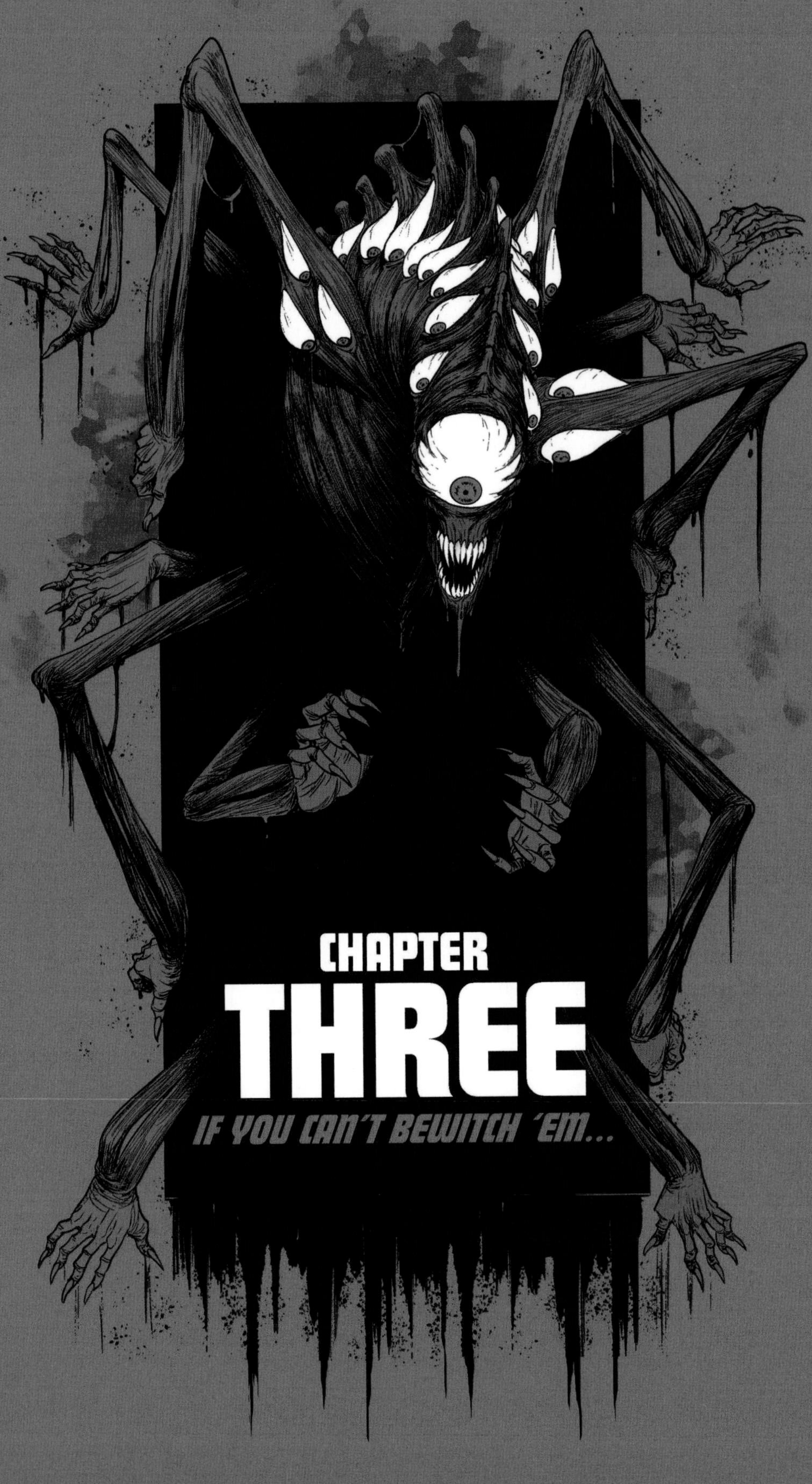

CHAPTER THREE

IF YOU CAN'T BEWITCH 'EM...

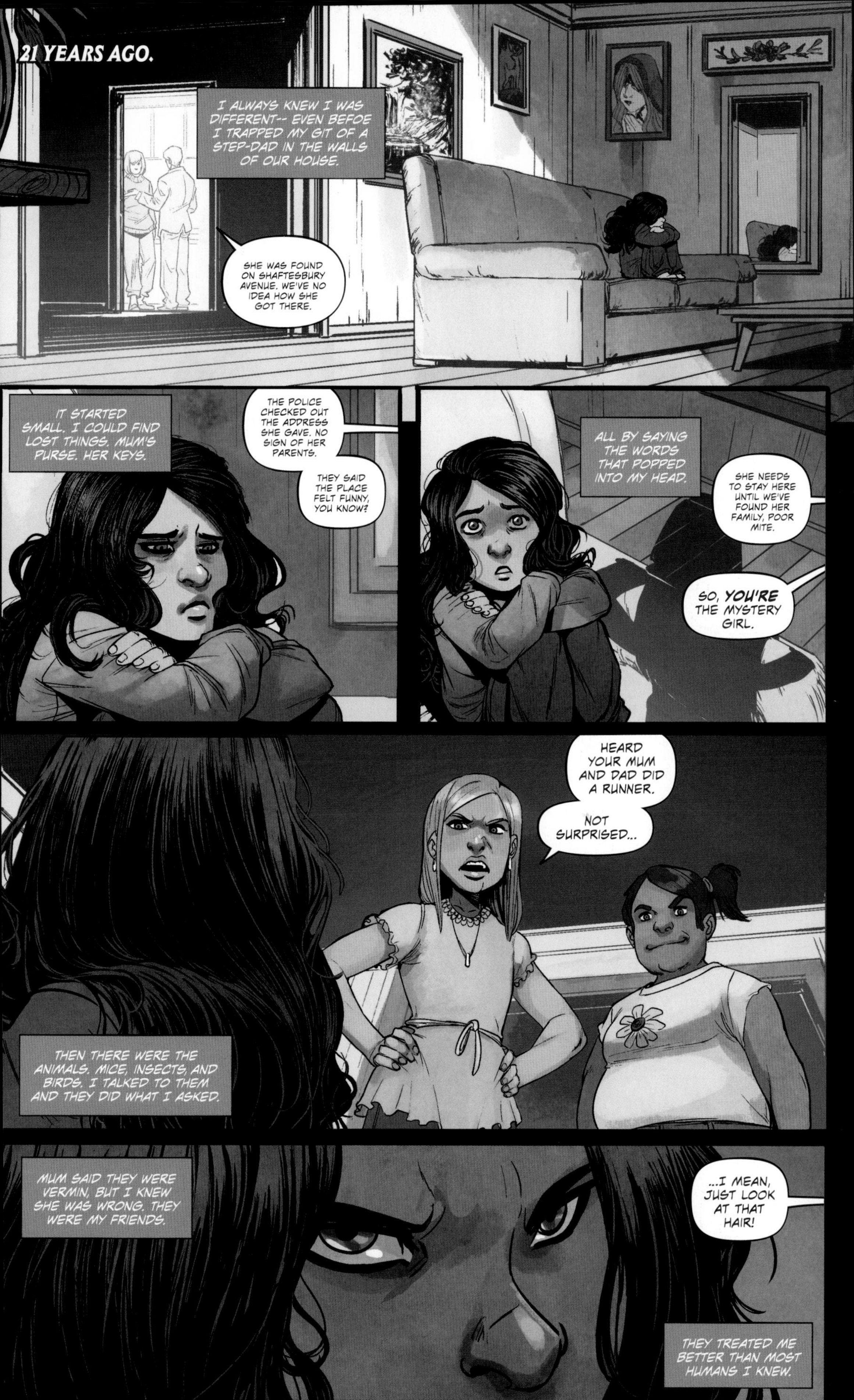
21 YEARS AGO.
I ALWAYS KNEW I WAS DIFFERENT-- EVEN BEFOE I TRAPPED MY GIT OF A STEP-DAD IN THE WALLS OF OUR HOUSE.
SHE WAS FOUND ON SHAFTESBURY AVENUE. WE'VE NO IDEA HOW SHE GOT THERE.
IT STARTED SMALL. I COULD FIND LOST THINGS. MUM'S PURSE. HER KEYS.
THE POLICE CHECKED OUT THE ADDRESS SHE GAVE. NO SIGN OF HER PARENTS.
THEY SAID THE PLACE FELT FUNNY, YOU KNOW?
ALL BY SAYING THE WORDS THAT POPPED INTO MY HEAD.
SHE NEEDS TO STAY HERE UNTIL WE'VE FOUND HER FAMILY, POOR MITE.
SO, YOU'RE THE MYSTERY GIRL.
HEARD YOUR MUM AND DAD DID A RUNNER.
NOT SURPRISED...
THEN THERE WERE THE ANIMALS. MICE, INSECTS, AND BIRDS. I TALKED TO THEM AND THEY DID WHAT I ASKED.
MUM SAID THEY WERE VERMIN, BUT I KNEW SHE WAS WRONG. THEY WERE MY FRIENDS.
...I MEAN, JUST LOOK AT THAT HAIR!
THEY TREATED ME BETTER THAN MOST HUMANS I KNEW.

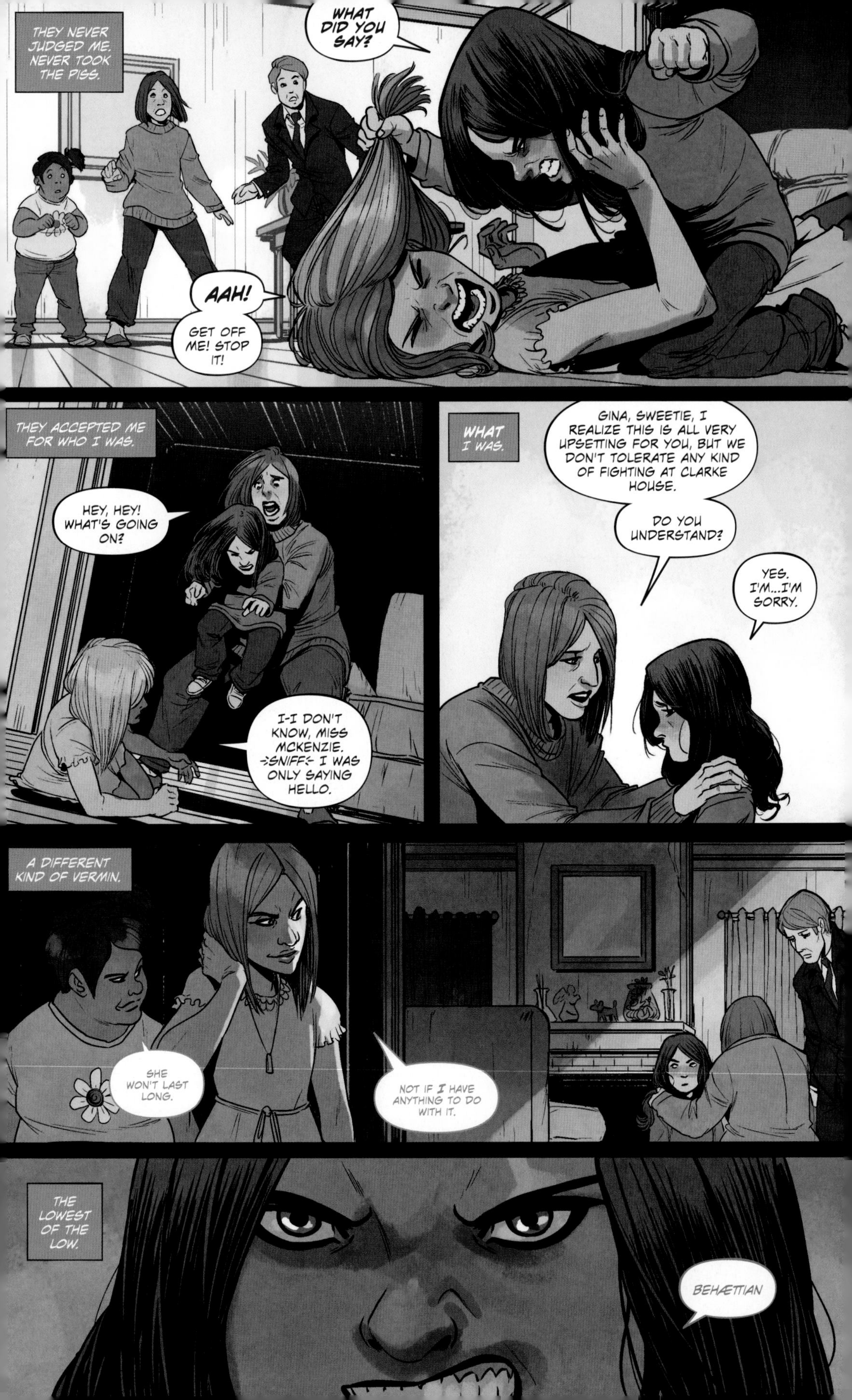
THEY NEVER JUDGED ME. NEVER TOOK THE PISS.
WHAT DID YOU SAY?
AAH!
GET OFF ME! STOP IT!
THEY ACCEPTED ME FOR WHO I WAS.
HEY, HEY! WHAT'S GOING ON?
I-I DON'T KNOW, MISS MCKENZIE. *SNIFF* I WAS ONLY SAYING HELLO.
WHAT I WAS.
GINA, SWEETIE, I REALIZE THIS IS ALL VERY UPSETTING FOR YOU, BUT WE DON'T TOLERATE ANY KIND OF FIGHTING AT CLARKE HOUSE.
DO YOU UNDERSTAND?
YES. I'M...I'M SORRY.
A DIFFERENT KIND OF VERMIN.
SHE WON'T LAST LONG.
NOT IF I HAVE ANYTHING TO DO WITH IT.
THE LOWEST OF THE LOW.
BEHÆTTIAN

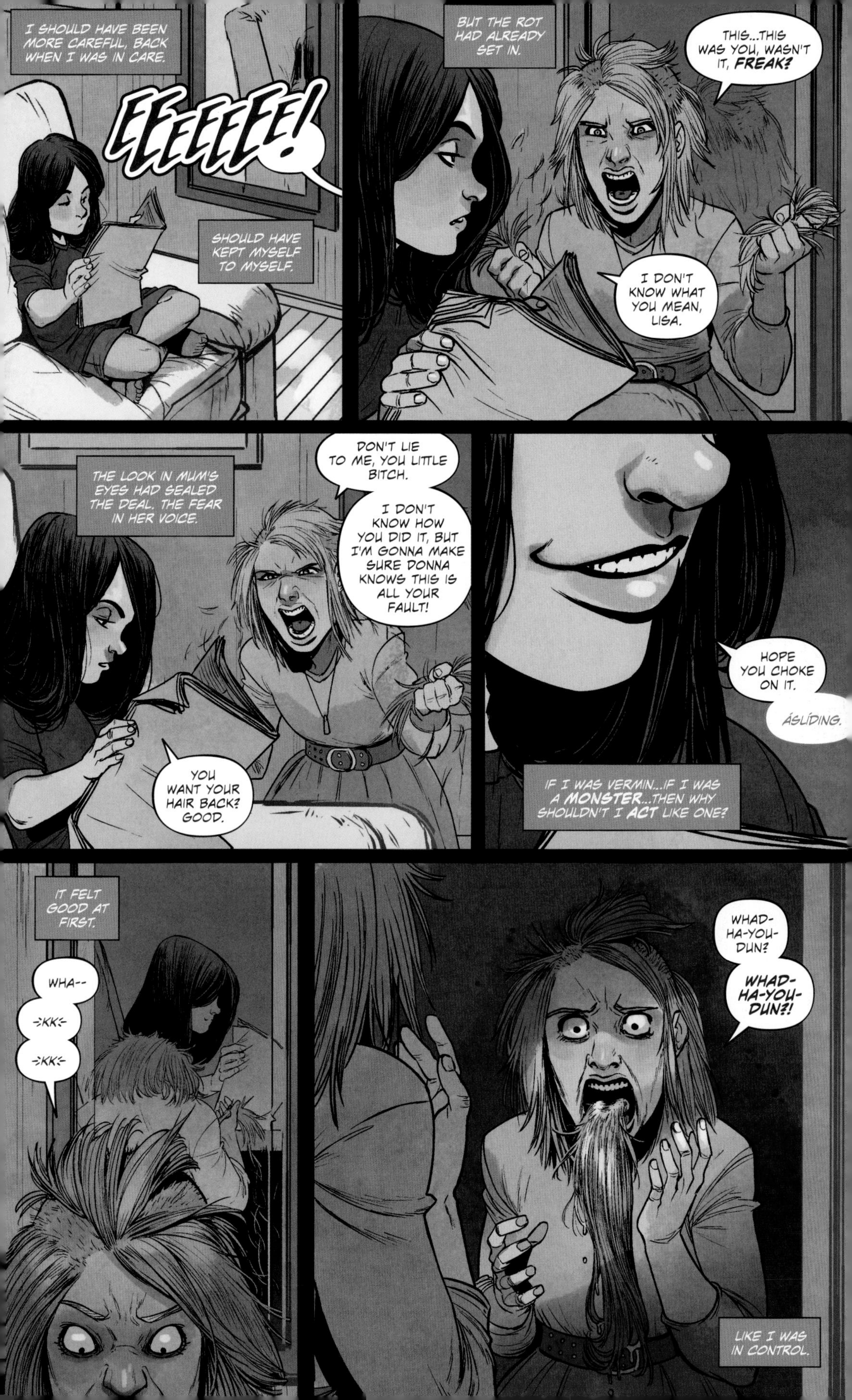
I SHOULD HAVE BEEN MORE CAREFUL, BACK WHEN I WAS IN CARE.
EEEEEEE!
SHOULD HAVE KEPT MYSELF TO MYSELF.
BUT THE ROT HAD ALREADY SET IN.
THIS...THIS WAS YOU, WASN'T IT, FREAK?
I DON'T KNOW WHAT YOU MEAN, LISA.
THE LOOK IN MUM'S EYES HAD SEALED THE DEAL. THE FEAR IN HER VOICE.
DON'T LIE TO ME, YOU LITTLE BITCH.
I DON'T KNOW HOW YOU DID IT, BUT I'M GONNA MAKE SURE DONNA KNOWS THIS IS ALL YOUR FAULT!
YOU WANT YOUR HAIR BACK? GOOD.
HOPE YOU CHOKE ON IT.
ÁSLÍDING.
IF I WAS VERMIN...IF I WAS A MONSTER...THEN WHY SHOULDN'T I ACT LIKE ONE?
IT FELT GOOD AT FIRST.
WHA--
KK
KK
WHAD-HA-YOU-DUN?
WHAD-HA-YOU-DUN?!
LIKE I WAS IN CONTROL.

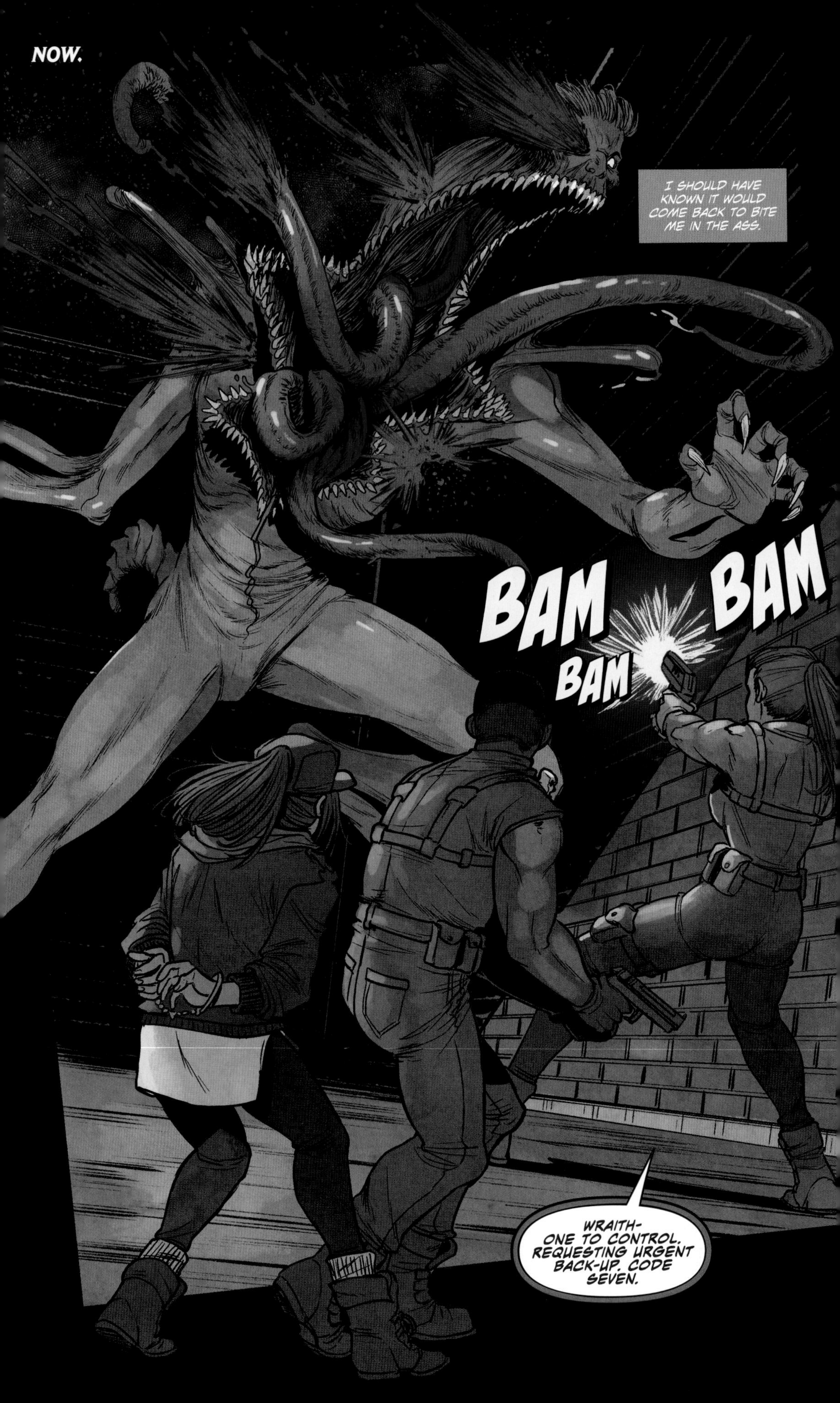
NOW.
I SHOULD HAVE KNOWN IT WOULD COME BACK TO BITE ME IN THE ASS.
BAM
BAM
BAM
WRAITH-ONE TO CONTROL. REQUESTING URGENT BACK-UP. CODE SEVEN.

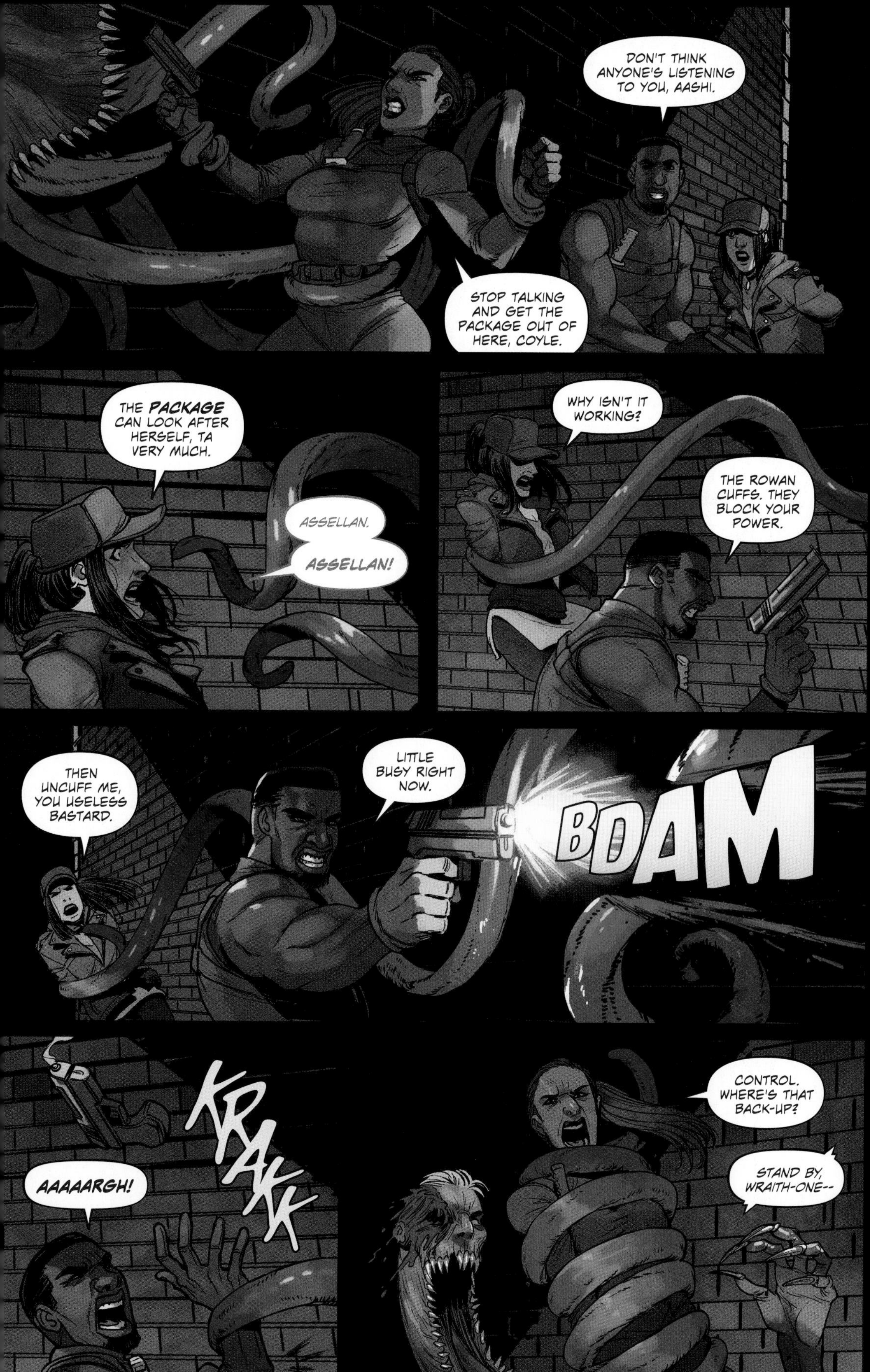
DON'T THINK ANYONE'S LISTENING TO YOU, AASHI.
STOP TALKING AND GET THE PACKAGE OUT OF HERE, COYLE.
THE **PACKAGE** CAN LOOK AFTER HERSELF, TA VERY MUCH.
ASSELLAN.
ASSELLAN!
WHY ISN'T IT WORKING?
THE ROWAN CUFFS. THEY BLOCK YOUR POWER.
THEN UNCUFF ME, YOU USELESS BASTARD.
LITTLE BUSY RIGHT NOW.
BDAM
KRAKK
AAAAARGH!
CONTROL. WHERE'S THAT BACK-UP?
STAND BY, WRAITH-ONE--

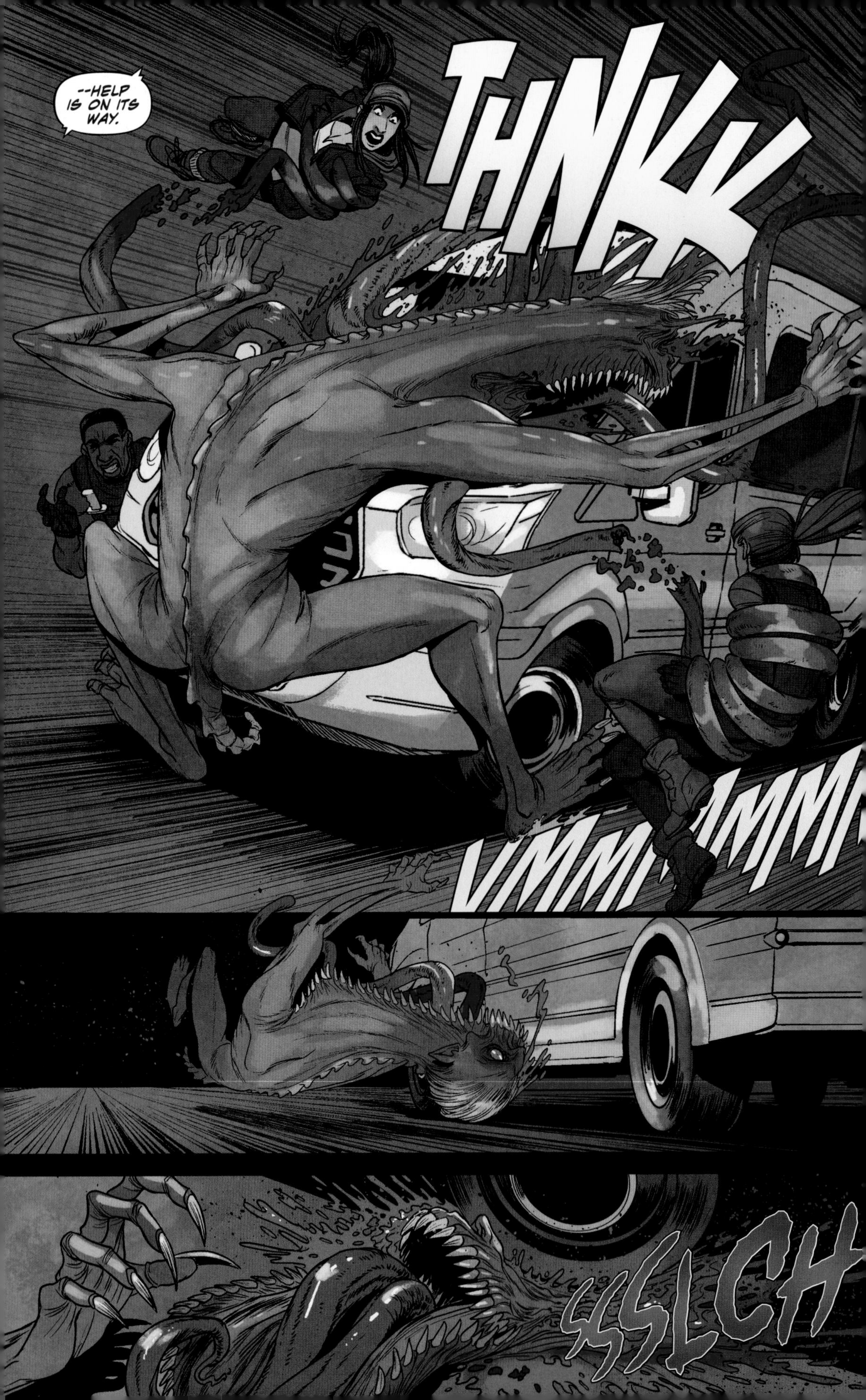
--HELP IS ON ITS WAY.
THNKK
VMMMMMMM
SSSLCH

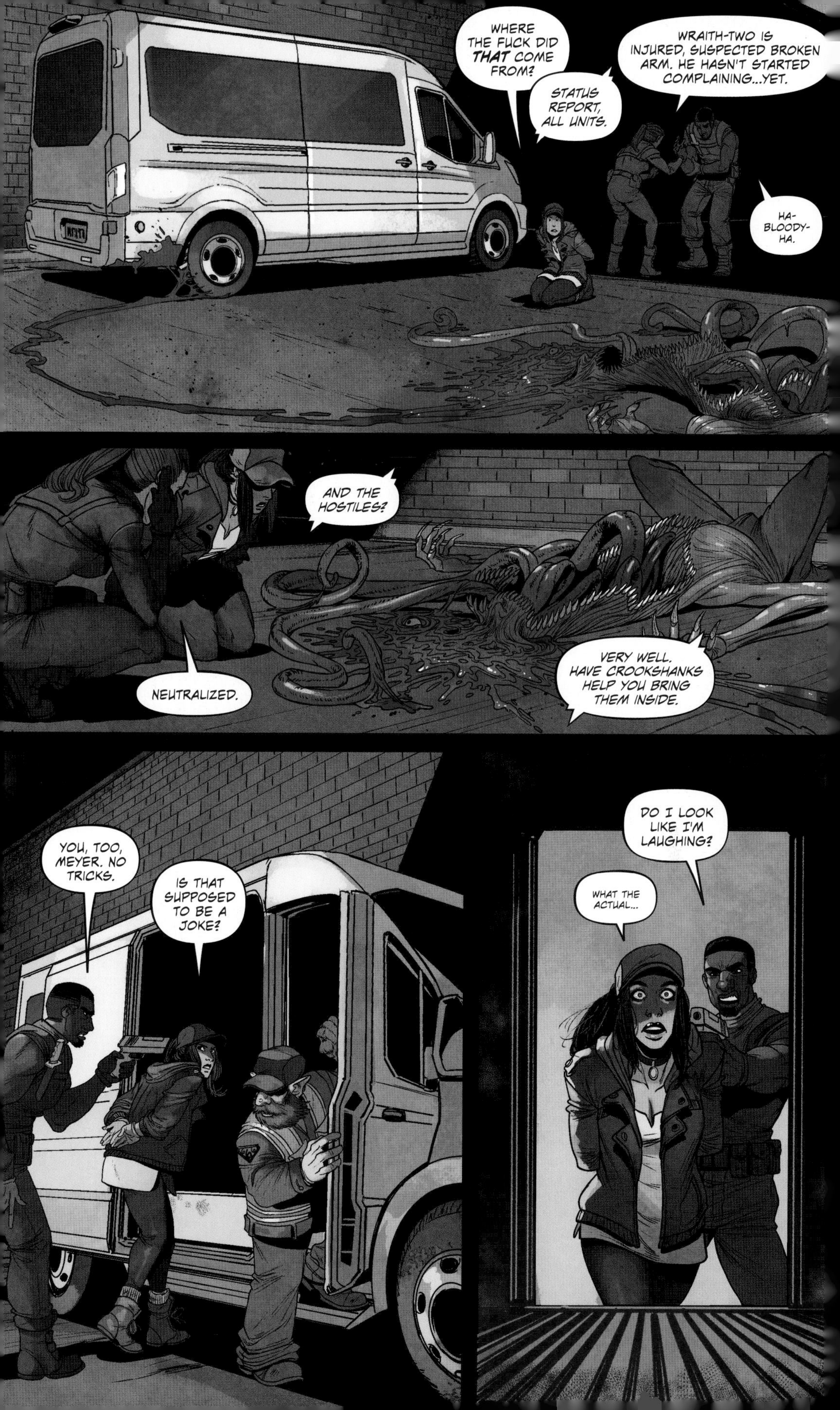
WHERE THE FUCK DID THAT COME FROM?
STATUS REPORT, ALL UNITS.
WRAITH-TWO IS INJURED, SUSPECTED BROKEN ARM. HE HASN'T STARTED COMPLAINING...YET.
HA-BLOODY-HA.
AND THE HOSTILES?
NEUTRALIZED.
VERY WELL. HAVE CROOKSHANKS HELP YOU BRING THEM INSIDE.
YOU, TOO, MEYER. NO TRICKS.
IS THAT SUPPOSED TO BE A JOKE?
DO I LOOK LIKE I'M LAUGHING?
WHAT THE ACTUAL...

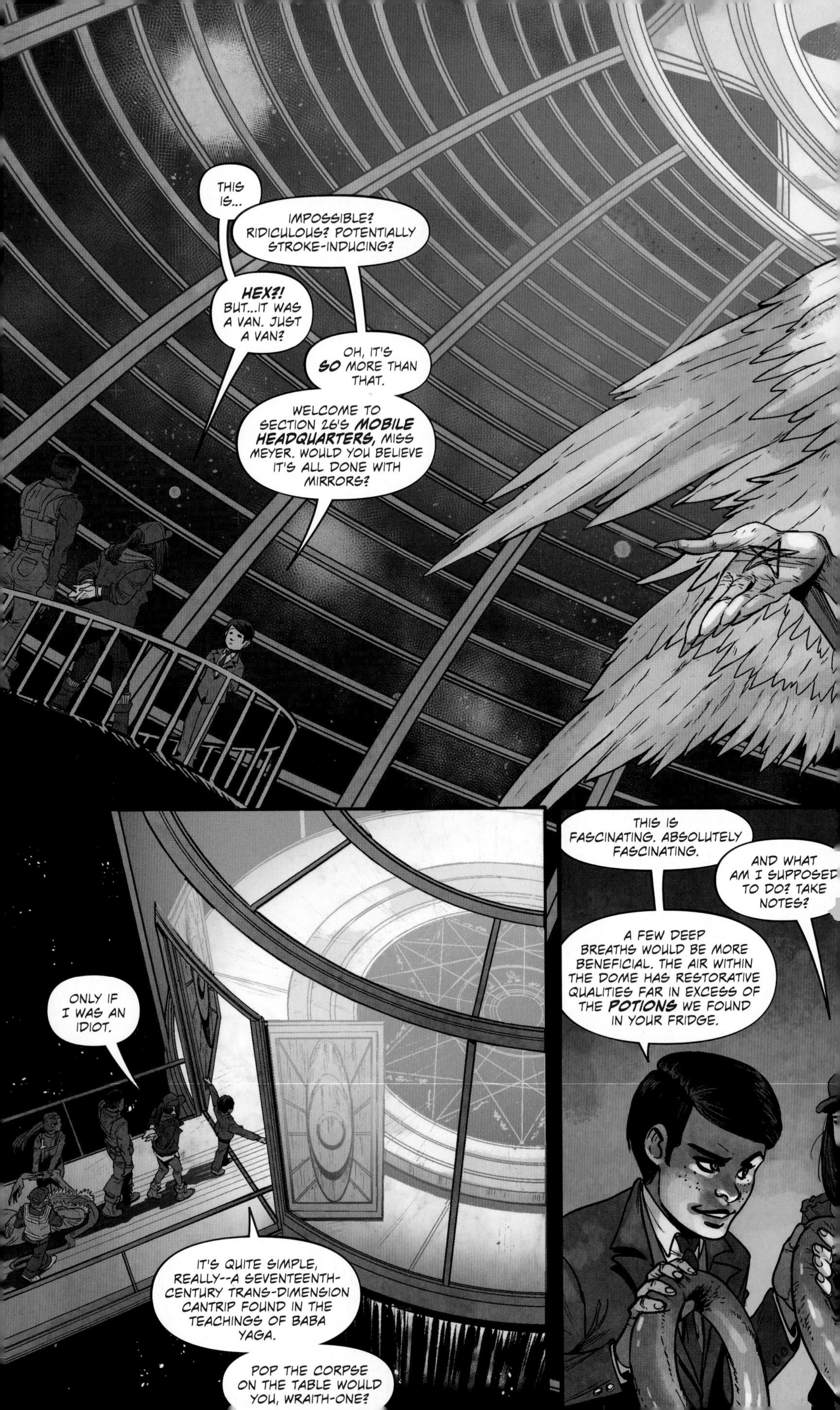
THIS IS...
IMPOSSIBLE? RIDICULOUS? POTENTIALLY STROKE-INDUCING?
HEX?! BUT...IT WAS A VAN. JUST A VAN?
OH, IT'S SO MORE THAN THAT.
WELCOME TO SECTION 26'S MOBILE HEADQUARTERS, MISS MEYER. WOULD YOU BELIEVE IT'S ALL DONE WITH MIRRORS?
ONLY IF I WAS AN IDIOT.
IT'S QUITE SIMPLE, REALLY--A SEVENTEENTH-CENTURY TRANS-DIMENSION CANTRIP FOUND IN THE TEACHINGS OF BABA YAGA.
POP THE CORPSE ON THE TABLE WOULD YOU, WRAITH-ONE?
THIS IS FASCINATING. ABSOLUTELY FASCINATING.
AND WHAT AM I SUPPOSED TO DO? TAKE NOTES?
A FEW DEEP BREATHS WOULD BE MORE BENEFICIAL. THE AIR WITHIN THE DOME HAS RESTORATIVE QUALITIES FAR IN EXCESS OF THE POTIONS WE FOUND IN YOUR FRIDGE.

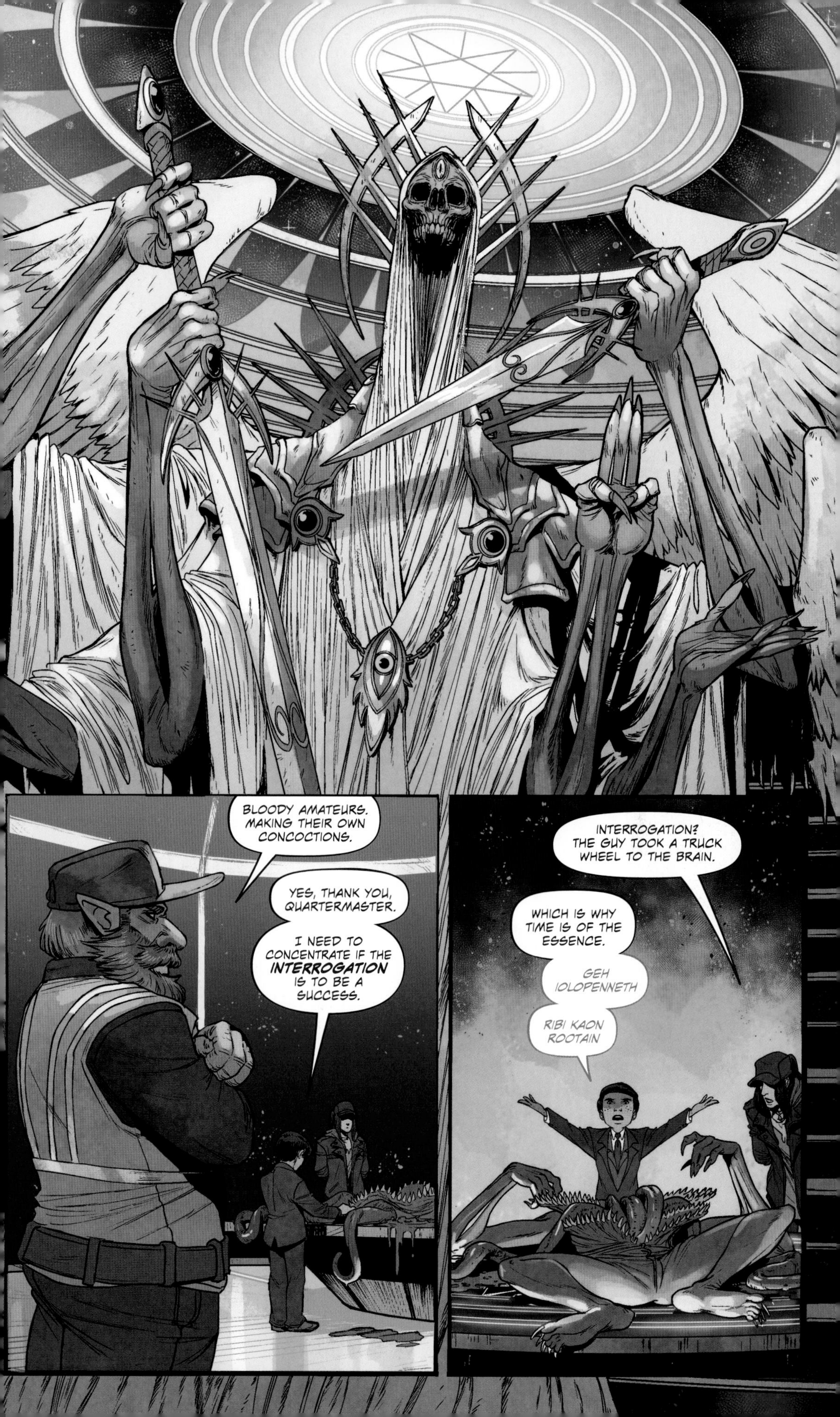
BLOODY AMATEURS. MAKING THEIR OWN CONCOCTIONS.
YES, THANK YOU, QUARTERMASTER.
I NEED TO CONCENTRATE IF THE INTERROGATION IS TO BE A SUCCESS.
INTERROGATION? THE GUY TOOK A TRUCK WHEEL TO THE BRAIN.
WHICH IS WHY TIME IS OF THE ESSENCE.
GEH IOLOPENNETH
RIBI KAON ROOTAIN

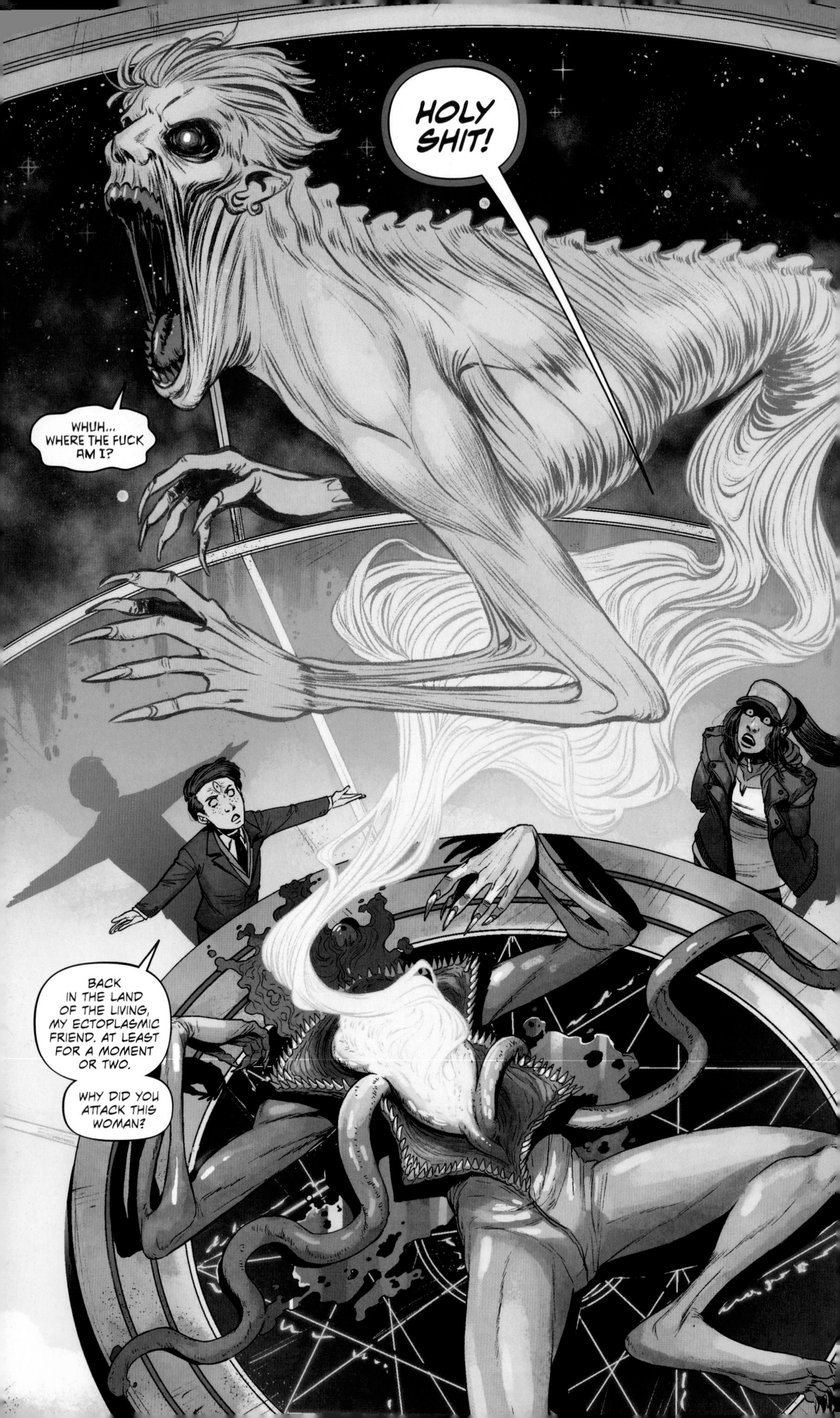
HOLY SHIT!
WHUH... WHERE THE FUCK AM I?
BACK IN THE LAND OF THE LIVING, MY ECTOPLASMIC FRIEND. AT LEAST FOR A MOMENT OR TWO.
WHY DID YOU ATTACK THIS WOMAN?

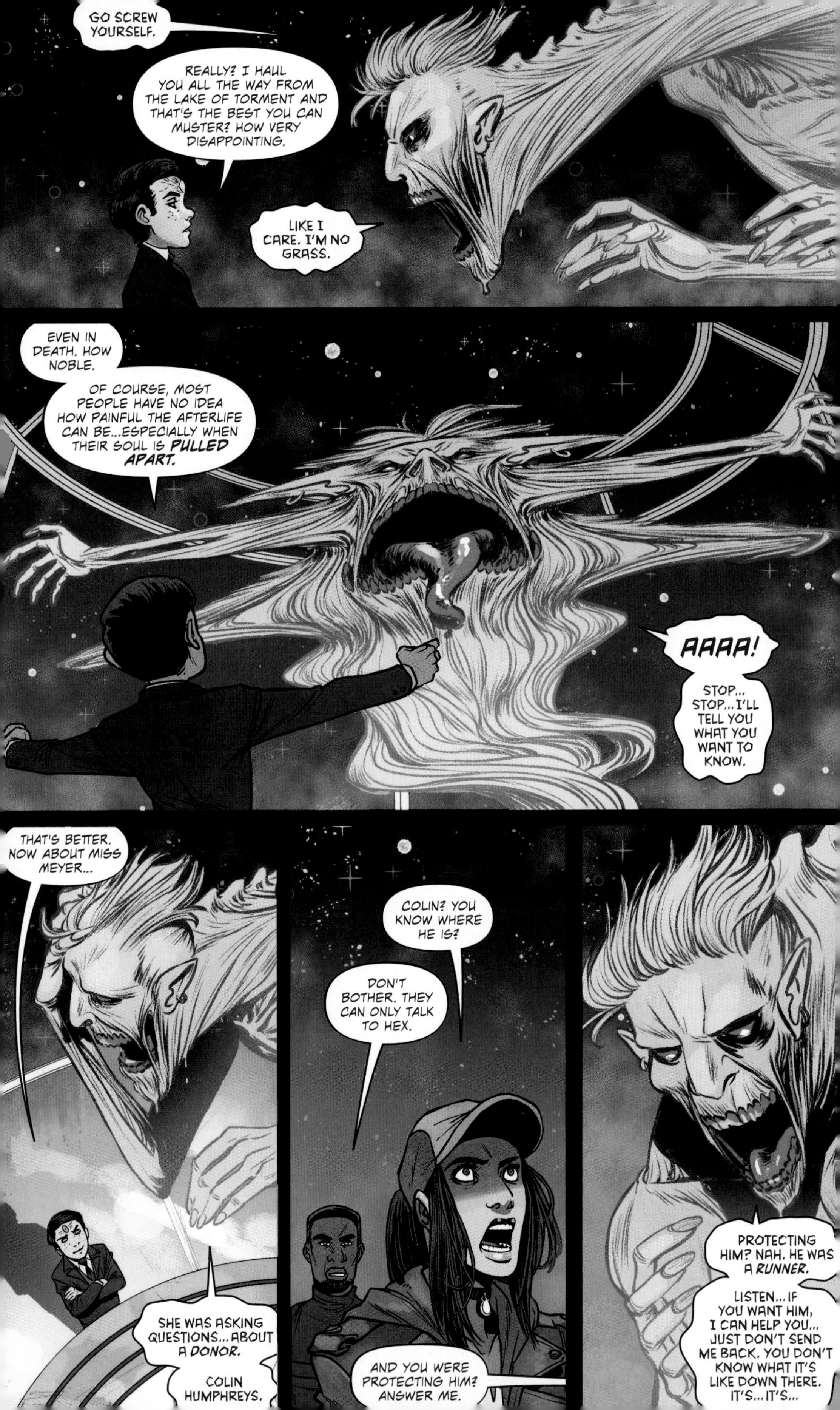
GO SCREW YOURSELF.
REALLY? I HAUL YOU ALL THE WAY FROM THE LAKE OF TORMENT AND THAT'S THE BEST YOU CAN MUSTER? HOW VERY DISAPPOINTING.
LIKE I CARE. I'M NO GRASS.
EVEN IN DEATH. HOW NOBLE.
OF COURSE, MOST PEOPLE HAVE NO IDEA HOW PAINFUL THE AFTERLIFE CAN BE...ESPECIALLY WHEN THEIR SOUL IS PULLED APART.
AAAA!
STOP... STOP...I'LL TELL YOU WHAT YOU WANT TO KNOW.
THAT'S BETTER. NOW ABOUT MISS MEYER...
SHE WAS ASKING QUESTIONS... ABOUT A DONOR.
COLIN HUMPHREYS.
COLIN? YOU KNOW WHERE HE IS?
DON'T BOTHER. THEY CAN ONLY TALK TO HEX.
AND YOU WERE PROTECTING HIM? ANSWER ME.
PROTECTING HIM? NAH. HE WAS A RUNNER.
LISTEN... IF YOU WANT HIM, I CAN HELP YOU... JUST DON'T SEND ME BACK. YOU DON'T KNOW WHAT IT'S LIKE DOWN THERE. IT'S... IT'S...

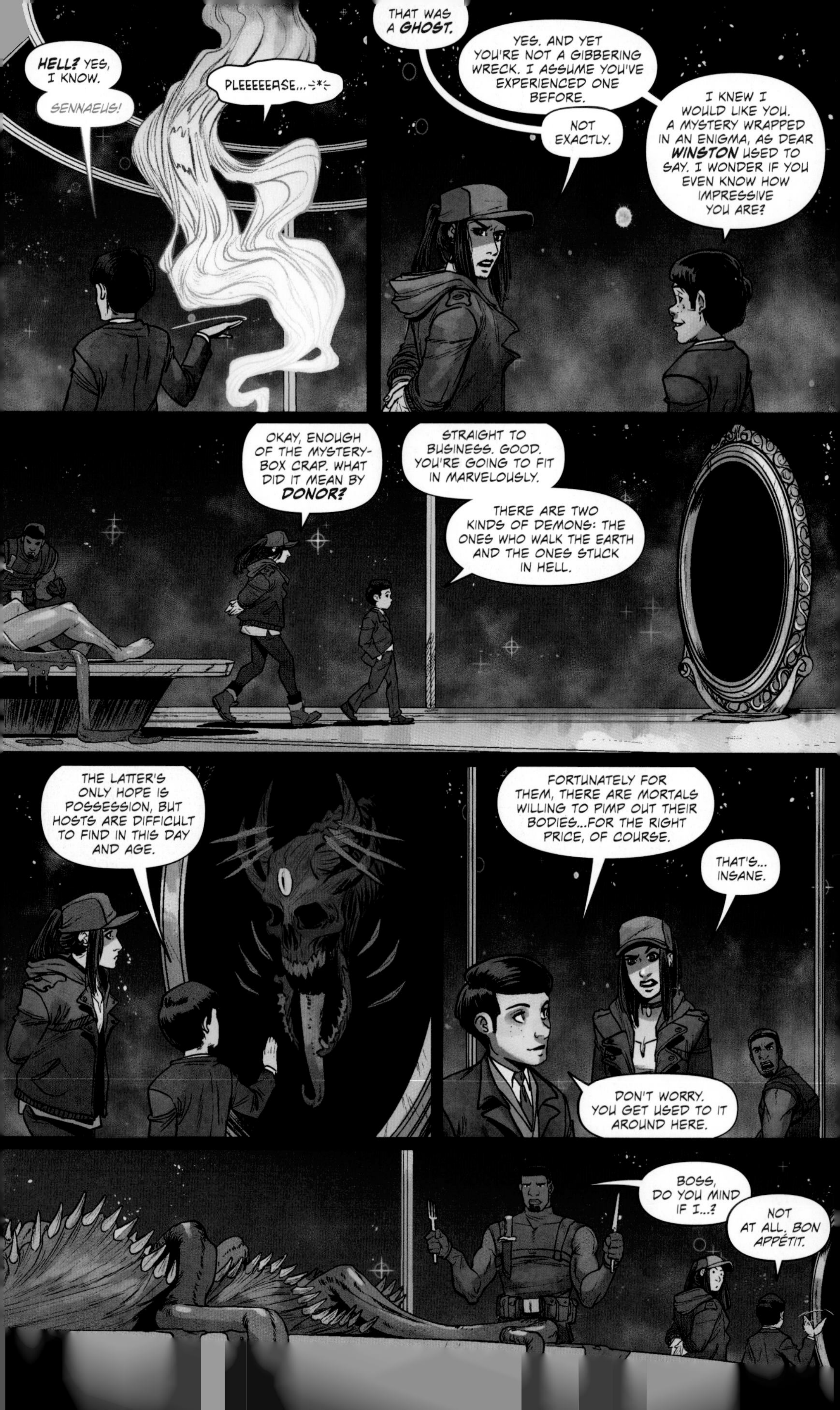
HELL? YES, I KNOW.
SENNAEUS!
PLEEEEEASE...
THAT WAS A GHOST.
YES. AND YET YOU'RE NOT A GIBBERING WRECK. I ASSUME YOU'VE EXPERIENCED ONE BEFORE.
NOT EXACTLY.
I KNEW I WOULD LIKE YOU. A MYSTERY WRAPPED IN AN ENIGMA, AS DEAR WINSTON USED TO SAY. I WONDER IF YOU EVEN KNOW HOW IMPRESSIVE YOU ARE?
OKAY, ENOUGH OF THE MYSTERY-BOX CRAP. WHAT DID IT MEAN BY DONOR?
STRAIGHT TO BUSINESS. GOOD. YOU'RE GOING TO FIT IN MARVELOUSLY.
THERE ARE TWO KINDS OF DEMONS: THE ONES WHO WALK THE EARTH AND THE ONES STUCK IN HELL.
THE LATTER'S ONLY HOPE IS POSSESSION, BUT HOSTS ARE DIFFICULT TO FIND IN THIS DAY AND AGE.
FORTUNATELY FOR THEM, THERE ARE MORTALS WILLING TO PIMP OUT THEIR BODIES...FOR THE RIGHT PRICE, OF COURSE.
THAT'S... INSANE.
DON'T WORRY. YOU GET USED TO IT AROUND HERE.
BOSS, DO YOU MIND IF I...?
NOT AT ALL, BON APPÉTIT.

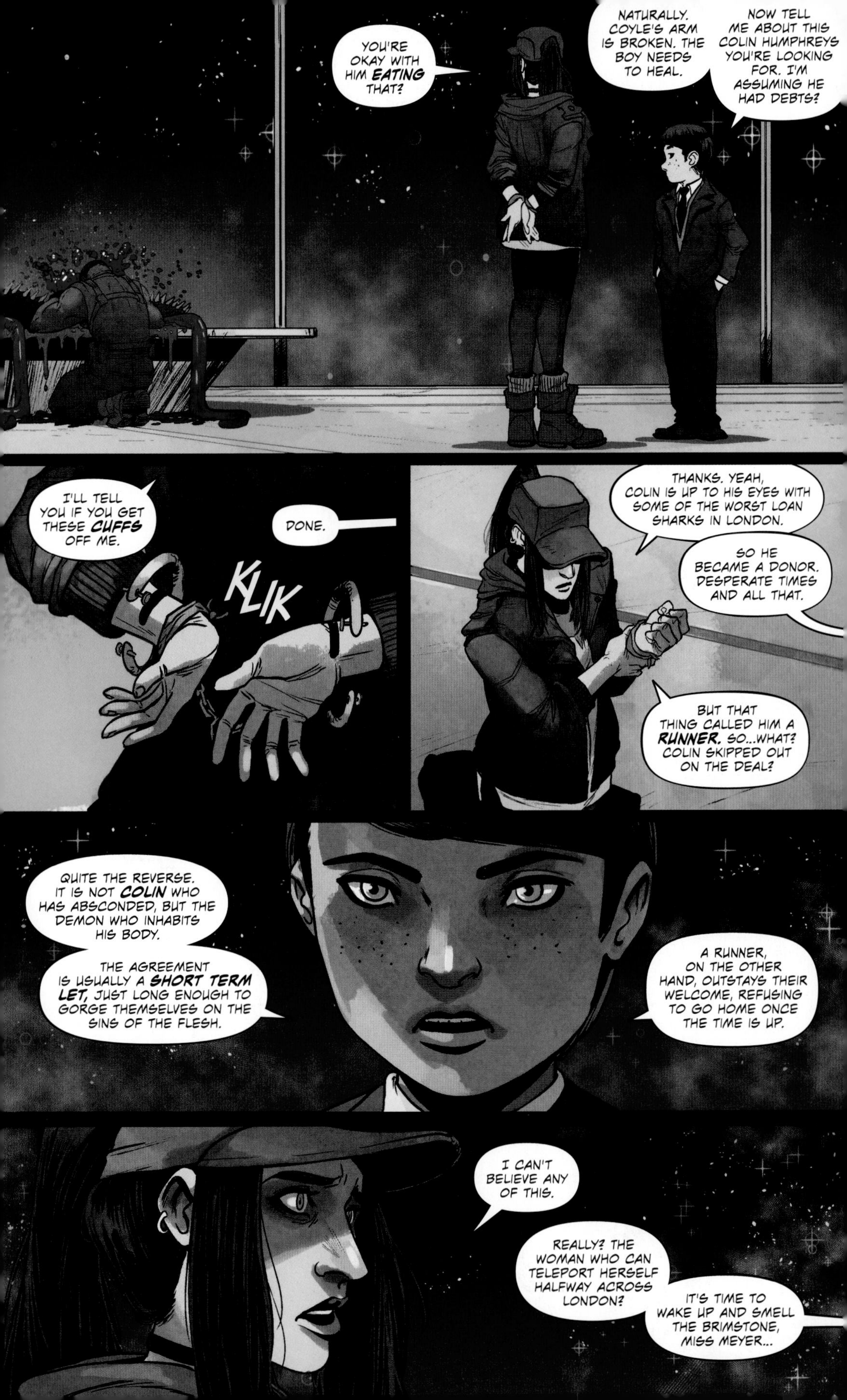
YOU'RE OKAY WITH HIM EATING THAT?
NATURALLY. COYLE'S ARM IS BROKEN. THE BOY NEEDS TO HEAL.
NOW TELL ME ABOUT THIS COLIN HUMPHREYS YOU'RE LOOKING FOR. I'M ASSUMING HE HAD DEBTS?
I'LL TELL YOU IF YOU GET THESE CUFFS OFF ME.
DONE.
KLIK
THANKS. YEAH, COLIN IS UP TO HIS EYES WITH SOME OF THE WORST LOAN SHARKS IN LONDON.
SO HE BECAME A DONOR. DESPERATE TIMES AND ALL THAT.
BUT THAT THING CALLED HIM A RUNNER. SO...WHAT? COLIN SKIPPED OUT ON THE DEAL?
QUITE THE REVERSE. IT IS NOT COLIN WHO HAS ABSCONDED, BUT THE DEMON WHO INHABITS HIS BODY.
THE AGREEMENT IS USUALLY A SHORT TERM LET, JUST LONG ENOUGH TO GORGE THEMSELVES ON THE SINS OF THE FLESH.
A RUNNER, ON THE OTHER HAND, OUTSTAYS THEIR WELCOME, REFUSING TO GO HOME ONCE THE TIME IS UP.
I CAN'T BELIEVE ANY OF THIS.
REALLY? THE WOMAN WHO CAN TELEPORT HERSELF HALFWAY ACROSS LONDON?
IT'S TIME TO WAKE UP AND SMELL THE BRIMSTONE, MISS MEYER...

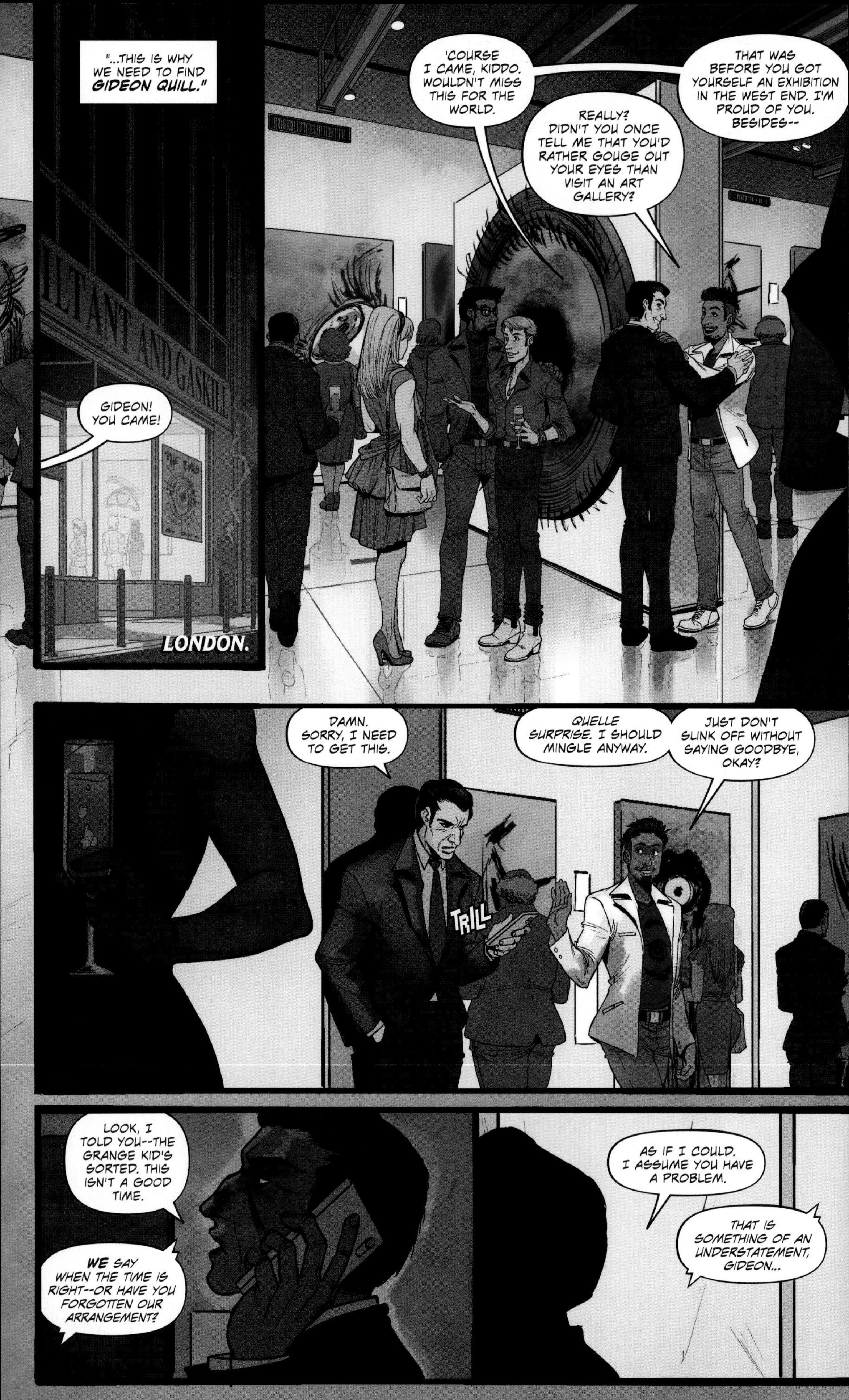
"...THIS IS WHY WE NEED TO FIND GIDEON QUILL."
ILTANT AND GASKILL
THE EYES
GIDEON! YOU CAME!
LONDON.
'COURSE I CAME, KIDDO. WOULDN'T MISS THIS FOR THE WORLD.
REALLY? DIDN'T YOU ONCE TELL ME THAT YOU'D RATHER GOUGE OUT YOUR EYES THAN VISIT AN ART GALLERY?
THAT WAS BEFORE YOU GOT YOURSELF AN EXHIBITION IN THE WEST END. I'M PROUD OF YOU. BESIDES--
DAMN. SORRY, I NEED TO GET THIS.
QUELLE SURPRISE. I SHOULD MINGLE ANYWAY.
JUST DON'T SLINK OFF WITHOUT SAYING GOODBYE, OKAY?
TRILL
LOOK, I TOLD YOU--THE GRANGE KID'S SORTED. THIS ISN'T A GOOD TIME.
WE SAY WHEN THE TIME IS RIGHT--OR HAVE YOU FORGOTTEN OUR ARRANGEMENT?
AS IF I COULD. I ASSUME YOU HAVE A PROBLEM.
THAT IS SOMETHING OF AN UNDERSTATEMENT, GIDEON...

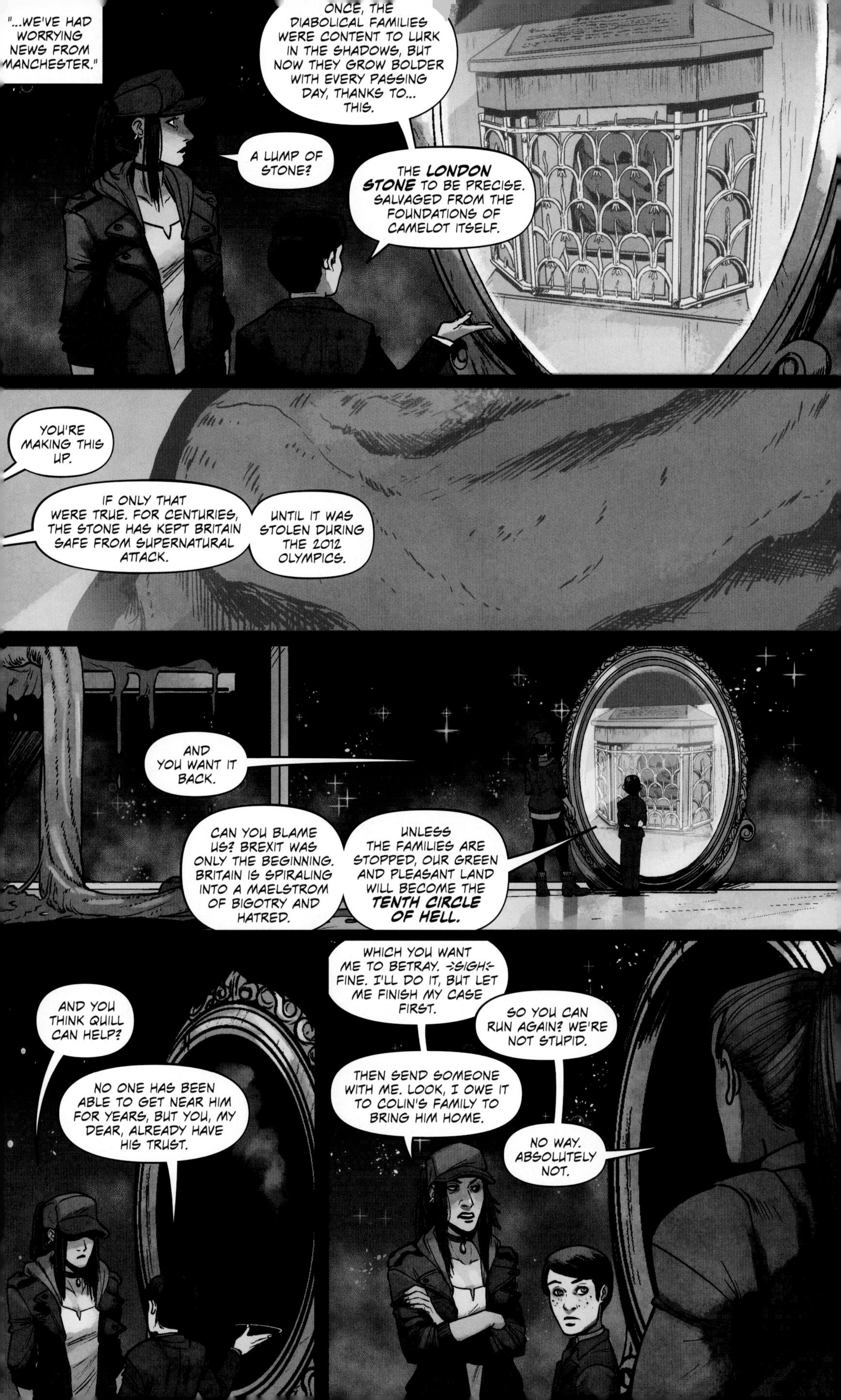
"...WE'VE HAD WORRYING NEWS FROM MANCHESTER."
ONCE, THE DIABOLICAL FAMILIES WERE CONTENT TO LURK IN THE SHADOWS, BUT NOW THEY GROW BOLDER WITH EVERY PASSING DAY, THANKS TO... THIS.
A LUMP OF STONE?
THE LONDON STONE TO BE PRECISE. SALVAGED FROM THE FOUNDATIONS OF CAMELOT ITSELF.
YOU'RE MAKING THIS UP.
IF ONLY THAT WERE TRUE. FOR CENTURIES, THE STONE HAS KEPT BRITAIN SAFE FROM SUPERNATURAL ATTACK.
UNTIL IT WAS STOLEN DURING THE 2012 OLYMPICS.
AND YOU WANT IT BACK.
CAN YOU BLAME US? BREXIT WAS ONLY THE BEGINNING. BRITAIN IS SPIRALING INTO A MAELSTROM OF BIGOTRY AND HATRED.
UNLESS THE FAMILIES ARE STOPPED, OUR GREEN AND PLEASANT LAND WILL BECOME THE TENTH CIRCLE OF HELL.
AND YOU THINK QUILL CAN HELP?
NO ONE HAS BEEN ABLE TO GET NEAR HIM FOR YEARS, BUT YOU, MY DEAR, ALREADY HAVE HIS TRUST.
WHICH YOU WANT ME TO BETRAY. -SIGH- FINE. I'LL DO IT, BUT LET ME FINISH MY CASE FIRST.
SO YOU CAN RUN AGAIN? WE'RE NOT STUPID.
THEN SEND SOMEONE WITH ME. LOOK, I OWE IT TO COLIN'S FAMILY TO BRING HIM HOME.
NO WAY. ABSOLUTELY NOT.

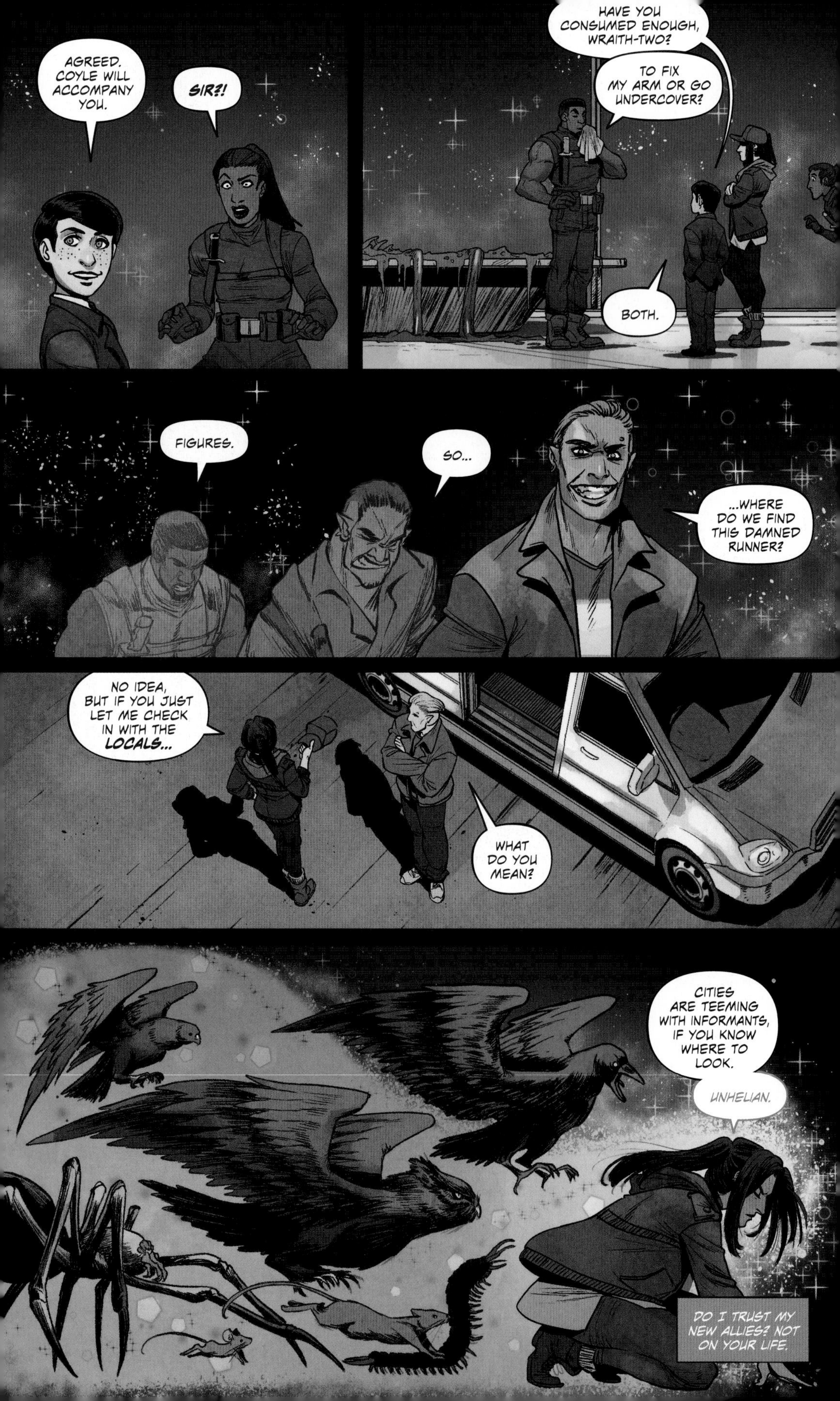
AGREED. COYLE WILL ACCOMPANY YOU.
SIR?!
HAVE YOU CONSUMED ENOUGH, WRAITH-TWO?
TO FIX MY ARM OR GO UNDERCOVER?
BOTH.
FIGURES.
SO...
...WHERE DO WE FIND THIS DAMNED RUNNER?
NO IDEA, BUT IF YOU JUST LET ME CHECK IN WITH THE LOCALS...
WHAT DO YOU MEAN?
CITIES ARE TEEMING WITH INFORMANTS, IF YOU KNOW WHERE TO LOOK.
UNHELIAN.
DO I TRUST MY NEW ALLIES? NOT ON YOUR LIFE.

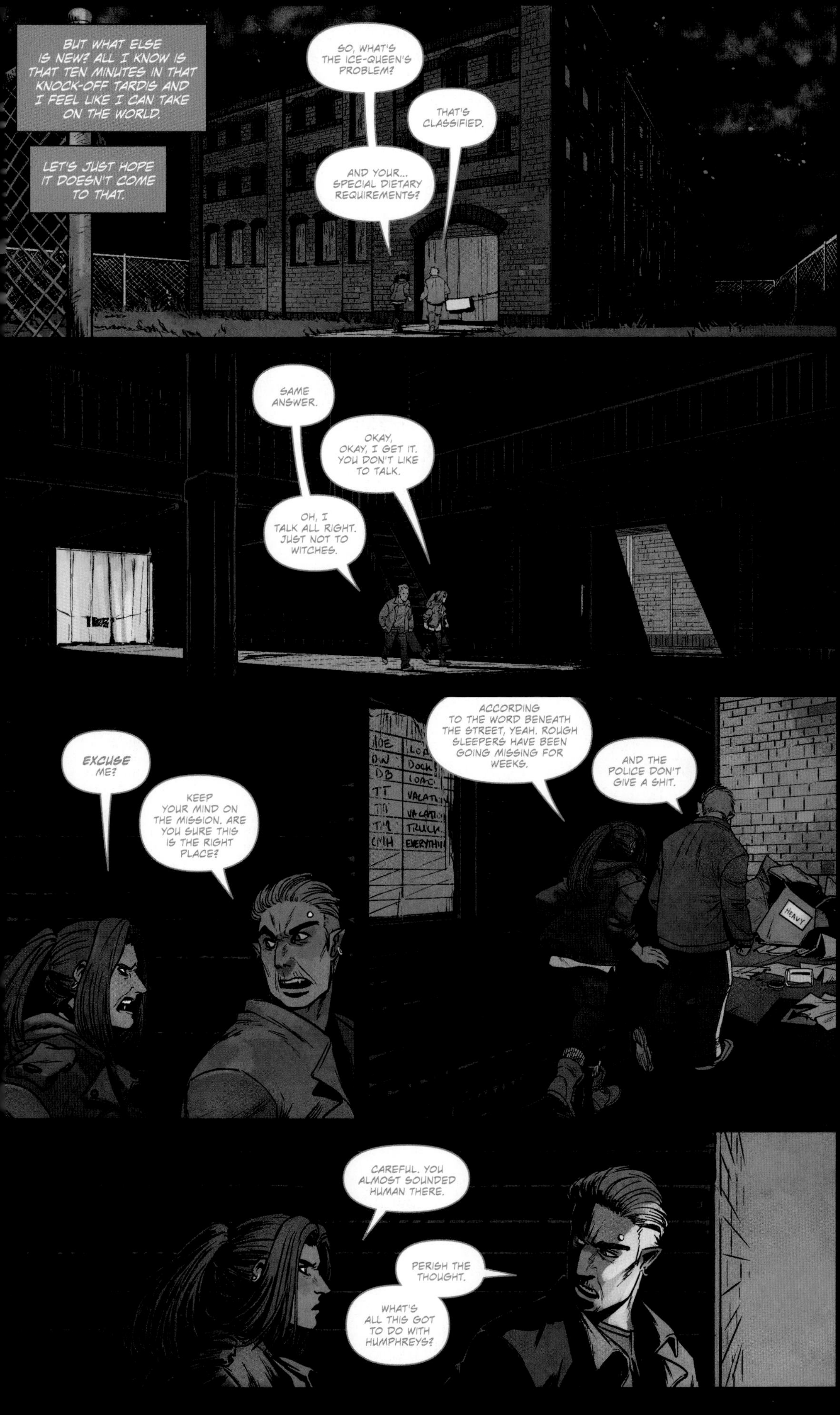
BUT WHAT ELSE IS NEW? ALL I KNOW IS THAT TEN MINUTES IN THAT KNOCK-OFF TARDIS AND I FEEL LIKE I CAN TAKE ON THE WORLD.
LET'S JUST HOPE IT DOESN'T COME TO THAT.
SO, WHAT'S THE ICE-QUEEN'S PROBLEM?
THAT'S CLASSIFIED.
AND YOUR... SPECIAL DIETARY REQUIREMENTS?
SAME ANSWER.
OKAY, OKAY, I GET IT. YOU DON'T LIKE TO TALK.
OH, I TALK ALL RIGHT. JUST NOT TO WITCHES.
ACCORDING TO THE WORD BENEATH THE STREET, YEAH. ROUGH SLEEPERS HAVE BEEN GOING MISSING FOR WEEKS.
AND THE POLICE DON'T GIVE A SHIT.
EXCUSE ME?
KEEP YOUR MIND ON THE MISSION. ARE YOU SURE THIS IS THE RIGHT PLACE?
HEAVY
CAREFUL. YOU ALMOST SOUNDED HUMAN THERE.
PERISH THE THOUGHT.
WHAT'S ALL THIS GOT TO DO WITH HUMPHREYS?

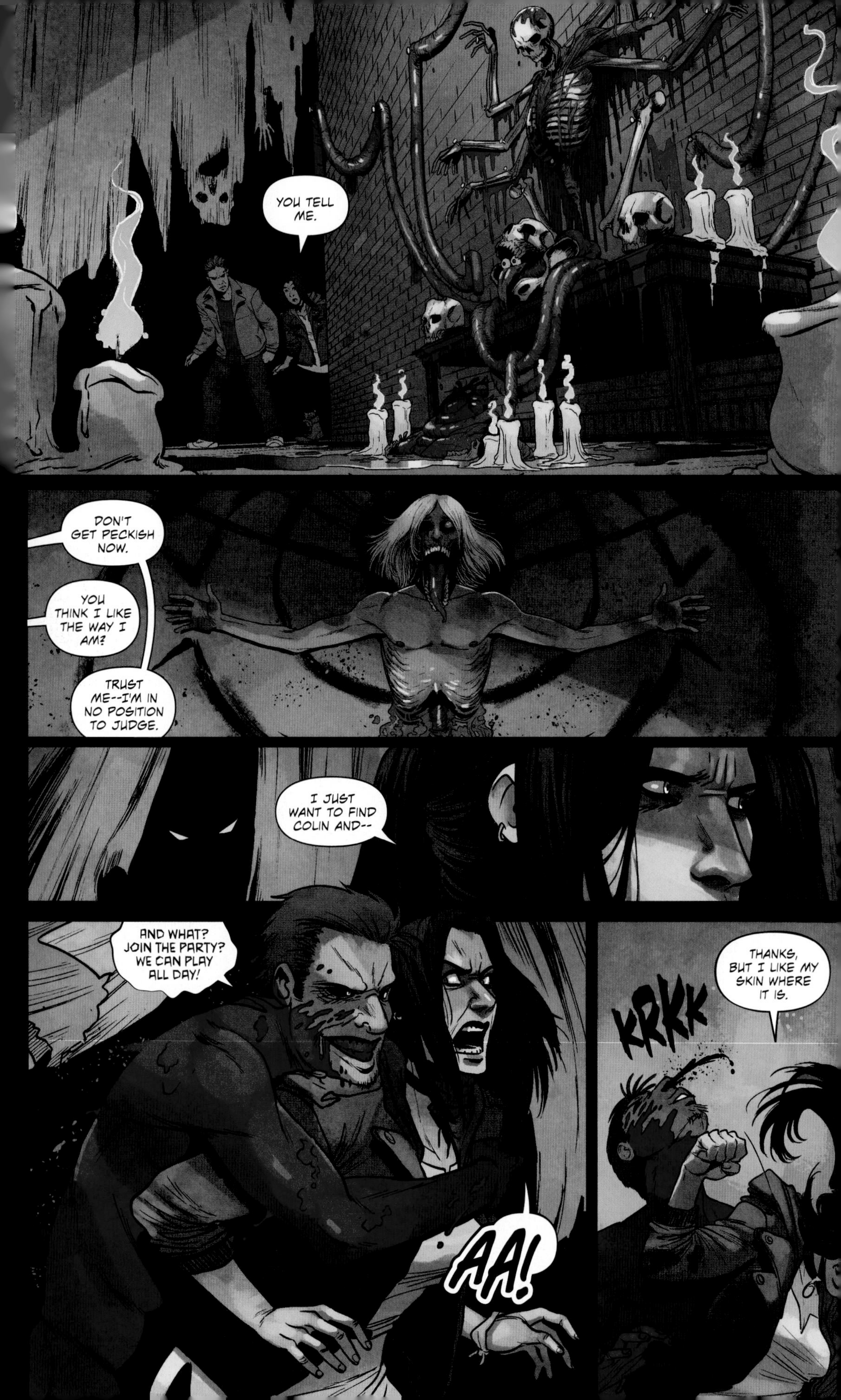
YOU TELL ME.
DON'T GET PECKISH NOW.
YOU THINK I LIKE THE WAY I AM?
TRUST ME--I'M IN NO POSITION TO JUDGE.
I JUST WANT TO FIND COLIN AND--
AND WHAT? JOIN THE PARTY? WE CAN PLAY ALL DAY!
AA!
KRKK
THANKS, BUT I LIKE MY SKIN WHERE IT IS.

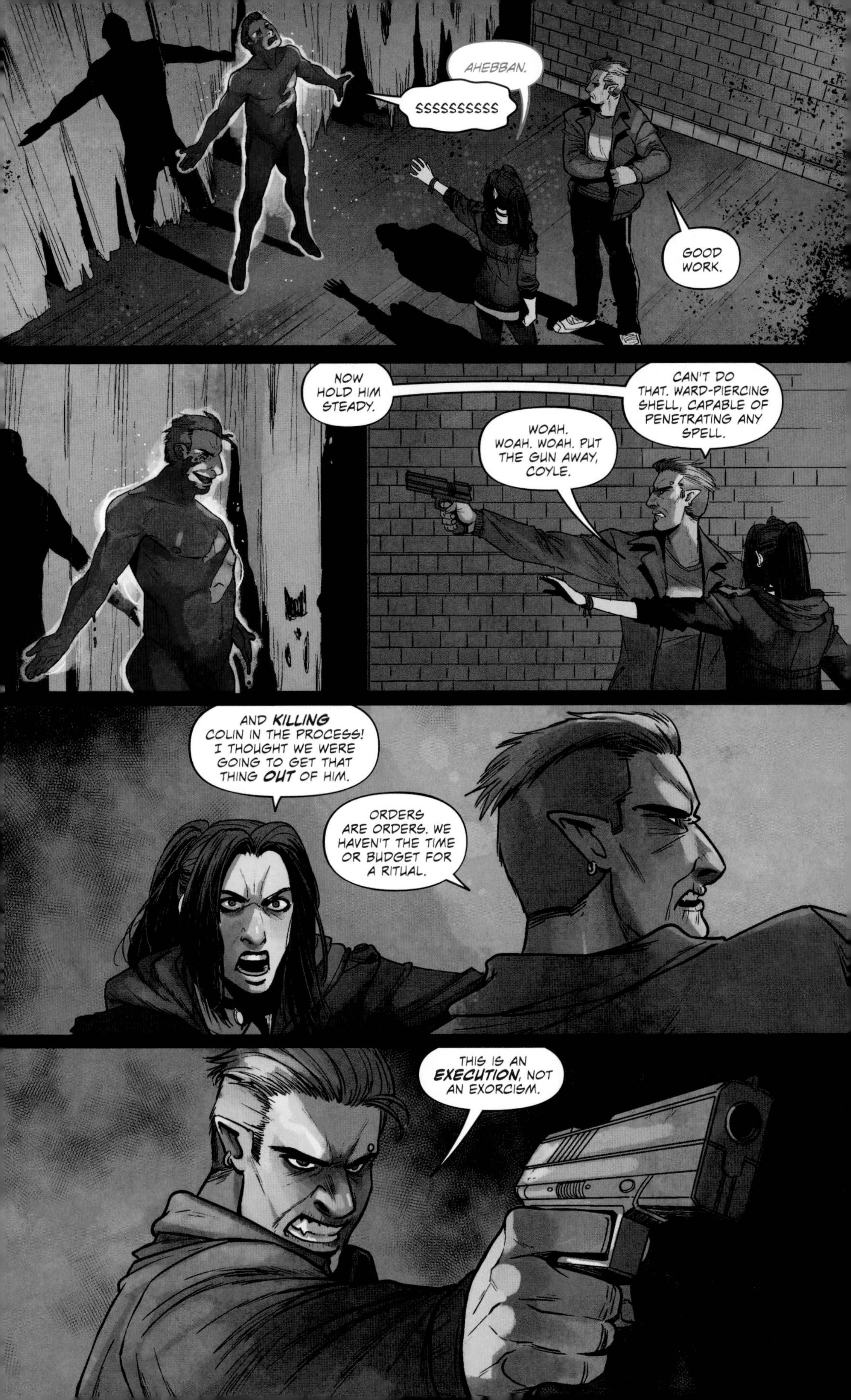
AHEBBAN.
SSSSSSSSSS
GOOD WORK.
NOW HOLD HIM STEADY.
CAN'T DO THAT. WARD-PIERCING SHELL, CAPABLE OF PENETRATING ANY SPELL.
WOAH. WOAH. WOAH. PUT THE GUN AWAY, COYLE.
AND KILLING COLIN IN THE PROCESS! I THOUGHT WE WERE GOING TO GET THAT THING OUT OF HIM.
ORDERS ARE ORDERS. WE HAVEN'T THE TIME OR BUDGET FOR A RITUAL.
THIS IS AN EXECUTION, NOT AN EXORCISM.

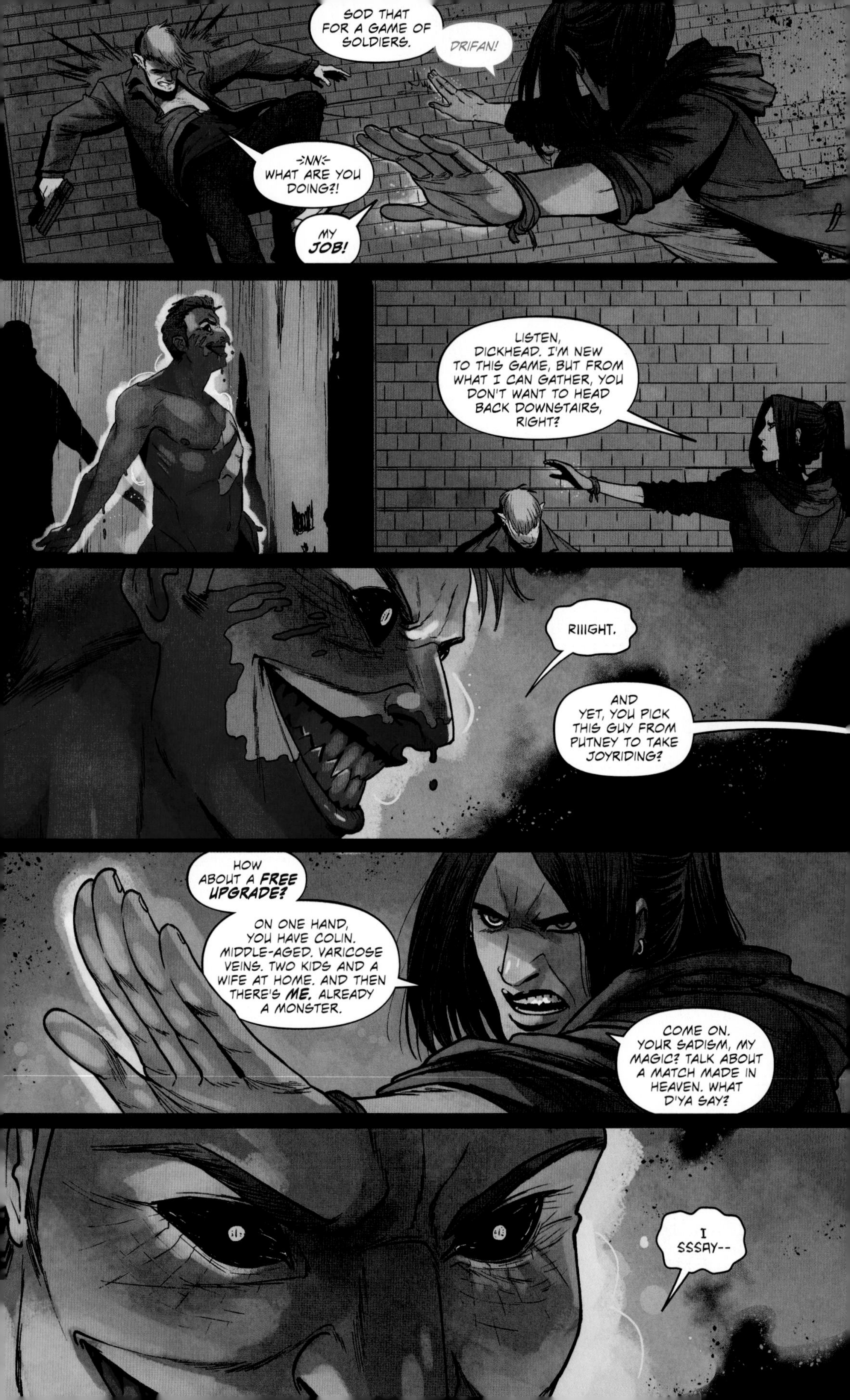
SOD THAT FOR A GAME OF SOLDIERS.
DRIFAN!
=NN= WHAT ARE YOU DOING?!
MY JOB!
LISTEN, DICKHEAD. I'M NEW TO THIS GAME, BUT FROM WHAT I CAN GATHER, YOU DON'T WANT TO HEAD BACK DOWNSTAIRS, RIGHT?
RIIIGHT.
AND YET, YOU PICK THIS GUY FROM PUTNEY TO TAKE JOYRIDING?
HOW ABOUT A FREE UPGRADE?
ON ONE HAND, YOU HAVE COLIN. MIDDLE-AGED. VARICOSE VEINS. TWO KIDS AND A WIFE AT HOME. AND THEN THERE'S ME. ALREADY A MONSTER.
COME ON. YOUR SADISM, MY MAGIC? TALK ABOUT A MATCH MADE IN HEAVEN. WHAT D'YA SAY?
I SSSAY--

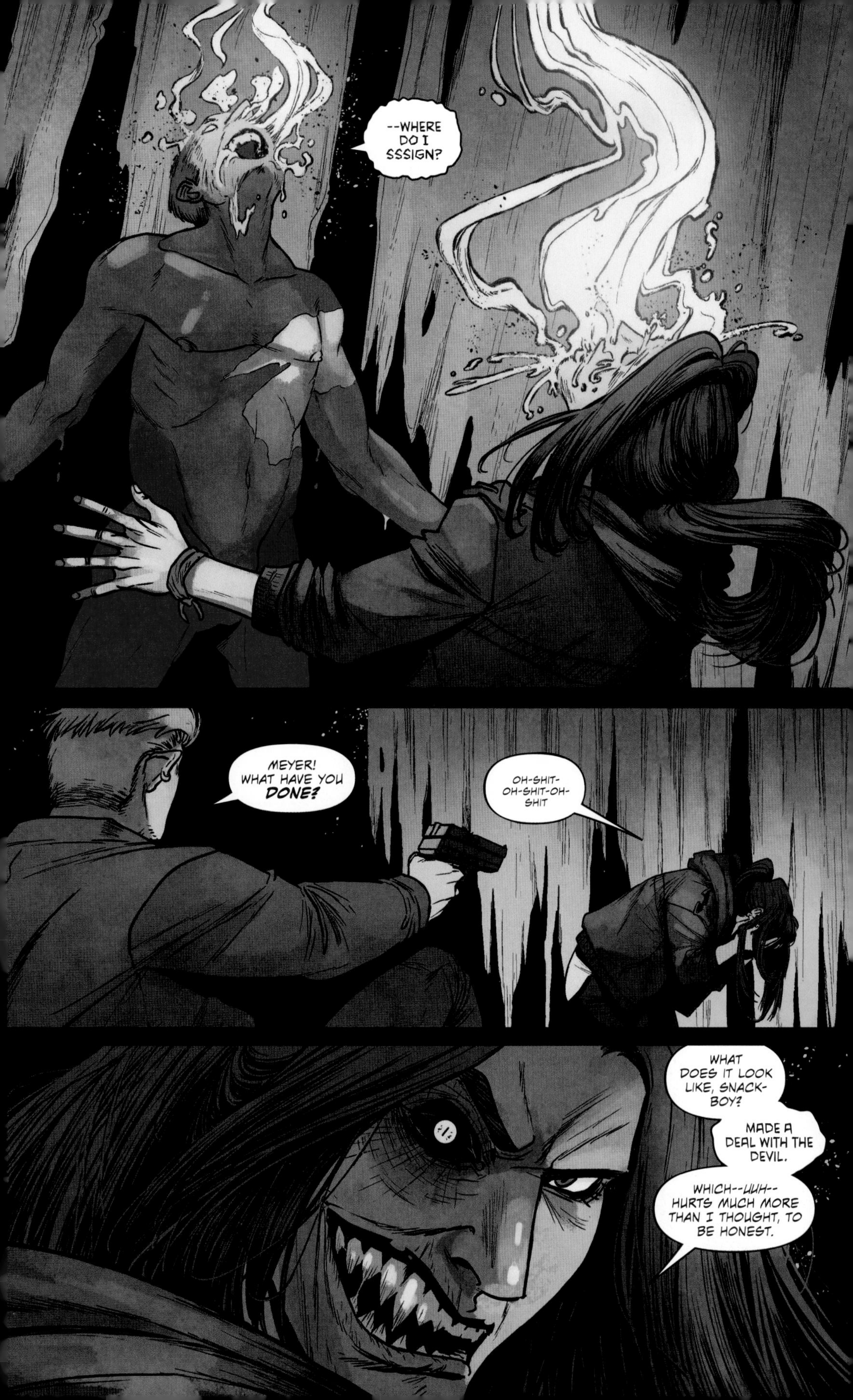
--WHERE DO I SSSIGN?
MEYER! WHAT HAVE YOU DONE?
OH-SHIT-OH-SHIT-OH-SHIT
WHAT DOES IT LOOK LIKE, SNACK-BOY?
MADE A DEAL WITH THE DEVIL.
WHICH--UUH--HURTS MUCH MORE THAN I THOUGHT, TO BE HONEST.

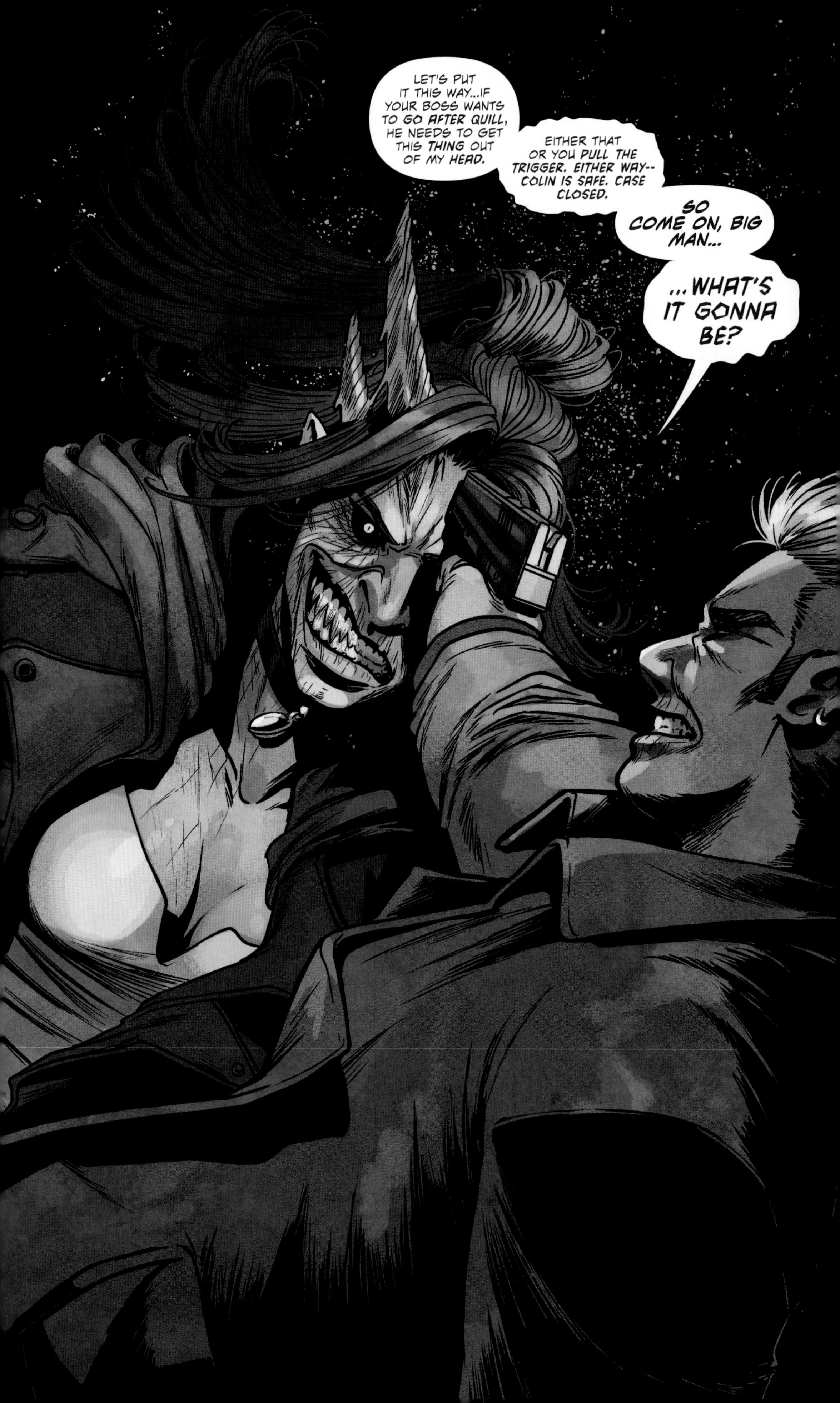
LET'S PUT IT THIS WAY...IF YOUR BOSS WANTS TO GO AFTER QUILL, HE NEEDS TO GET THIS THING OUT OF MY HEAD.
EITHER THAT OR YOU PULL THE TRIGGER. EITHER WAY-- COLIN IS SAFE. CASE CLOSED.
SO COME ON, BIG MAN...
...WHAT'S IT GONNA BE?

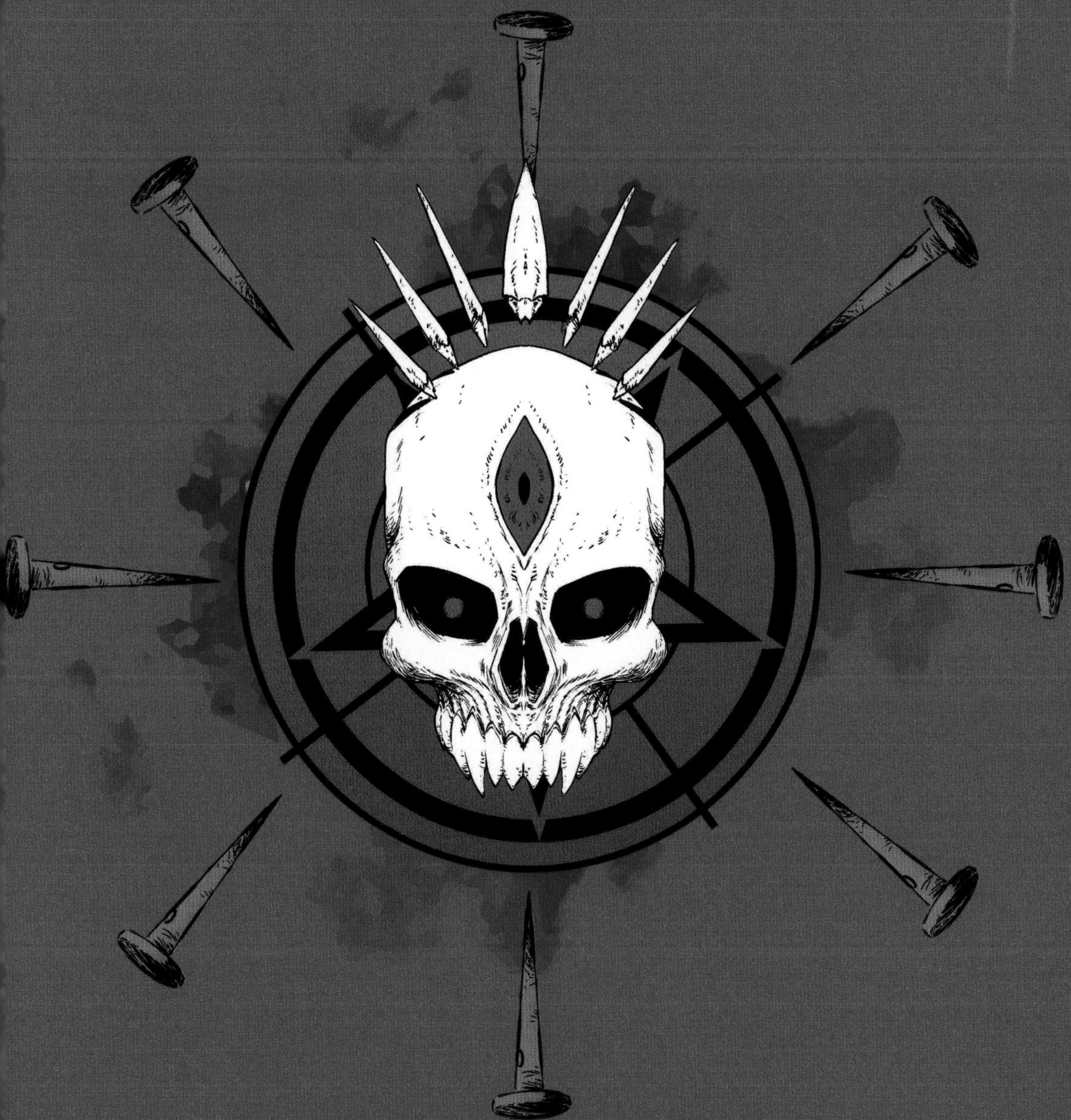

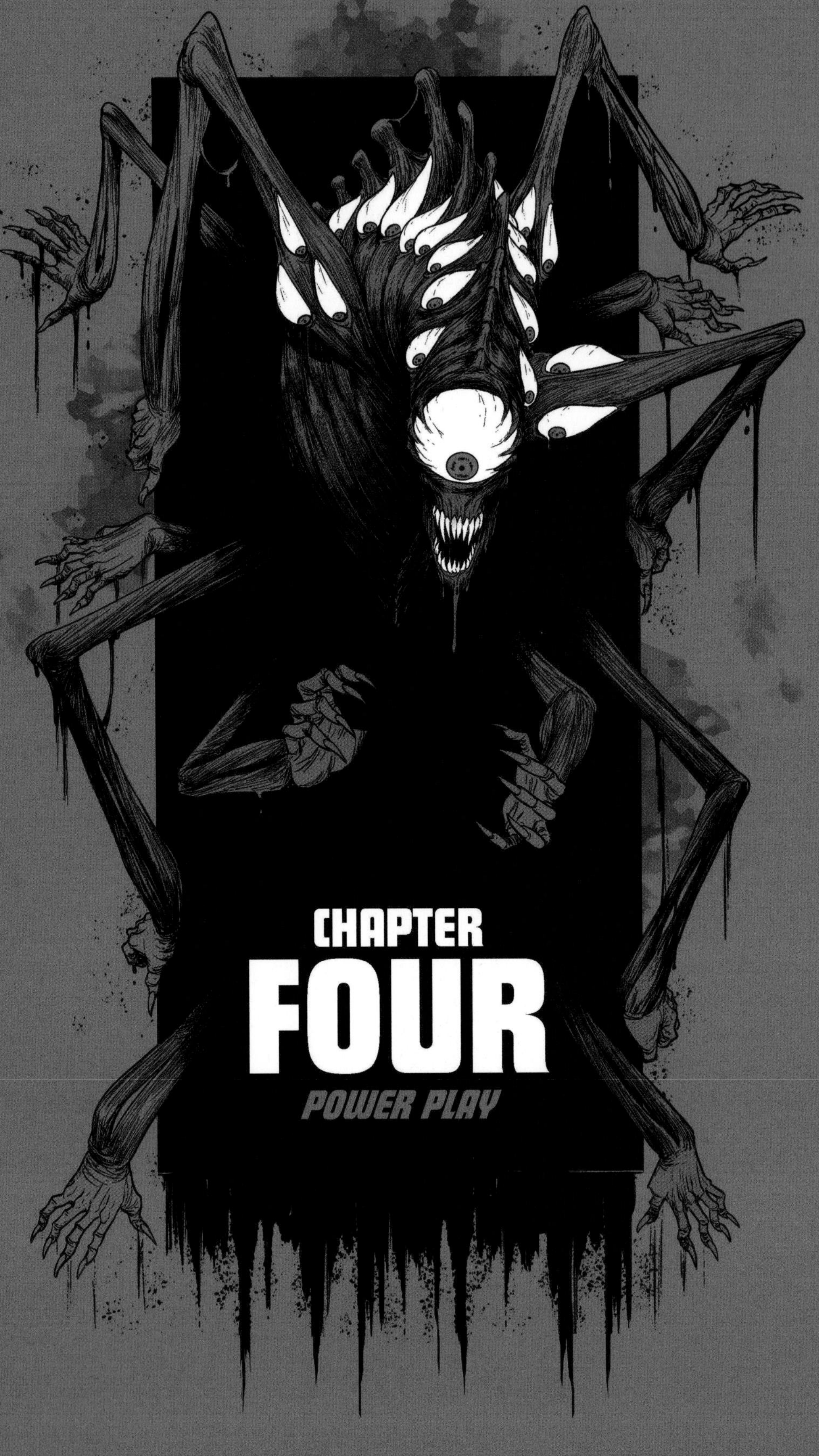

CHAPTER FOUR

POWER PLAY

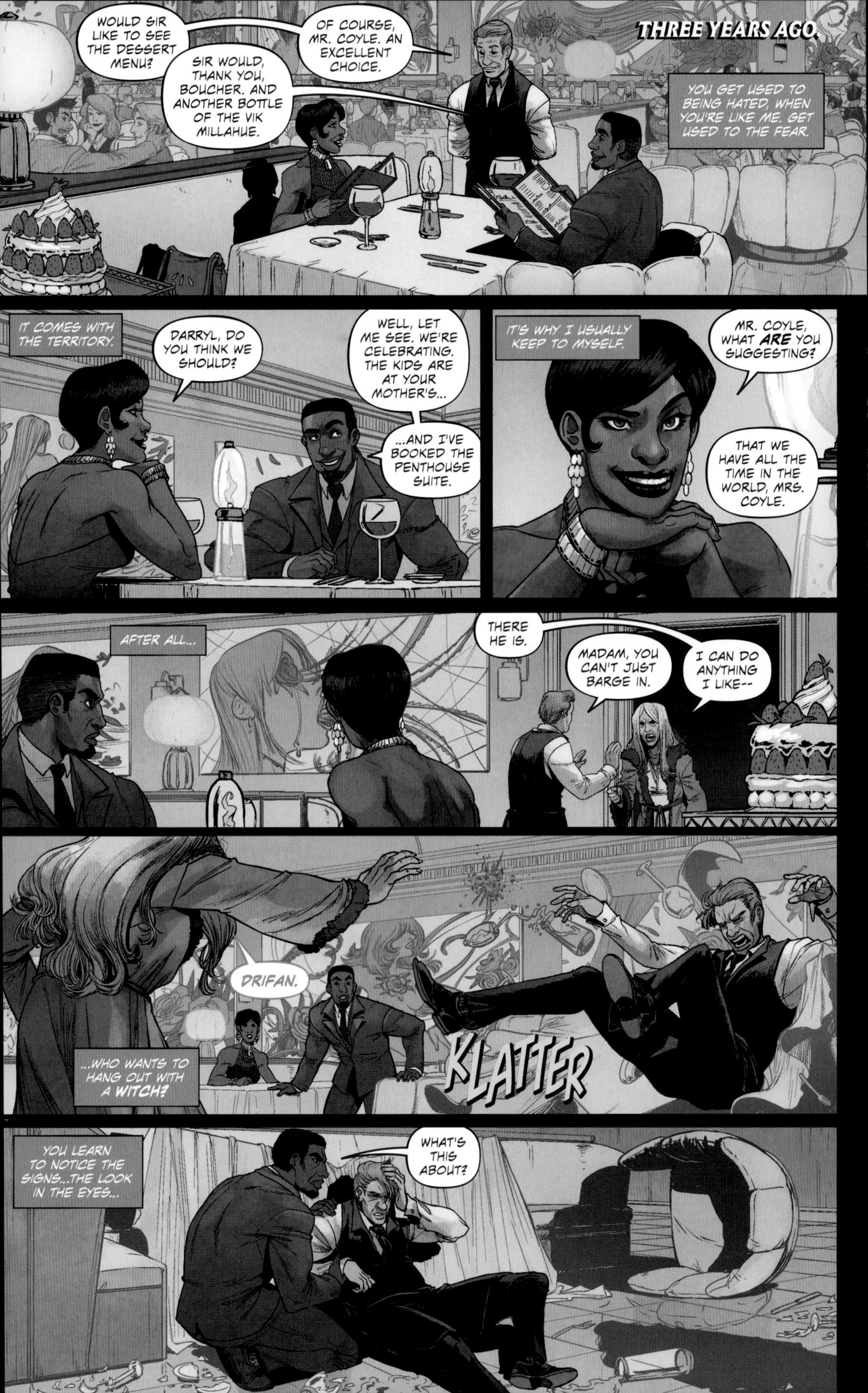
THREE YEARS AGO.
WOULD SIR LIKE TO SEE THE DESSERT MENU?
OF COURSE, MR. COYLE. AN EXCELLENT CHOICE.
SIR WOULD, THANK YOU, BOUCHER. AND ANOTHER BOTTLE OF THE VIK MILLAHUE.
YOU GET USED TO BEING HATED, WHEN YOU'RE LIKE ME. GET USED TO THE FEAR.
IT COMES WITH THE TERRITORY.
DARRYL, DO YOU THINK WE SHOULD?
WELL, LET ME SEE. WE'RE CELEBRATING. THE KIDS ARE AT YOUR MOTHER'S...
...AND I'VE BOOKED THE PENTHOUSE SUITE.
IT'S WHY I USUALLY KEEP TO MYSELF.
MR. COYLE, WHAT ARE YOU SUGGESTING?
THAT WE HAVE ALL THE TIME IN THE WORLD, MRS. COYLE.
AFTER ALL...
THERE HE IS.
MADAM, YOU CAN'T JUST BARGE IN.
I CAN DO ANYTHING I LIKE--
DRIFAN.
...WHO WANTS TO HANG OUT WITH A WITCH?
KLATTER
YOU LEARN TO NOTICE THE SIGNS...THE LOOK IN THE EYES...
WHAT'S THIS ABOUT?

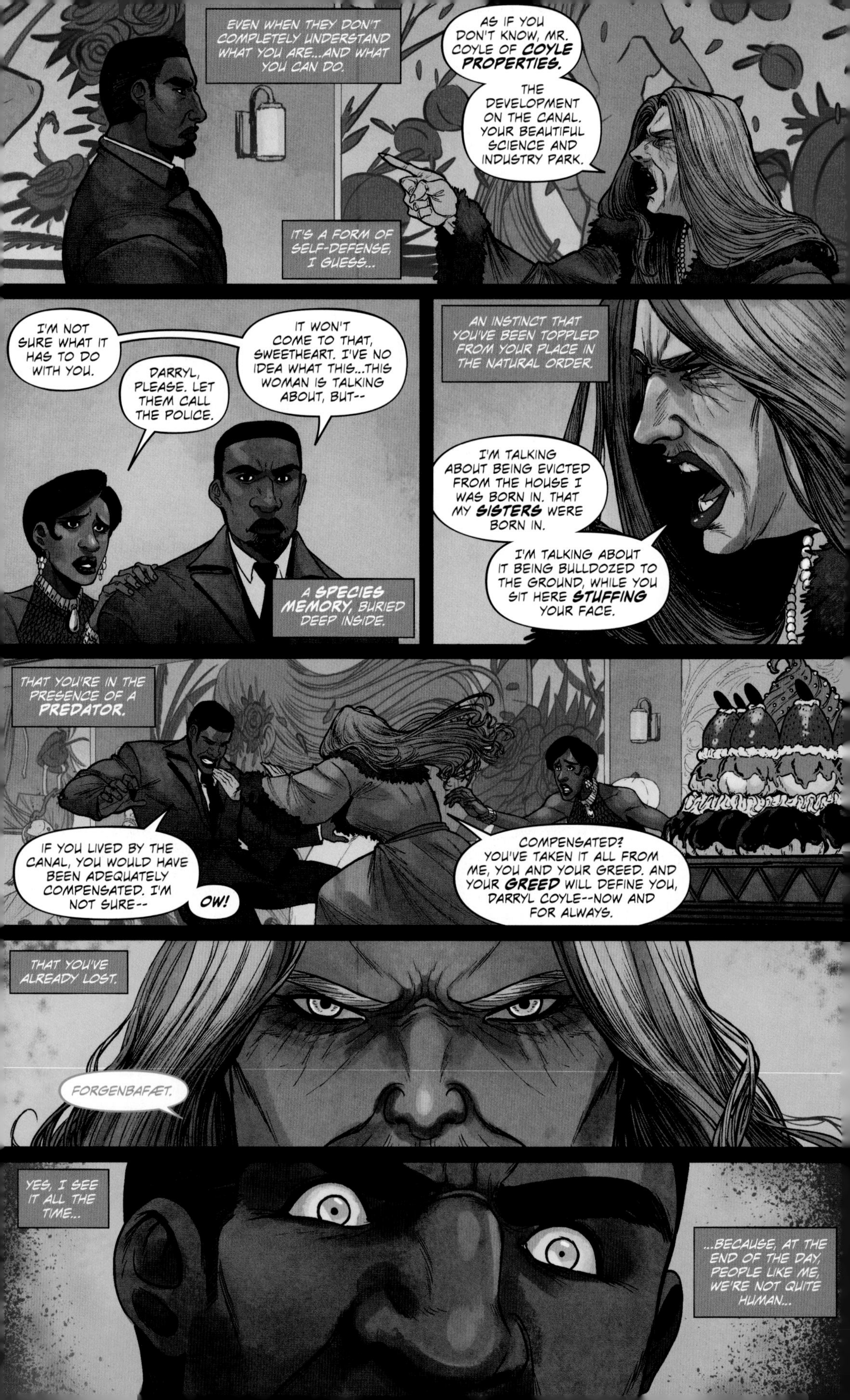
EVEN WHEN THEY DON'T COMPLETELY UNDERSTAND WHAT YOU ARE...AND WHAT YOU CAN DO.
AS IF YOU DON'T KNOW, MR. COYLE OF COYLE PROPERTIES.
THE DEVELOPMENT ON THE CANAL. YOUR BEAUTIFUL SCIENCE AND INDUSTRY PARK.
IT'S A FORM OF SELF-DEFENSE, I GUESS...
I'M NOT SURE WHAT IT HAS TO DO WITH YOU.
DARRYL, PLEASE. LET THEM CALL THE POLICE.
IT WON'T COME TO THAT, SWEETHEART. I'VE NO IDEA WHAT THIS...THIS WOMAN IS TALKING ABOUT, BUT--
A SPECIES MEMORY, BURIED DEEP INSIDE.
AN INSTINCT THAT YOU'VE BEEN TOPPLED FROM YOUR PLACE IN THE NATURAL ORDER.
I'M TALKING ABOUT BEING EVICTED FROM THE HOUSE I WAS BORN IN. THAT MY SISTERS WERE BORN IN.
I'M TALKING ABOUT IT BEING BULLDOZED TO THE GROUND, WHILE YOU SIT HERE STUFFING YOUR FACE.
THAT YOU'RE IN THE PRESENCE OF A PREDATOR.
IF YOU LIVED BY THE CANAL, YOU WOULD HAVE BEEN ADEQUATELY COMPENSATED. I'M NOT SURE--
OW!
COMPENSATED? YOU'VE TAKEN IT ALL FROM ME, YOU AND YOUR GREED. AND YOUR GREED WILL DEFINE YOU, DARRYL COYLE--NOW AND FOR ALWAYS.
THAT YOU'VE ALREADY LOST.
FORGENBAFÆT.
YES, I SEE IT ALL THE TIME...
...BECAUSE, AT THE END OF THE DAY, PEOPLE LIKE ME, WE'RE NOT QUITE HUMAN...

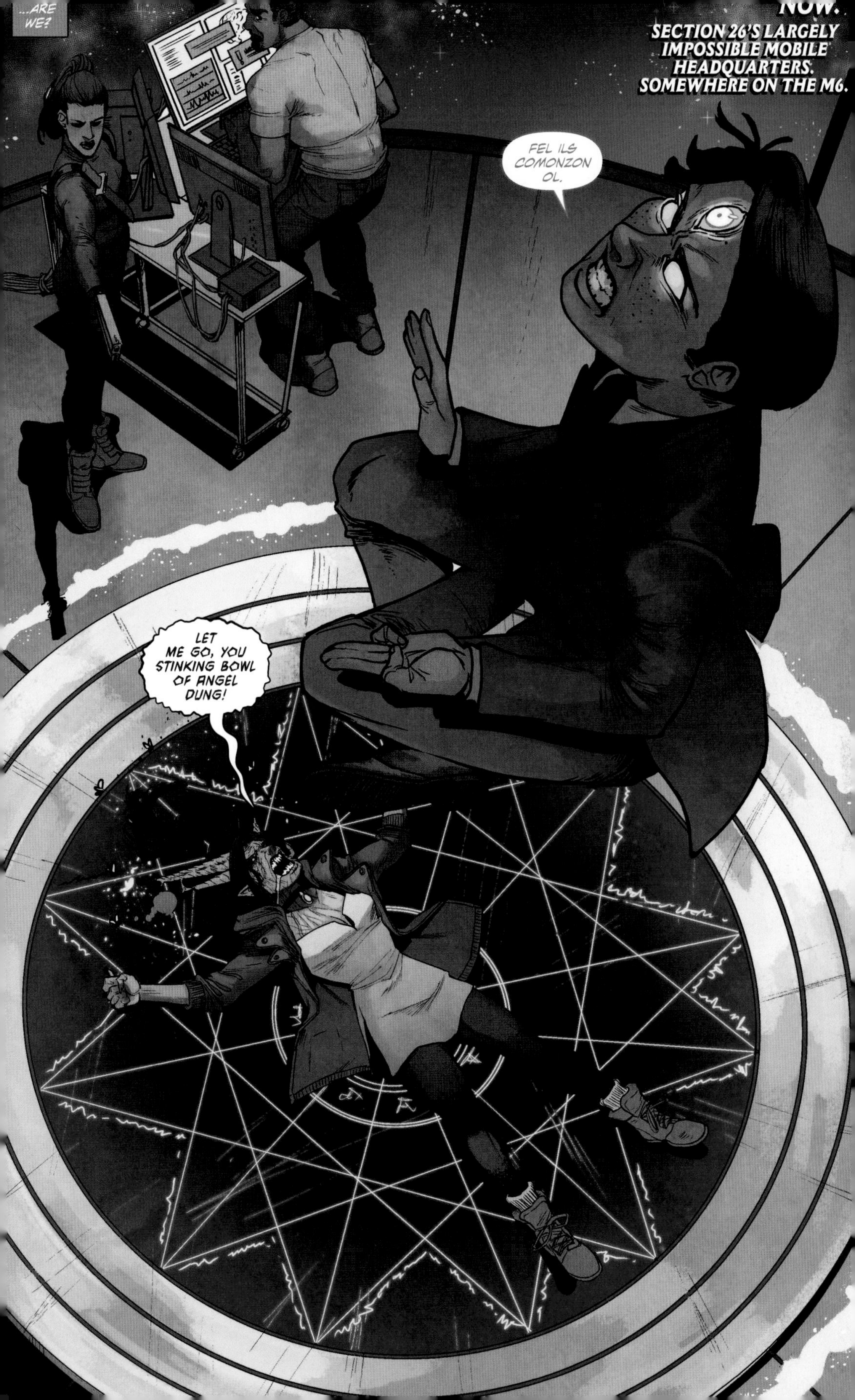
...ARE WE?
NOW.
SECTION 26'S LARGELY IMPOSSIBLE MOBILE HEADQUARTERS. SOMEWHERE ON THE M6.
FEL ILS COMONZON OL.
LET ME GO, YOU STINKING BOWL OF ANGEL DUNG!

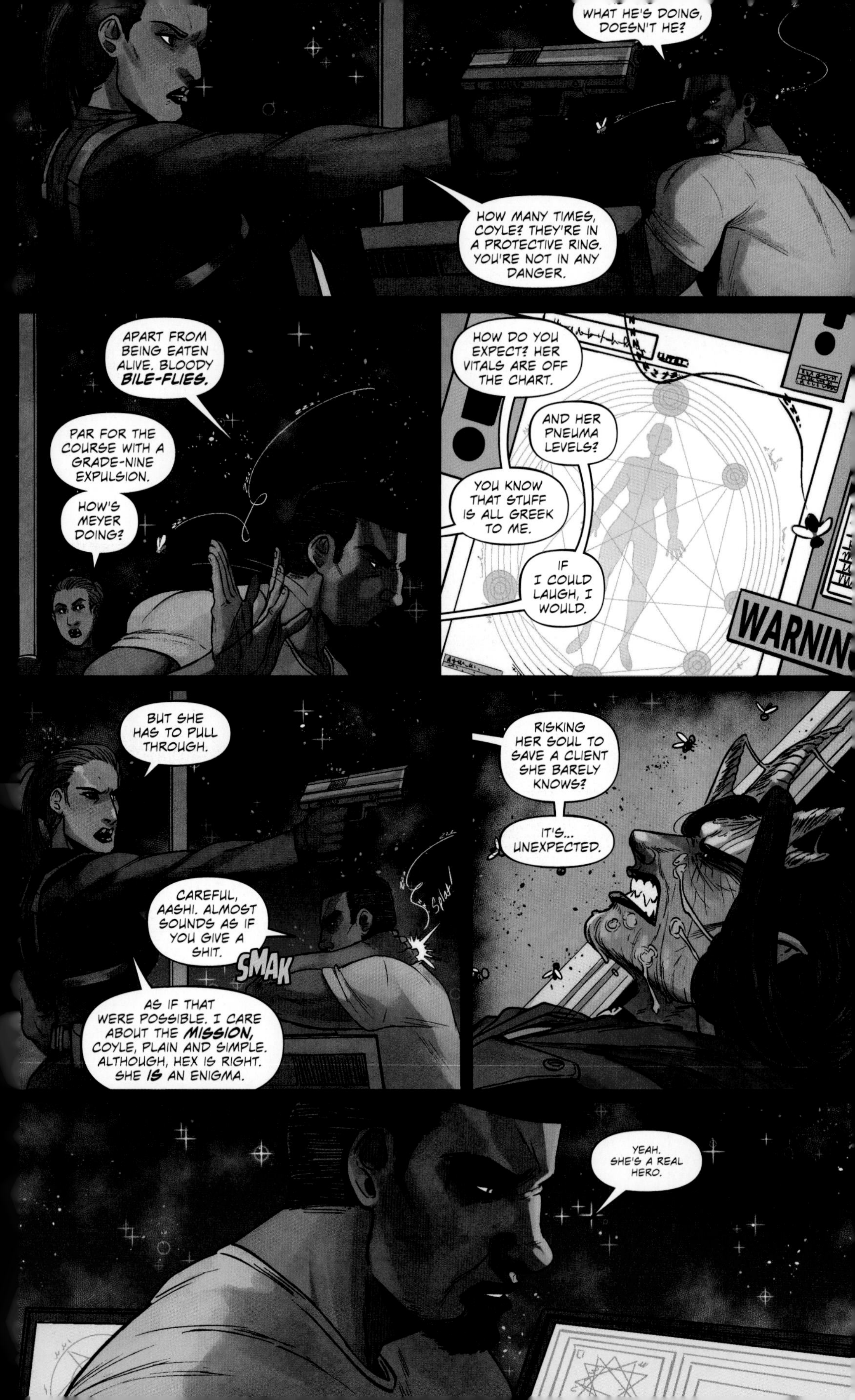

WHAT HE'S DOING, DOESN'T HE?
HOW MANY TIMES, COYLE? THEY'RE IN A PROTECTIVE RING. YOU'RE NOT IN ANY DANGER.
APART FROM BEING EATEN ALIVE. BLOODY BILE-FLIES.
PAR FOR THE COURSE WITH A GRADE-NINE EXPULSION.
HOW'S MEYER DOING?
HOW DO YOU EXPECT? HER VITALS ARE OFF THE CHART.
AND HER PNEUMA LEVELS?
YOU KNOW THAT STUFF IS ALL GREEK TO ME.
IF I COULD LAUGH, I WOULD.
WARNIN
BUT SHE HAS TO PULL THROUGH.
CAREFUL, AASHI. ALMOST SOUNDS AS IF YOU GIVE A SHIT.
SMAK
Splat!
AS IF THAT WERE POSSIBLE. I CARE ABOUT THE MISSION, COYLE, PLAIN AND SIMPLE. ALTHOUGH, HEX IS RIGHT. SHE IS AN ENIGMA.
RISKING HER SOUL TO SAVE A CLIENT SHE BARELY KNOWS?
IT'S... UNEXPECTED.
YEAH. SHE'S A REAL HERO.

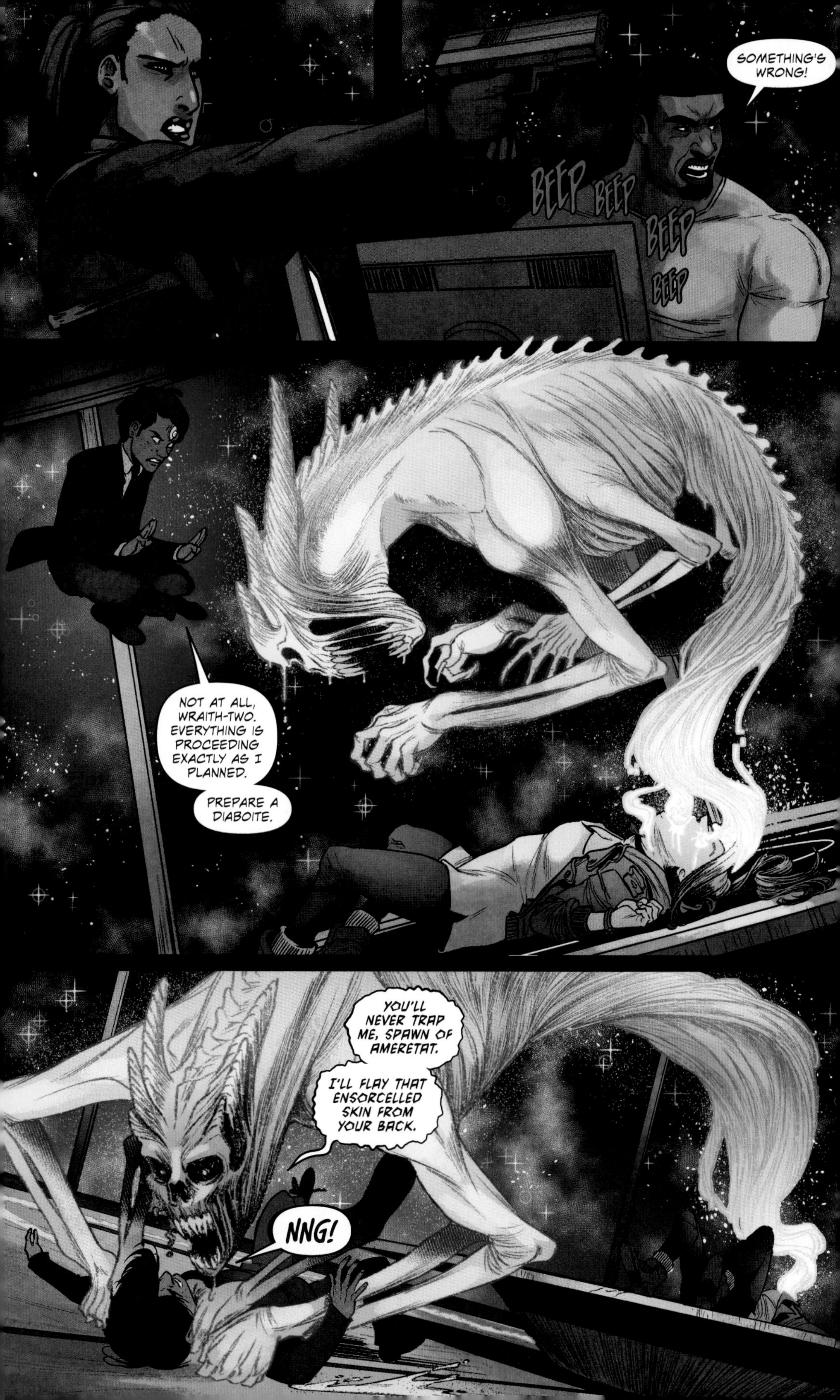
SOMETHING'S WRONG!
BEEP BEEP BEEP BEEP
NOT AT ALL, WRAITH-TWO. EVERYTHING IS PROCEEDING EXACTLY AS I PLANNED.
PREPARE A DIABOITE.
YOU'LL NEVER TRAP ME, SPAWN OF AMERETAT.
I'LL FLAY THAT ENSORCELLED SKIN FROM YOUR BACK.
NNG!

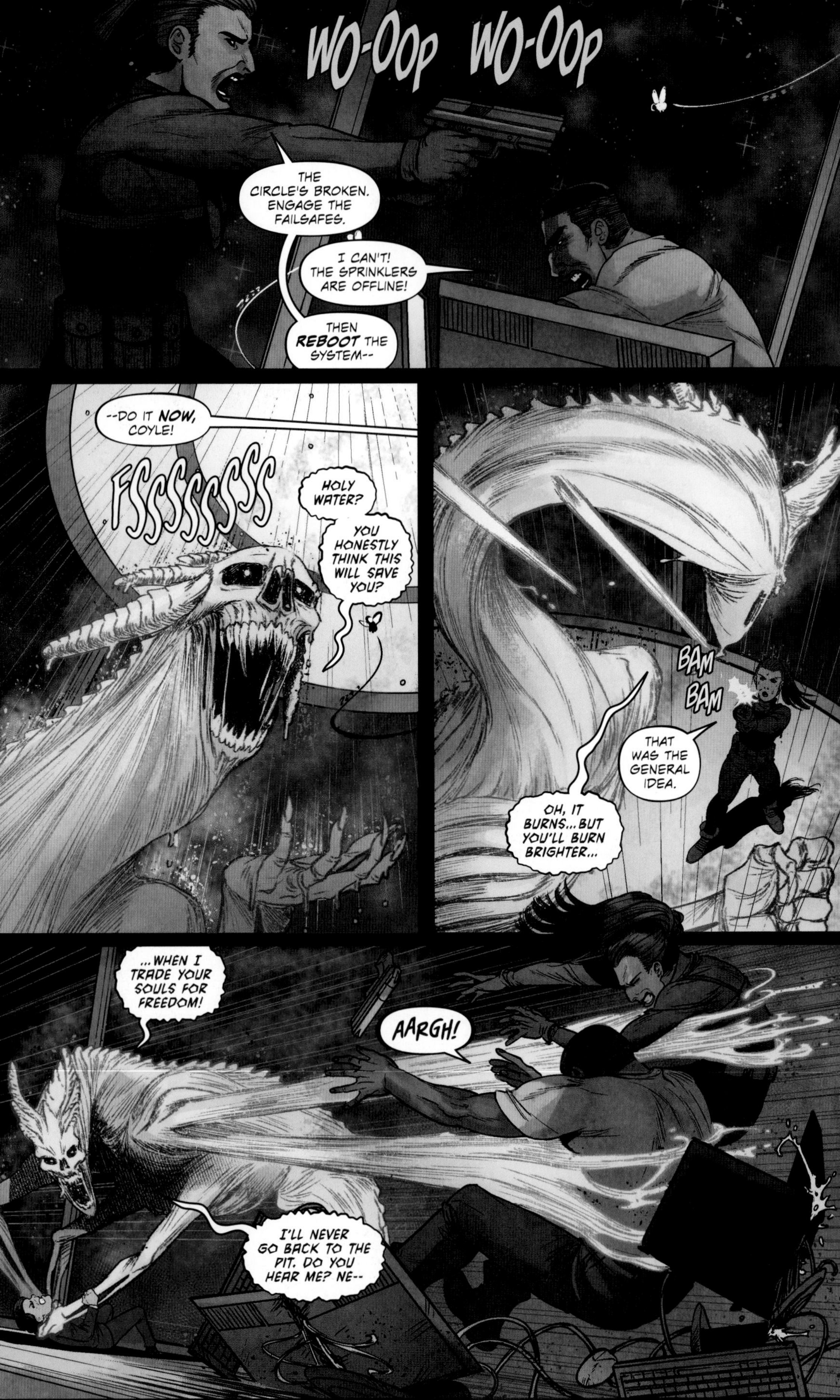
WO-OOP WO-OOP
THE CIRCLE'S BROKEN. ENGAGE THE FAILSAFES.
I CAN'T! THE SPRINKLERS ARE OFFLINE!
THEN **REBOOT** THE SYSTEM--
--DO IT **NOW**, COYLE!
FSSSSSSSS
HOLY WATER?
YOU HONESTLY THINK THIS WILL SAVE YOU?
BAM
BAM
THAT WAS THE GENERAL IDEA.
OH, IT BURNS...BUT YOU'LL BURN BRIGHTER...
...WHEN I TRADE YOUR SOULS FOR FREEDOM!
AARGH!
I'LL NEVER GO BACK TO THE PIT. DO YOU HEAR ME? NE--

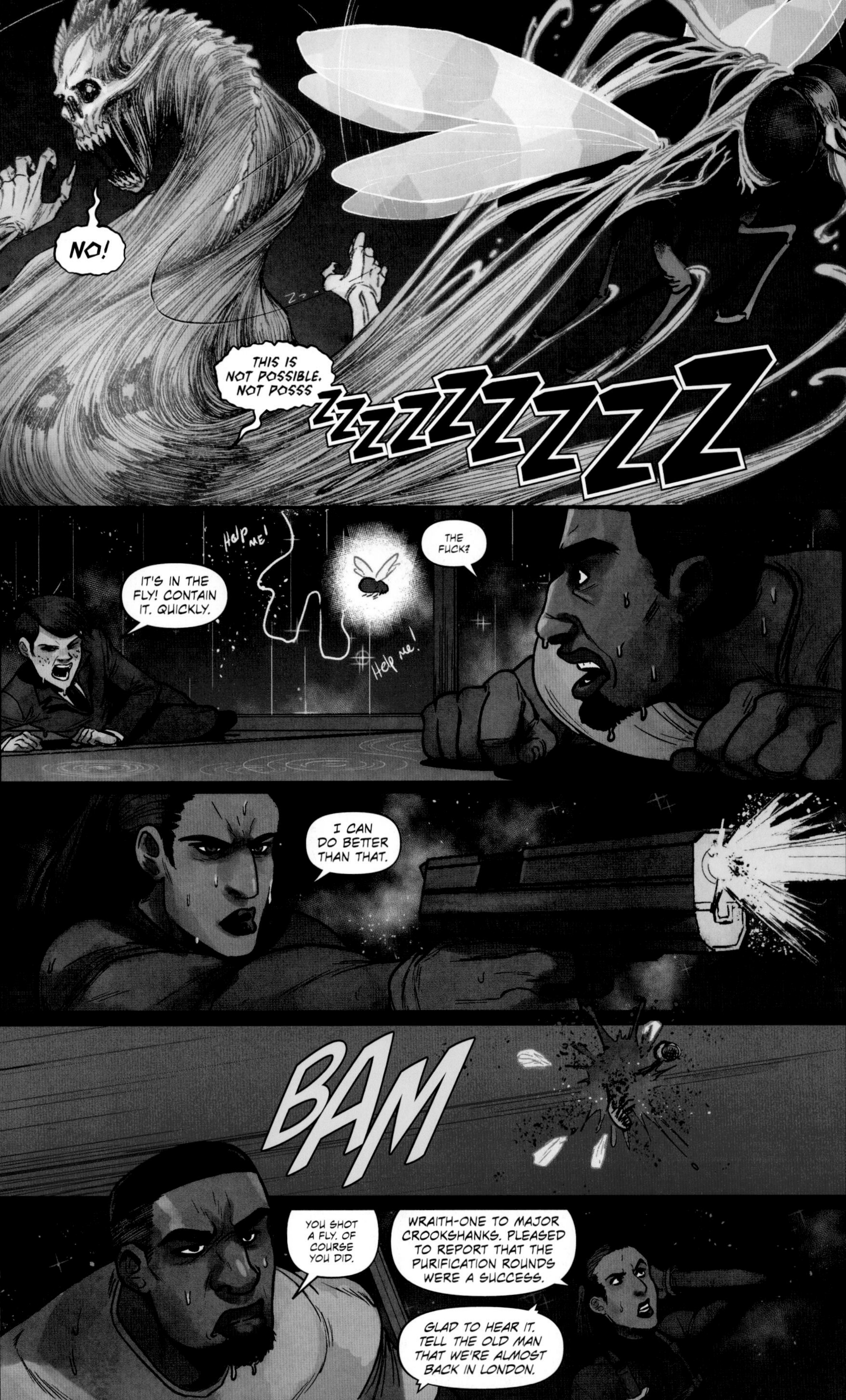

NO!
THIS IS NOT POSSIBLE. NOT POSSS
ZZZZZZZZZZZ
IT'S IN THE FLY! CONTAIN IT. QUICKLY.
Help me!
Help me!
THE FUCK?
I CAN DO BETTER THAN THAT.
BAM
YOU SHOT A FLY. OF COURSE YOU DID.
WRAITH-ONE TO MAJOR CROOKSHANKS. PLEASED TO REPORT THAT THE PURIFICATION ROUNDS WERE A SUCCESS.
GLAD TO HEAR IT. TELL THE OLD MAN THAT WE'RE ALMOST BACK IN LONDON.

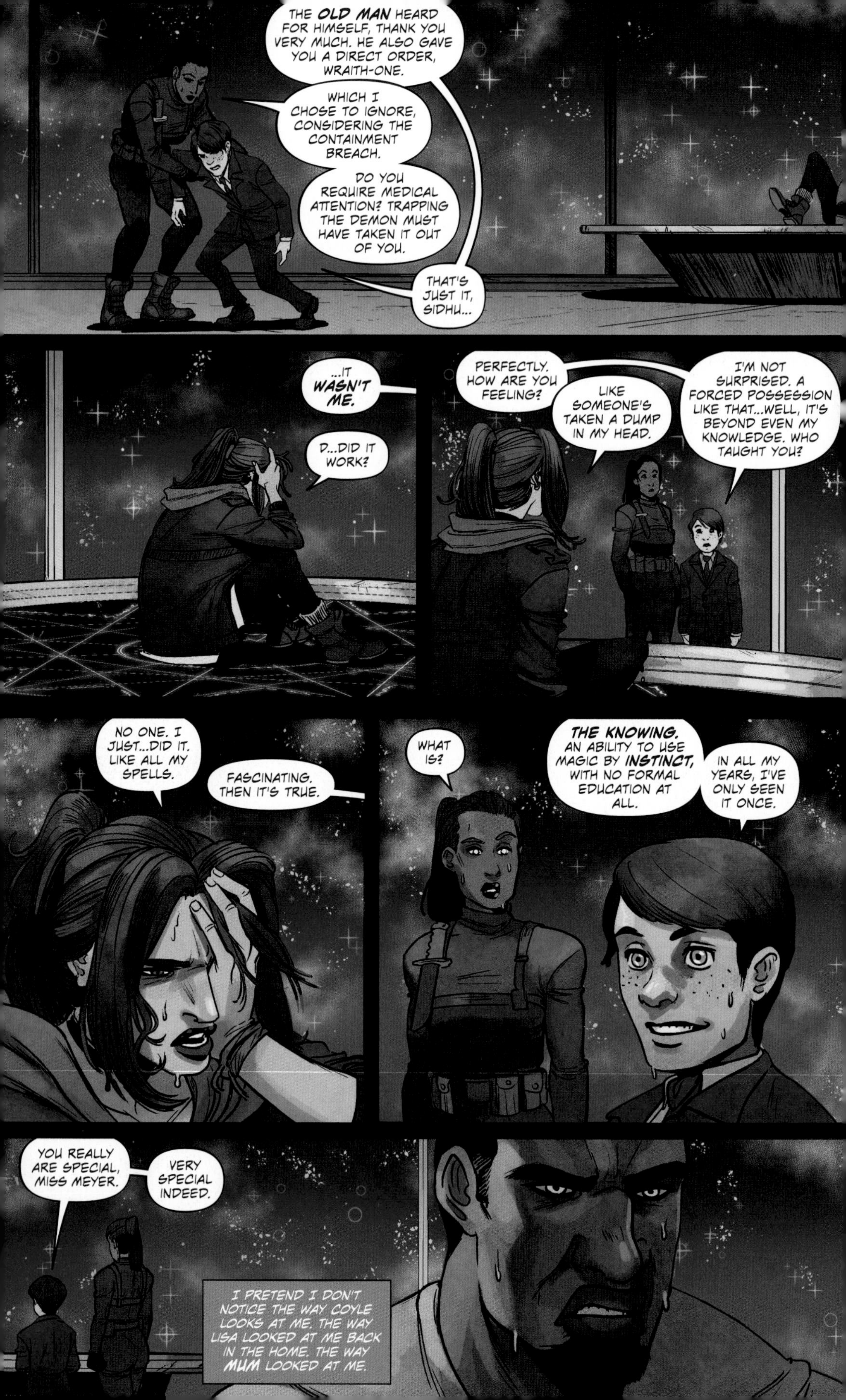

THE **OLD MAN** HEARD FOR HIMSELF, THANK YOU VERY MUCH. HE ALSO GAVE YOU A DIRECT ORDER, WRAITH-ONE.
WHICH I CHOSE TO IGNORE, CONSIDERING THE CONTAINMENT BREACH.
DO YOU REQUIRE MEDICAL ATTENTION? TRAPPING THE DEMON MUST HAVE TAKEN IT OUT OF YOU.
THAT'S JUST IT, SIDHU...
...IT ***WASN'T ME.***
D...DID IT WORK?
PERFECTLY. HOW ARE YOU FEELING?
LIKE SOMEONE'S TAKEN A DUMP IN MY HEAD.
I'M NOT SURPRISED. A FORCED POSSESSION LIKE THAT...WELL, IT'S BEYOND EVEN MY KNOWLEDGE. WHO TAUGHT YOU?
NO ONE. I JUST...DID IT. LIKE ALL MY SPELLS.
FASCINATING. THEN IT'S TRUE.
WHAT IS?
THE KNOWING. AN ABILITY TO USE MAGIC BY ***INSTINCT,*** WITH NO FORMAL EDUCATION AT ALL.
IN ALL MY YEARS, I'VE ONLY SEEN IT ONCE.
YOU REALLY ARE SPECIAL, MISS MEYER.
VERY SPECIAL INDEED.
I PRETEND I DON'T NOTICE THE WAY COYLE LOOKS AT ME. THE WAY LISA LOOKED AT ME BACK IN THE HOME. THE WAY **MUM** LOOKED AT ME.

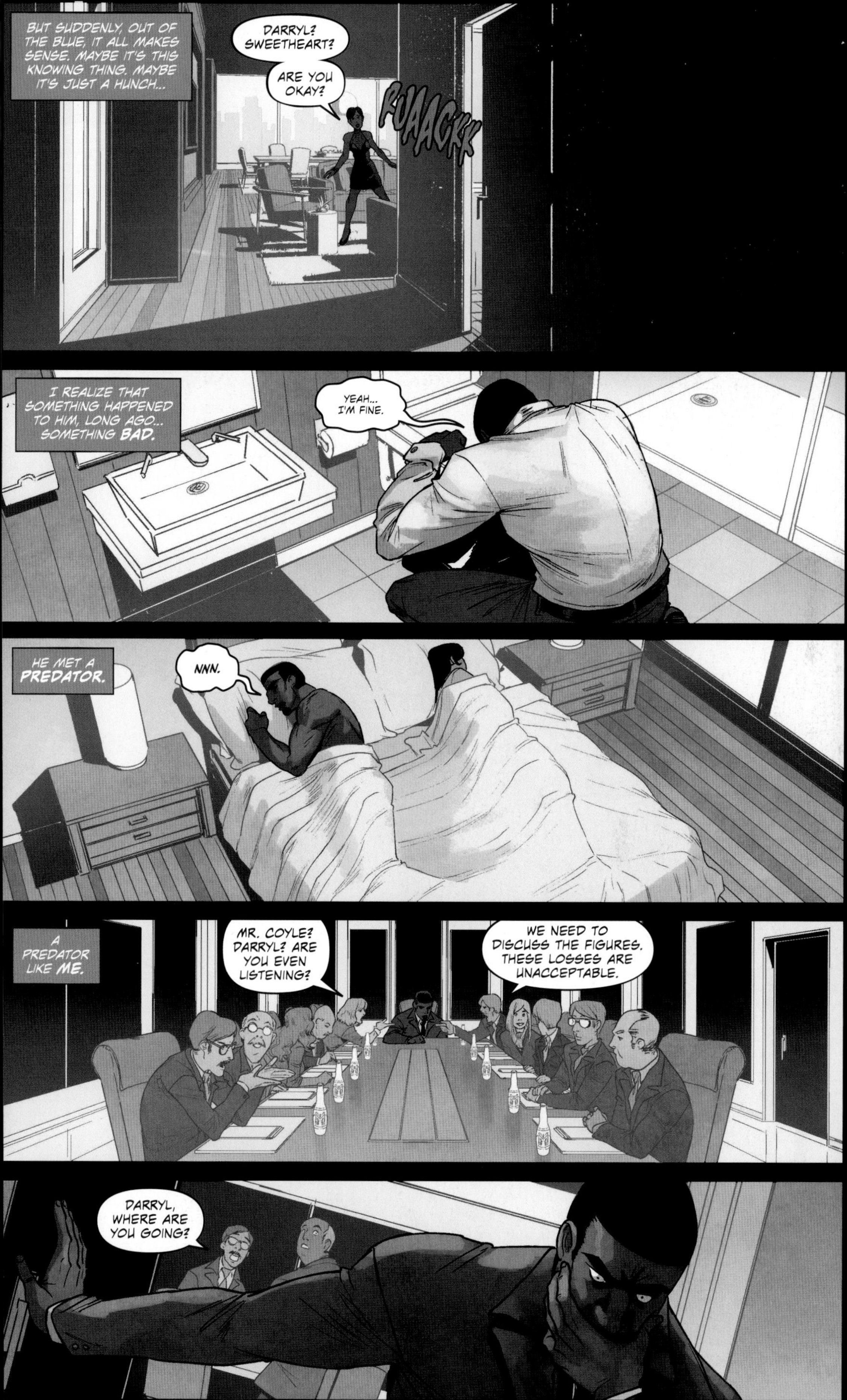
BUT SUDDENLY, OUT OF THE BLUE, IT ALL MAKES SENSE. MAYBE IT'S THIS KNOWING THING. MAYBE IT'S JUST A HUNCH...
DARRYL? SWEETHEART?
ARE YOU OKAY?
FUAAACKK
I REALIZE THAT SOMETHING HAPPENED TO HIM, LONG AGO... SOMETHING BAD.
YEAH... I'M FINE.
HE MET A PREDATOR.
NNN.
A PREDATOR LIKE ME.
MR. COYLE? DARRYL? ARE YOU EVEN LISTENING?
WE NEED TO DISCUSS THE FIGURES. THESE LOSSES ARE UNACCEPTABLE.
DARRYL, WHERE ARE YOU GOING?

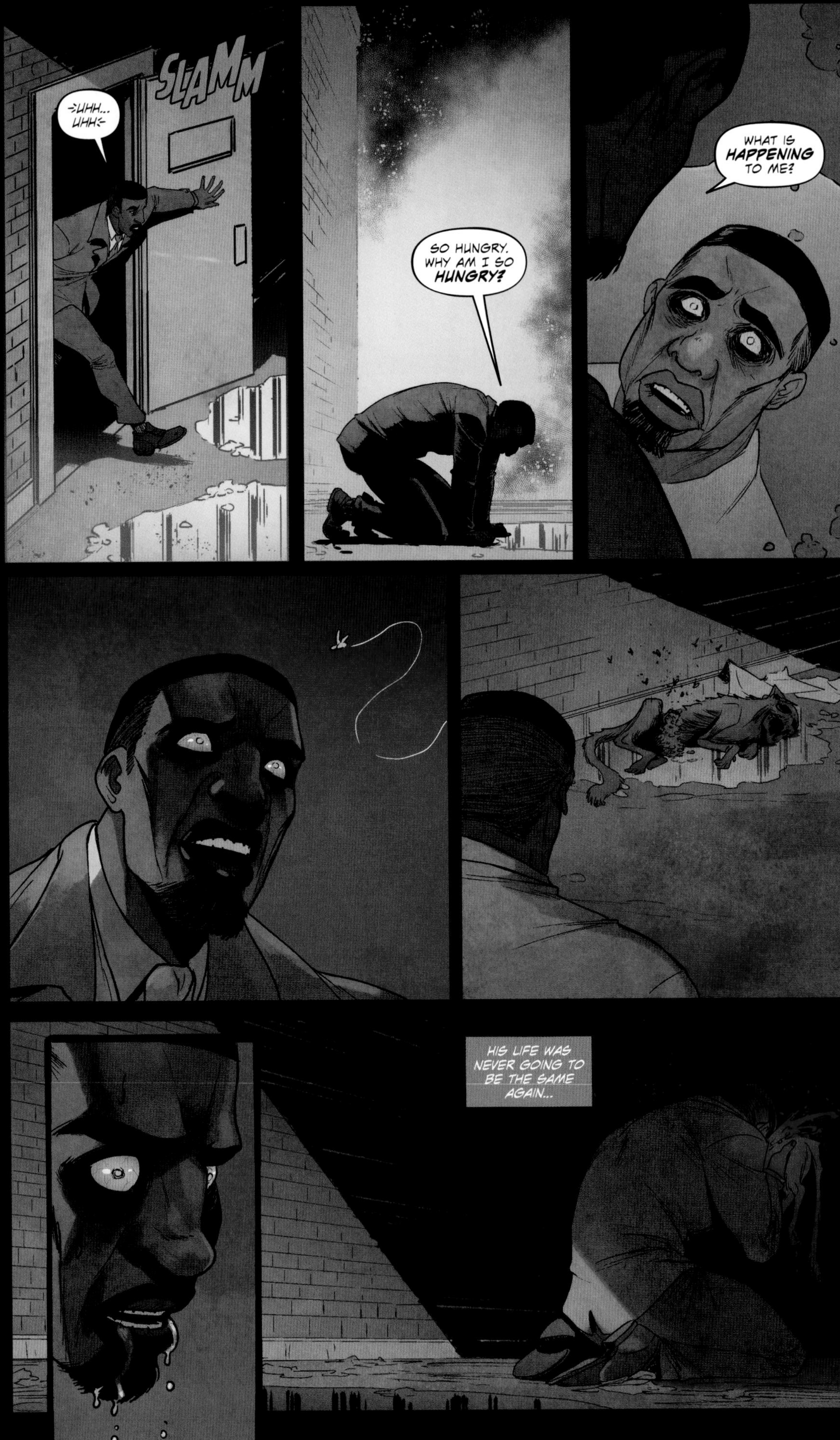
SLAMM
-UHH... UHH-
SO HUNGRY. WHY AM I SO HUNGRY?
WHAT IS HAPPENING TO ME?
HIS LIFE WAS NEVER GOING TO BE THE SAME AGAIN...

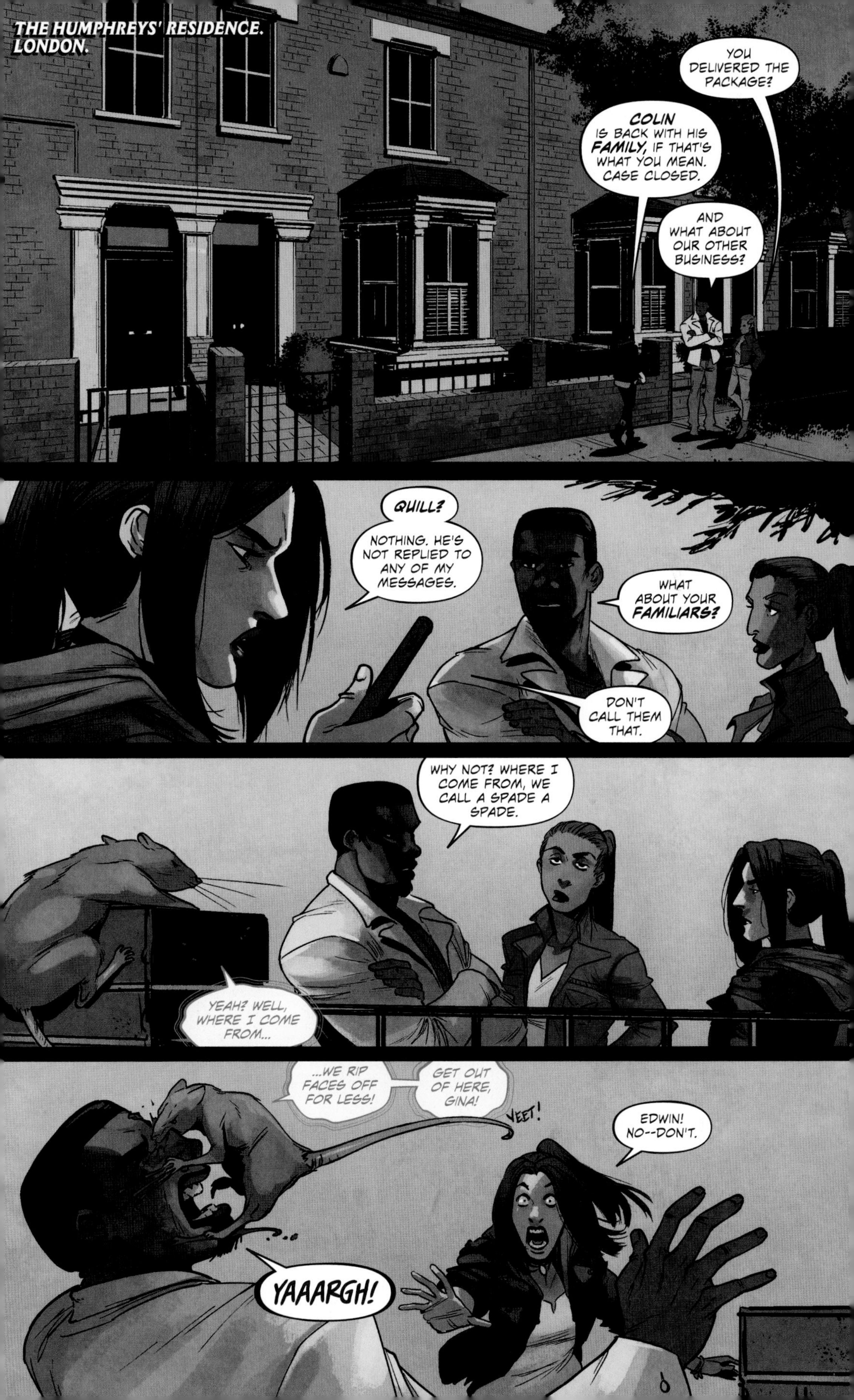
THE HUMPHREYS' RESIDENCE. LONDON.
YOU DELIVERED THE PACKAGE?
COLIN IS BACK WITH HIS FAMILY, IF THAT'S WHAT YOU MEAN. CASE CLOSED.
AND WHAT ABOUT OUR OTHER BUSINESS?
QUILL?
NOTHING. HE'S NOT REPLIED TO ANY OF MY MESSAGES.
WHAT ABOUT YOUR FAMILIARS?
DON'T CALL THEM THAT.
WHY NOT? WHERE I COME FROM, WE CALL A SPADE A SPADE.
YEAH? WELL, WHERE I COME FROM...
...WE RIP FACES OFF FOR LESS!
GET OUT OF HERE, GINA!
YEET!
EDWIN! NO--DON'T.
YAAARGH!

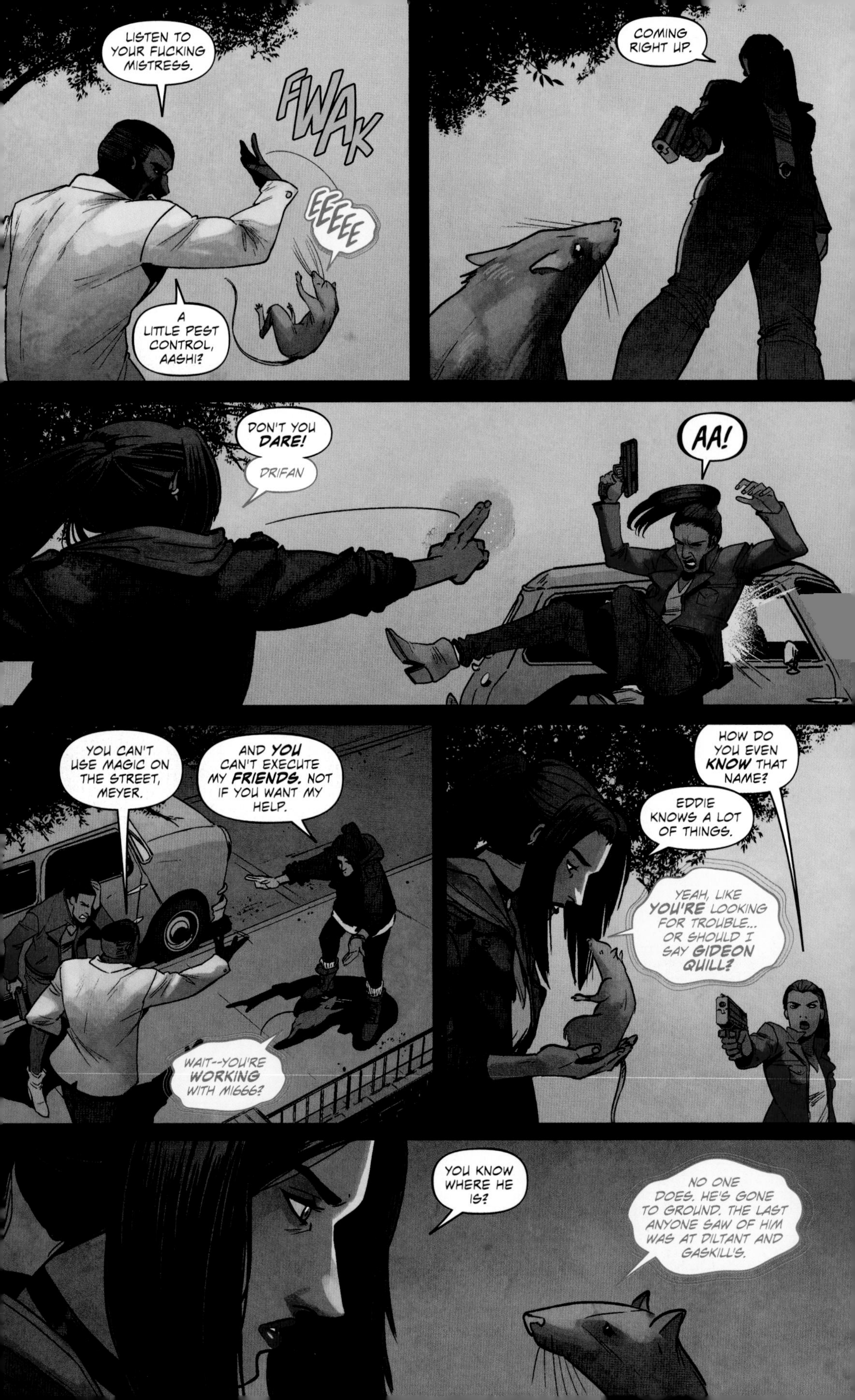
LISTEN TO YOUR FUCKING MISTRESS.
FWAK
EEEEE
A LITTLE PEST CONTROL, AASHI?
COMING RIGHT UP.
DON'T YOU DARE!
DRIFAN
AA!
YOU CAN'T USE MAGIC ON THE STREET, MEYER.
AND YOU CAN'T EXECUTE MY FRIENDS. NOT IF YOU WANT MY HELP.
WAIT--YOU'RE WORKING WITH MI666?
HOW DO YOU EVEN KNOW THAT NAME?
EDDIE KNOWS A LOT OF THINGS.
YEAH, LIKE YOU'RE LOOKING FOR TROUBLE... OR SHOULD I SAY GIDEON QUILL?
YOU KNOW WHERE HE IS?
NO ONE DOES. HE'S GONE TO GROUND. THE LAST ANYONE SAW OF HIM WAS AT DILTANT AND GASKILL'S.

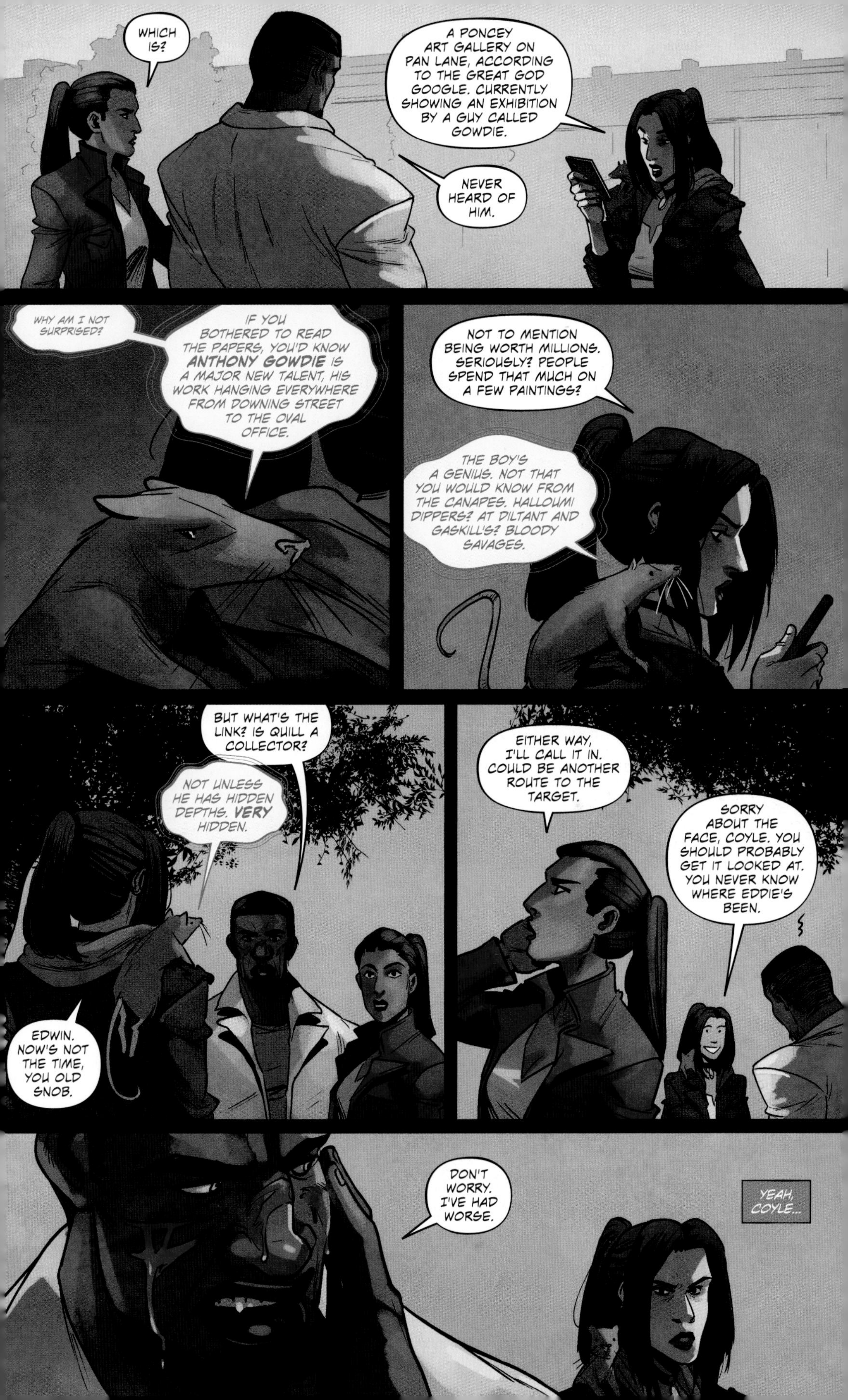
WHICH IS?
A PONCEY ART GALLERY ON PAN LANE, ACCORDING TO THE GREAT GOD GOOGLE. CURRENTLY SHOWING AN EXHIBITION BY A GUY CALLED GOWDIE.
NEVER HEARD OF HIM.
WHY AM I NOT SURPRISED?
IF YOU BOTHERED TO READ THE PAPERS, YOU'D KNOW ANTHONY GOWDIE IS A MAJOR NEW TALENT, HIS WORK HANGING EVERYWHERE FROM DOWNING STREET TO THE OVAL OFFICE.
NOT TO MENTION BEING WORTH MILLIONS. SERIOUSLY? PEOPLE SPEND THAT MUCH ON A FEW PAINTINGS?
THE BOY'S A GENIUS. NOT THAT YOU WOULD KNOW FROM THE CANAPES. HALLOUMI DIPPERS? AT DILTANT AND GASKILL'S? BLOODY SAVAGES.
BUT WHAT'S THE LINK? IS QUILL A COLLECTOR?
NOT UNLESS HE HAS HIDDEN DEPTHS. VERY HIDDEN.
EDWIN. NOW'S NOT THE TIME, YOU OLD SNOB.
EITHER WAY, I'LL CALL IT IN. COULD BE ANOTHER ROUTE TO THE TARGET.
SORRY ABOUT THE FACE, COYLE. YOU SHOULD PROBABLY GET IT LOOKED AT. YOU NEVER KNOW WHERE EDDIE'S BEEN.
DON'T WORRY. I'VE HAD WORSE.
YEAH, COYLE...

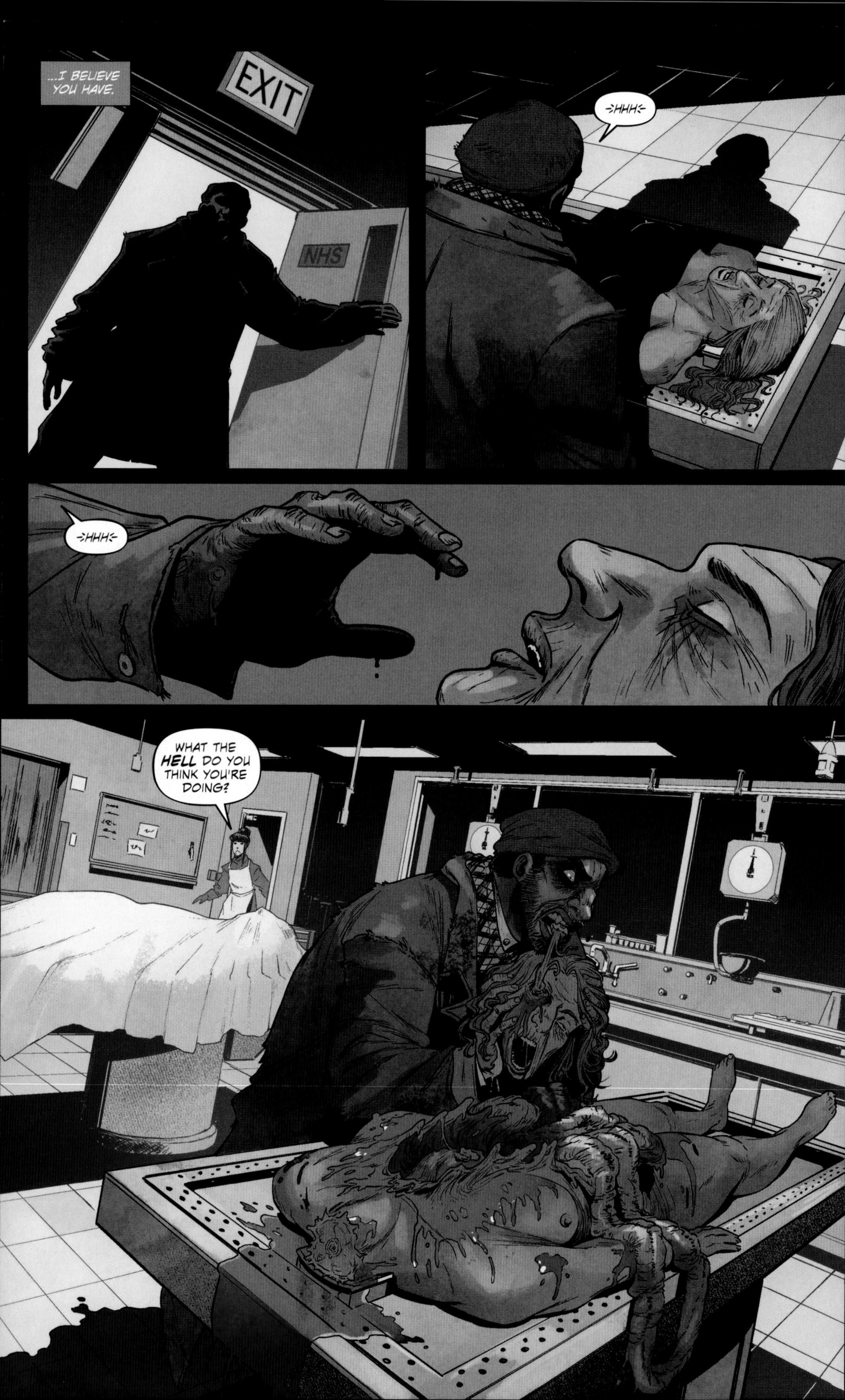
...I BELIEVE YOU HAVE.
EXIT
NHS
-:HHH:-
-:HHH:-
WHAT THE HELL DO YOU THINK YOU'RE DOING?

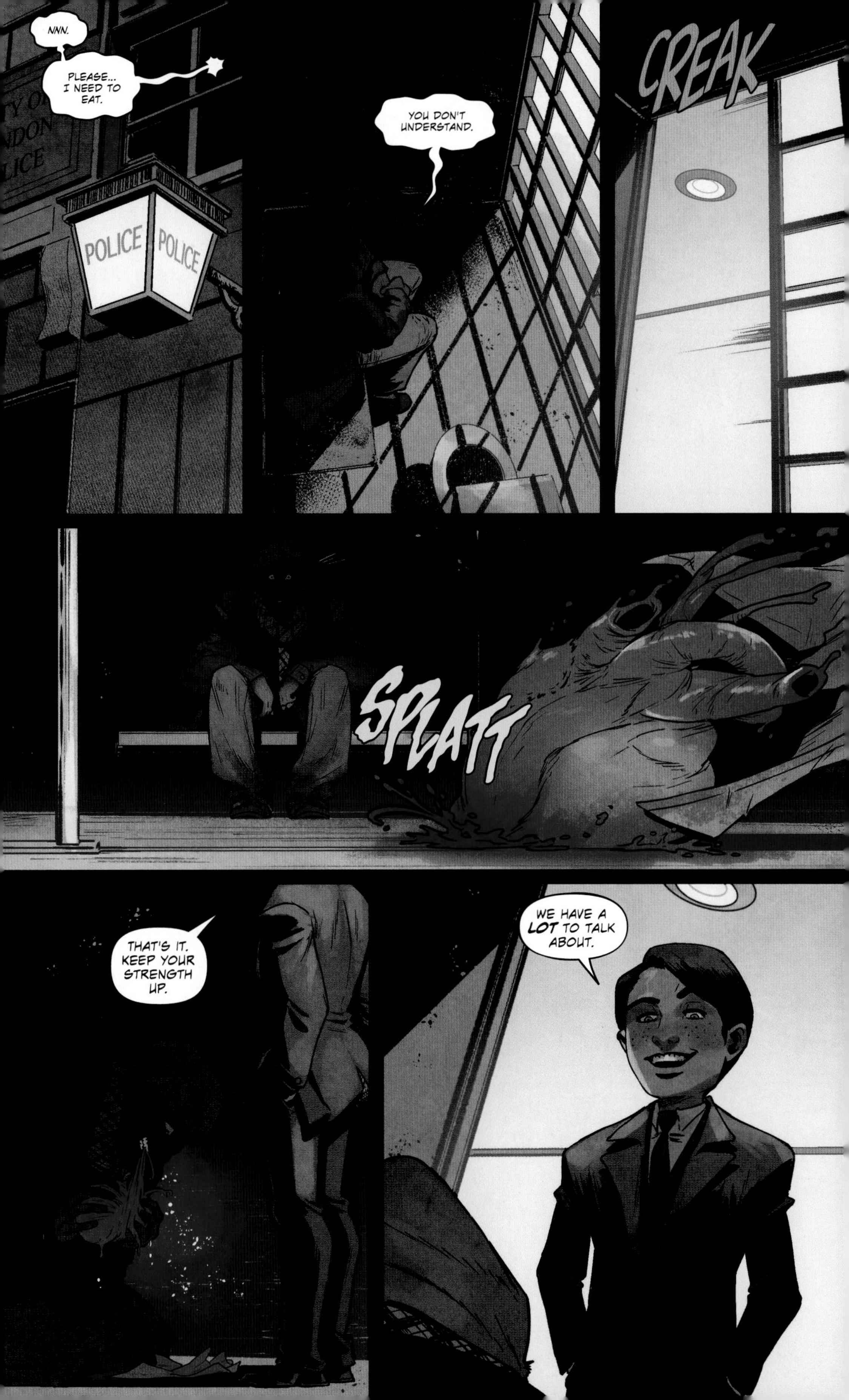
NNN.
PLEASE... I NEED TO EAT.
POLICE POLICE
YOU DON'T UNDERSTAND.
CREAK
SPLATT
THAT'S IT. KEEP YOUR STRENGTH UP.
WE HAVE A LOT TO TALK ABOUT.

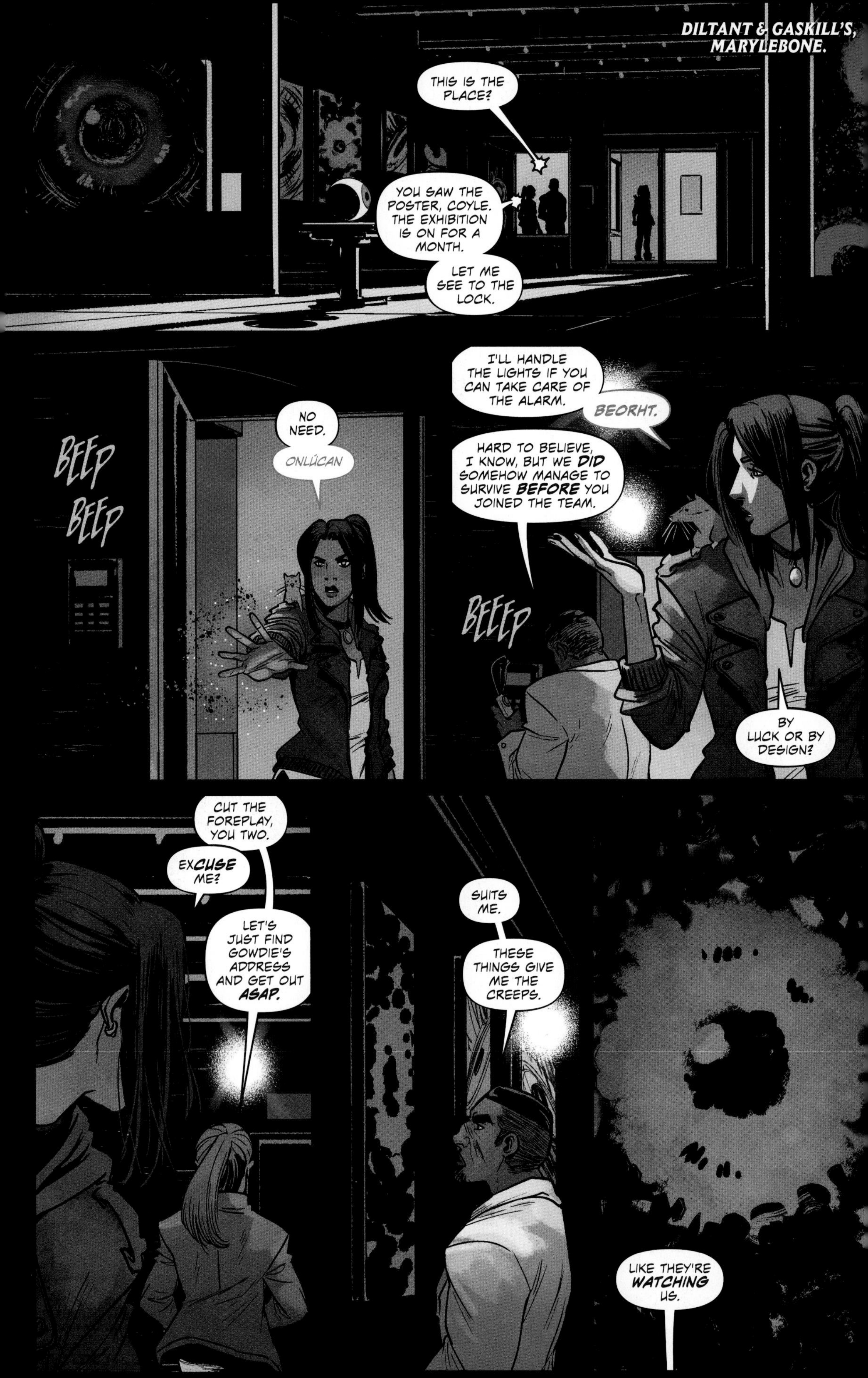
DILTANT & GASKILL'S, MARYLEBONE.
THIS IS THE PLACE?
YOU SAW THE POSTER, COYLE. THE EXHIBITION IS ON FOR A MONTH.
LET ME SEE TO THE LOCK.
BEEP BEEP
NO NEED.
ONLŪCAN
I'LL HANDLE THE LIGHTS IF YOU CAN TAKE CARE OF THE ALARM.
BEORHT.
HARD TO BELIEVE, I KNOW, BUT WE DID SOMEHOW MANAGE TO SURVIVE BEFORE YOU JOINED THE TEAM.
BEEEP
BY LUCK OR BY DESIGN?
CUT THE FOREPLAY, YOU TWO.
EXCUSE ME?
LET'S JUST FIND GOWDIE'S ADDRESS AND GET OUT ASAP.
SUITS ME.
THESE THINGS GIVE ME THE CREEPS.
LIKE THEY'RE WATCHING US.

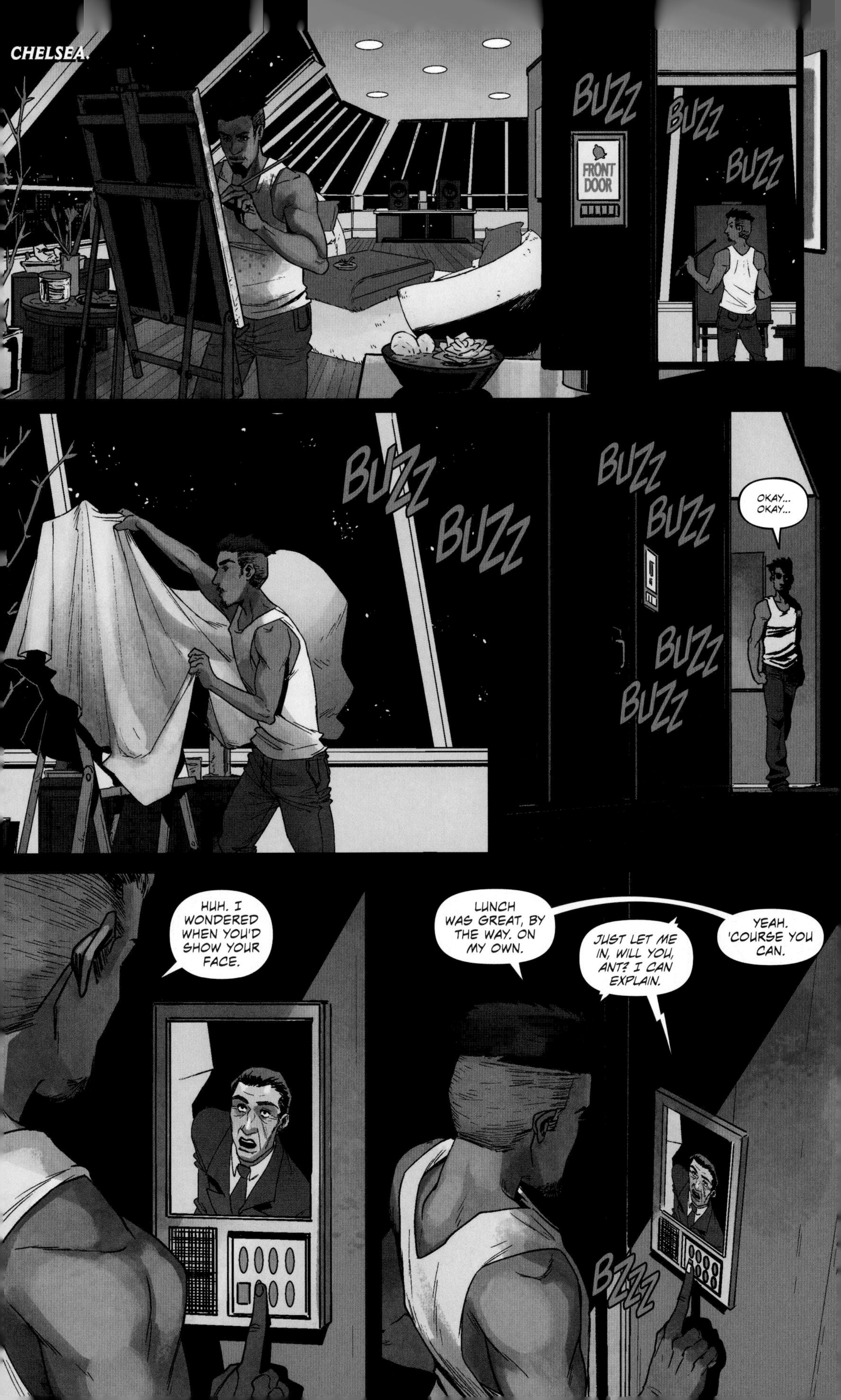
CHELSEA.
BUZZ
FRONT DOOR
BUZZ
BUZZ
BUZZ
BUZZ
BUZZ
BUZZ
OKAY... OKAY...
BUZZ
BUZZ
HUH. I WONDERED WHEN YOU'D SHOW YOUR FACE.
LUNCH WAS GREAT, BY THE WAY. ON MY OWN.
JUST LET ME IN, WILL YOU, ANT? I CAN EXPLAIN.
YEAH. 'COURSE YOU CAN.
BZZZ

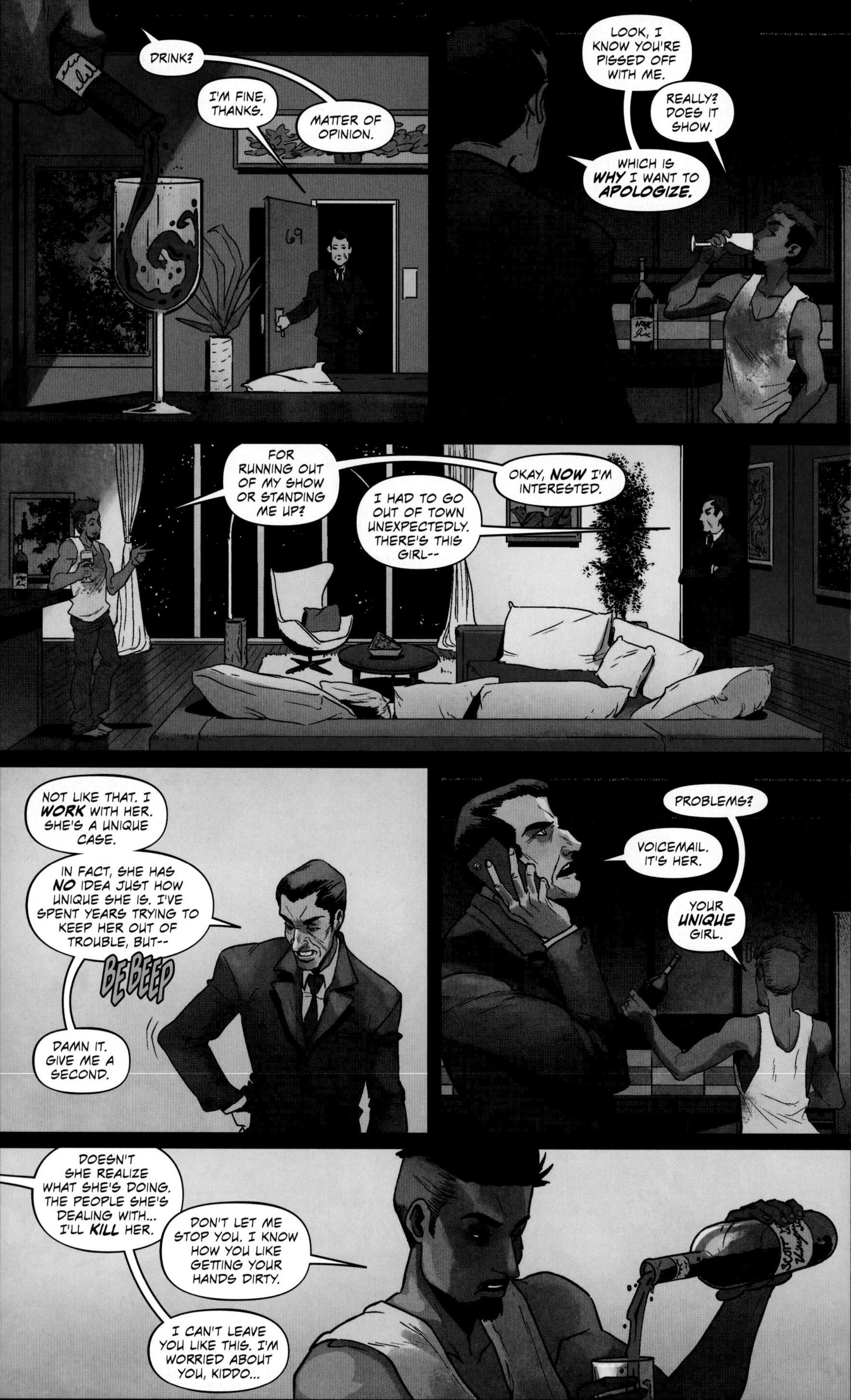
DRINK?
I'M FINE, THANKS.
MATTER OF OPINION.
LOOK, I KNOW YOU'RE PISSED OFF WITH ME.
REALLY? DOES IT SHOW.
WHICH IS WHY I WANT TO APOLOGIZE.
FOR RUNNING OUT OF MY SHOW OR STANDING ME UP?
I HAD TO GO OUT OF TOWN UNEXPECTEDLY. THERE'S THIS GIRL--
OKAY, NOW I'M INTERESTED.
NOT LIKE THAT. I WORK WITH HER. SHE'S A UNIQUE CASE.
IN FACT, SHE HAS NO IDEA JUST HOW UNIQUE SHE IS. I'VE SPENT YEARS TRYING TO KEEP HER OUT OF TROUBLE, BUT--
BE BEEP
DAMN IT. GIVE ME A SECOND.
PROBLEMS?
VOICEMAIL. IT'S HER.
YOUR UNIQUE GIRL.
DOESN'T SHE REALIZE WHAT SHE'S DOING. THE PEOPLE SHE'S DEALING WITH... I'LL KILL HER.
DON'T LET ME STOP YOU. I KNOW HOW YOU LIKE GETTING YOUR HANDS DIRTY.
I CAN'T LEAVE YOU LIKE THIS. I'M WORRIED ABOUT YOU, KIDDO...

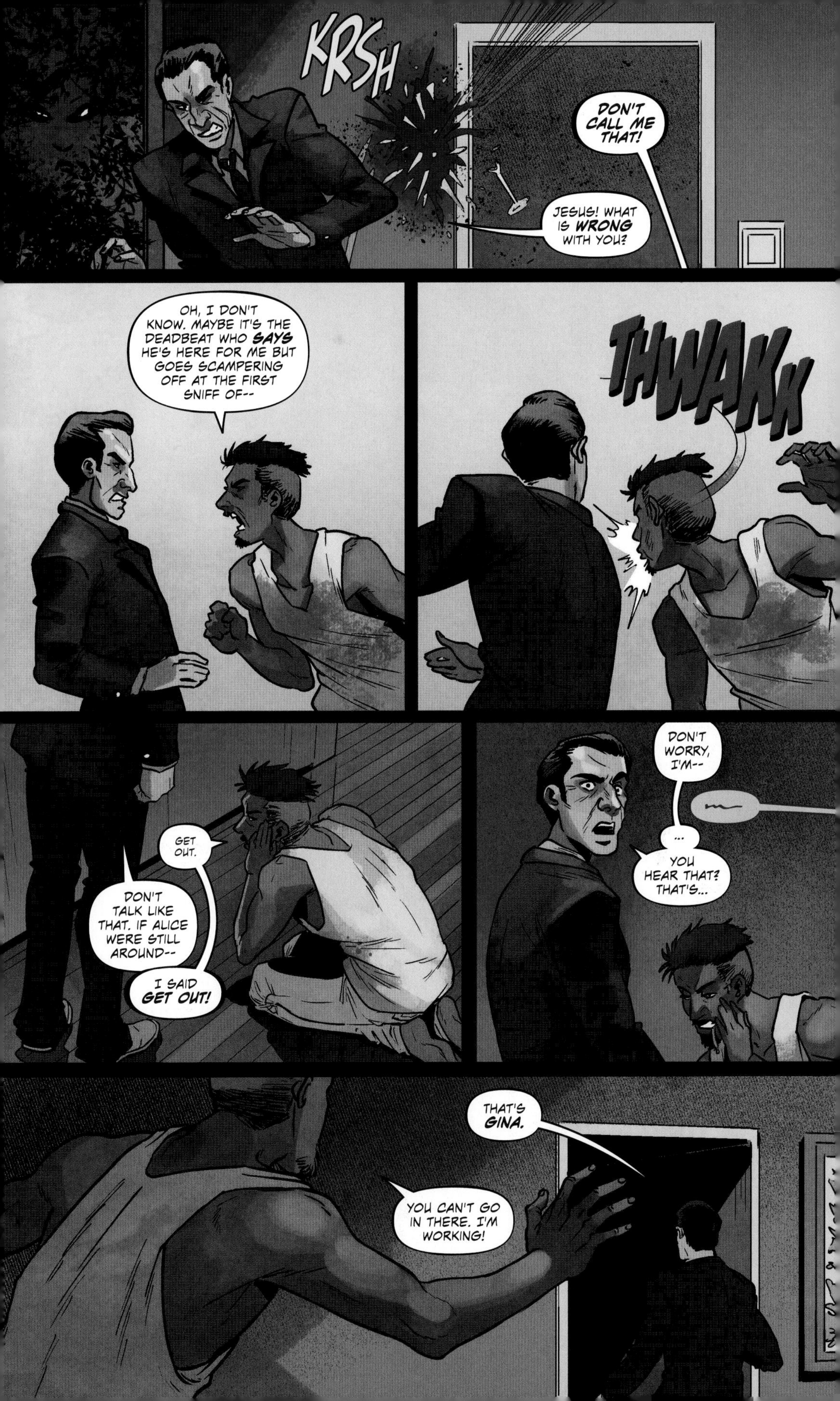
KRSH
DON'T CALL ME THAT!
JESUS! WHAT IS WRONG WITH YOU?
OH, I DON'T KNOW. MAYBE IT'S THE DEADBEAT WHO SAYS HE'S HERE FOR ME BUT GOES SCAMPERING OFF AT THE FIRST SNIFF OF--
THWAKK
GET OUT.
DON'T TALK LIKE THAT. IF ALICE WERE STILL AROUND--
I SAID GET OUT!
DON'T WORRY, I'M--
...
YOU HEAR THAT? THAT'S...
THAT'S GINA.
YOU CAN'T GO IN THERE. I'M WORKING!

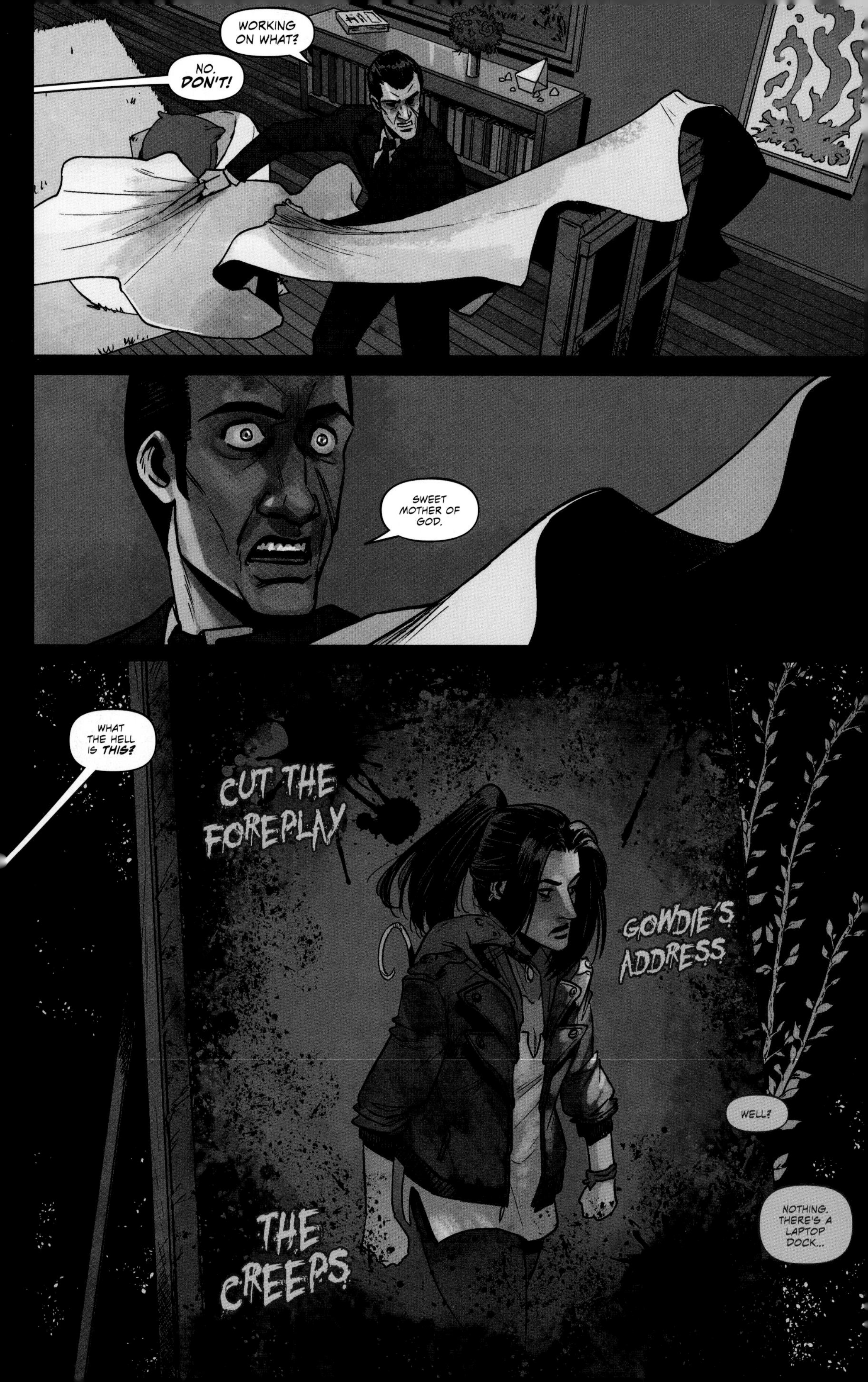
WORKING ON WHAT?
NO. DON'T!
SWEET MOTHER OF GOD.
WHAT THE HELL IS THIS?
CUT THE FOREPLAY
GOWDIE'S ADDRESS
THE CREEPS
WELL?
NOTHING. THERE'S A LAPTOP DOCK...

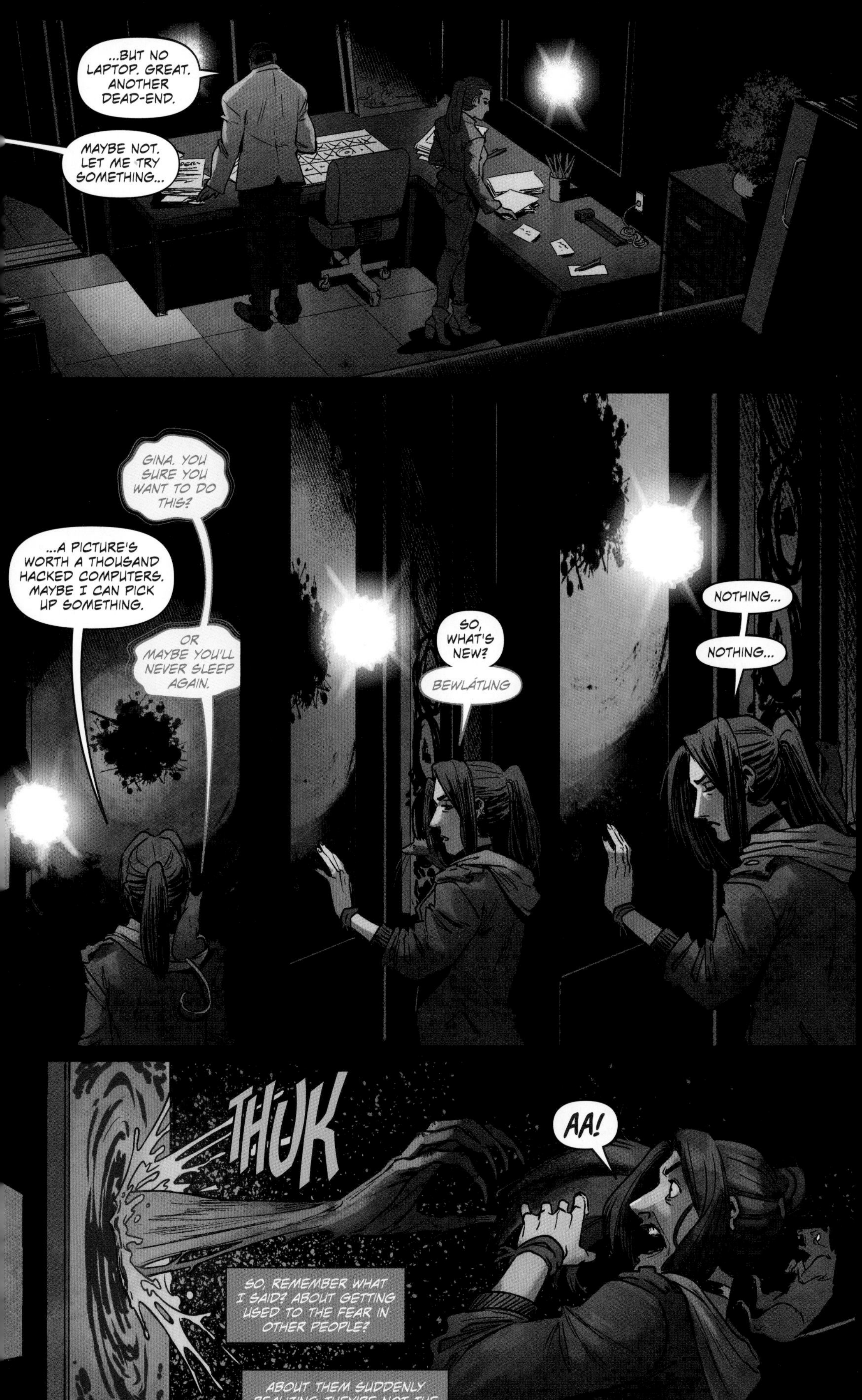
...BUT NO LAPTOP. GREAT. ANOTHER DEAD-END.
MAYBE NOT. LET ME TRY SOMETHING...
GINA. YOU SURE YOU WANT TO DO THIS?
...A PICTURE'S WORTH A THOUSAND HACKED COMPUTERS. MAYBE I CAN PICK UP SOMETHING.
OR MAYBE YOU'LL NEVER SLEEP AGAIN.
SO, WHAT'S NEW?
BEWLÁTUNG
NOTHING...
NOTHING...
THUK
AA!
SO, REMEMBER WHAT I SAID? ABOUT GETTING USED TO THE FEAR IN OTHER PEOPLE?
ABOUT THEM SUDDENLY REALIZING THEY'RE NOT THE MOST TERRIFYING CREATURE IN THE ROOM?

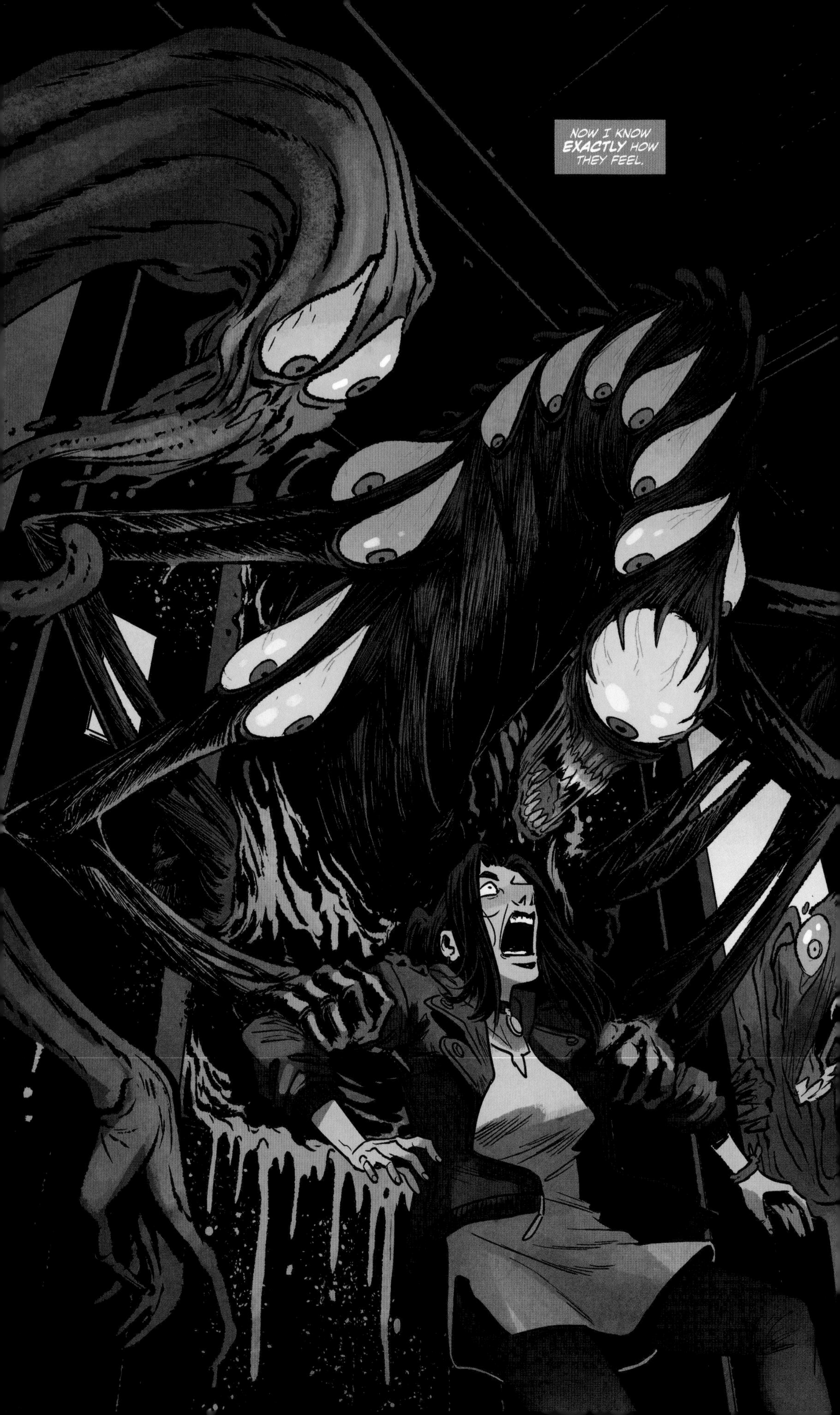
NOW I KNOW **EXACTLY** HOW THEY FEEL.

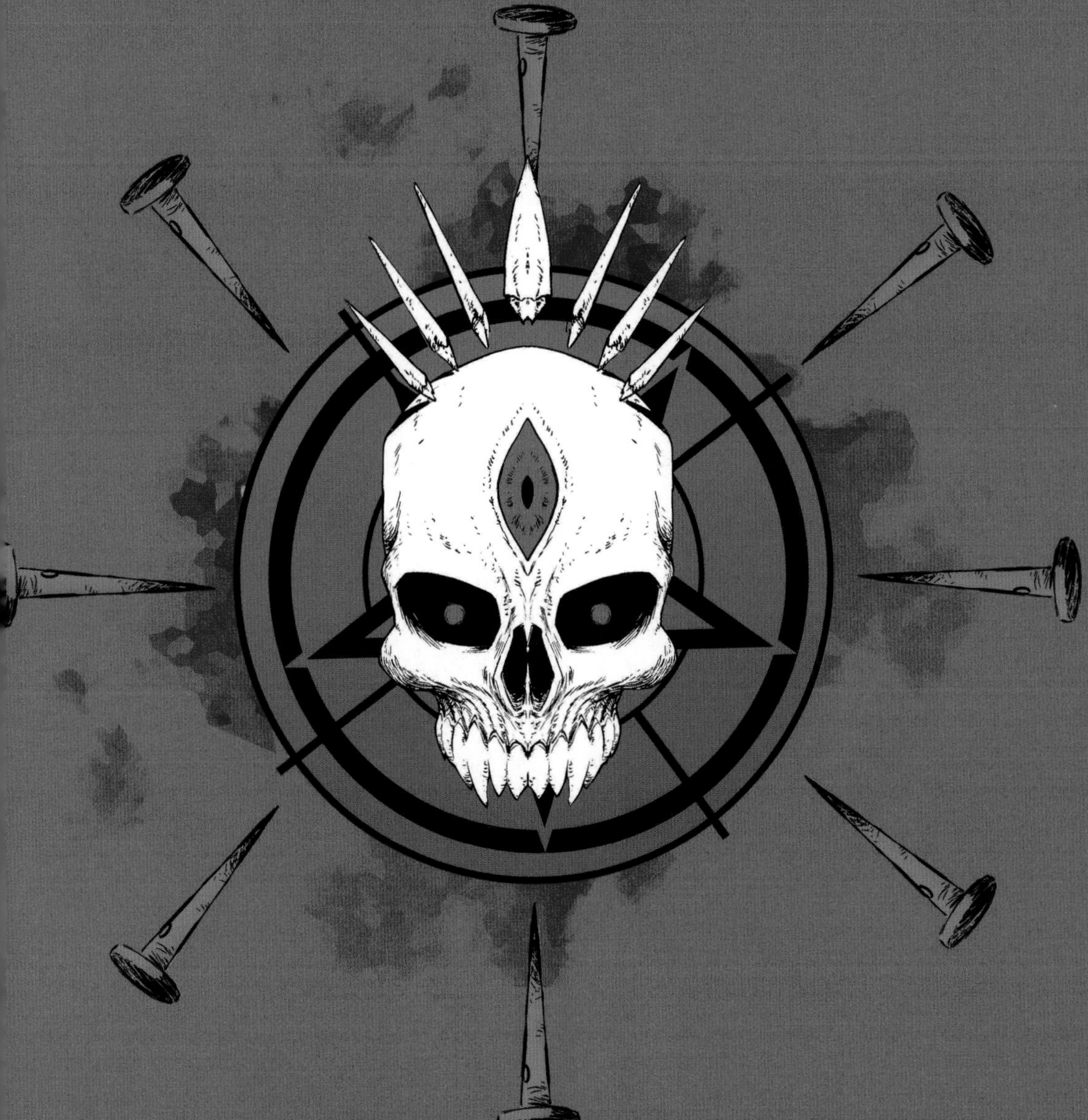

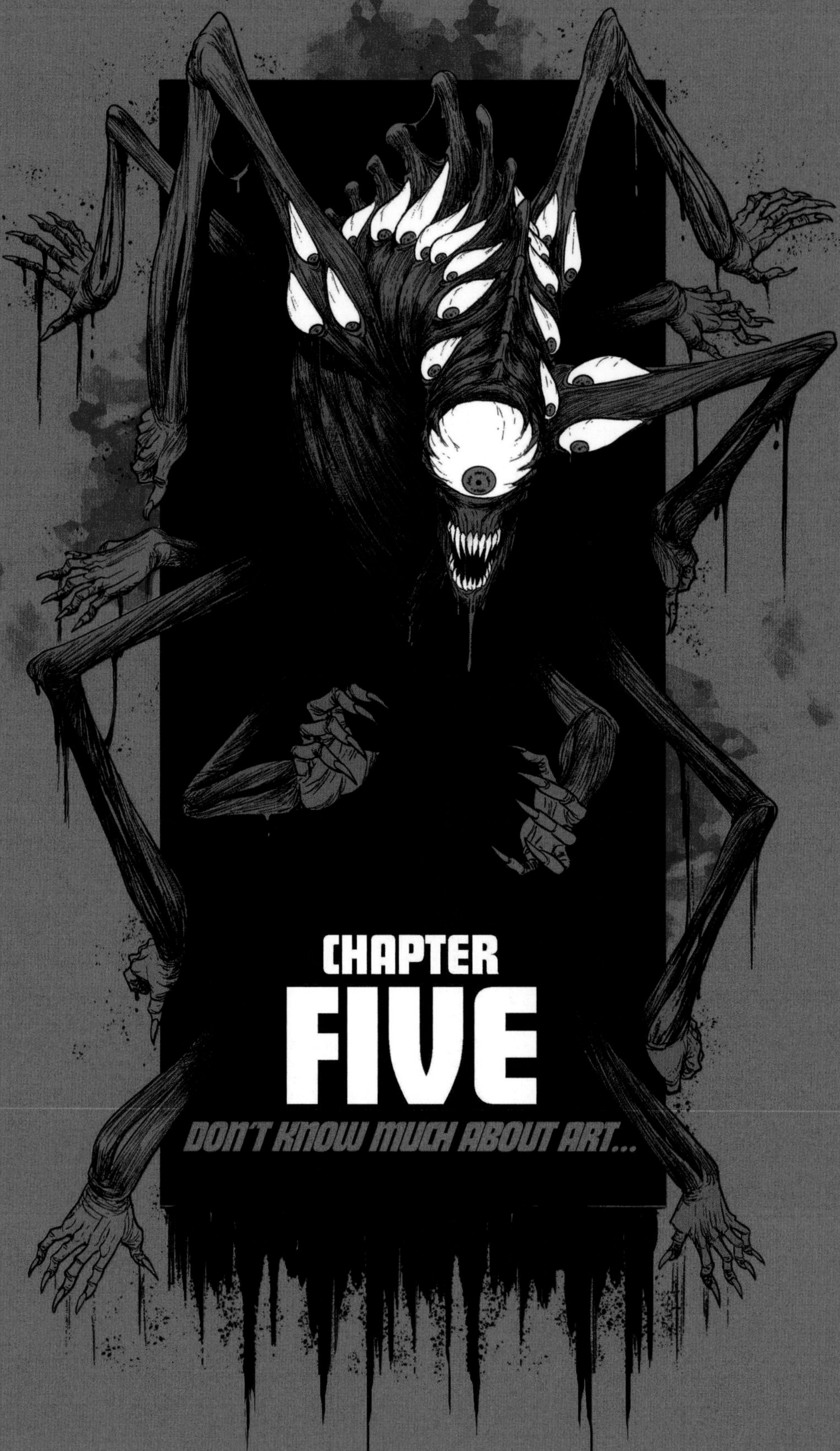

CHAPTER FIVE

DON'T KNOW MUCH ABOUT ART...

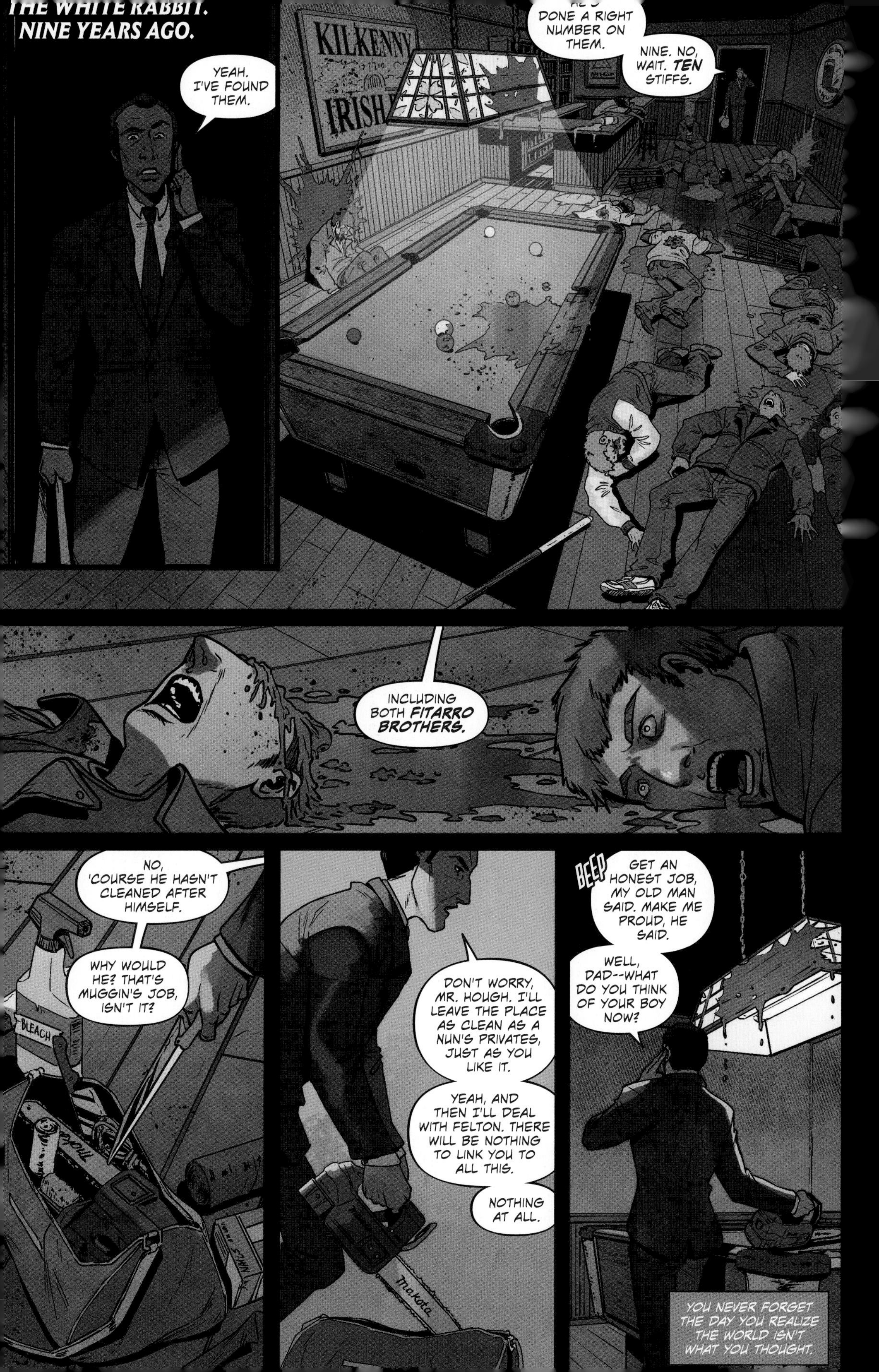
THE WHITE RABBIT. NINE YEARS AGO.
YEAH. I'VE FOUND THEM.
DONE A RIGHT NUMBER ON THEM.
NINE. NO, WAIT. TEN STIFFS.
KILKENNY
IRISH
INCLUDING BOTH FITARRO BROTHERS.
NO, 'COURSE HE HASN'T CLEANED AFTER HIMSELF.
WHY WOULD HE? THAT'S MUGGIN'S JOB, ISN'T IT?
BLEACH
DON'T WORRY, MR. HOUGH. I'LL LEAVE THE PLACE AS CLEAN AS A NUN'S PRIVATES, JUST AS YOU LIKE IT.
YEAH, AND THEN I'LL DEAL WITH FELTON. THERE WILL BE NOTHING TO LINK YOU TO ALL THIS.
NOTHING AT ALL.
makota
BEEP
GET AN HONEST JOB, MY OLD MAN SAID. MAKE ME PROUD, HE SAID.
WELL, DAD--WHAT DO YOU THINK OF YOUR BOY NOW?
YOU NEVER FORGET THE DAY YOU REALIZE THE WORLD ISN'T WHAT YOU THOUGHT.

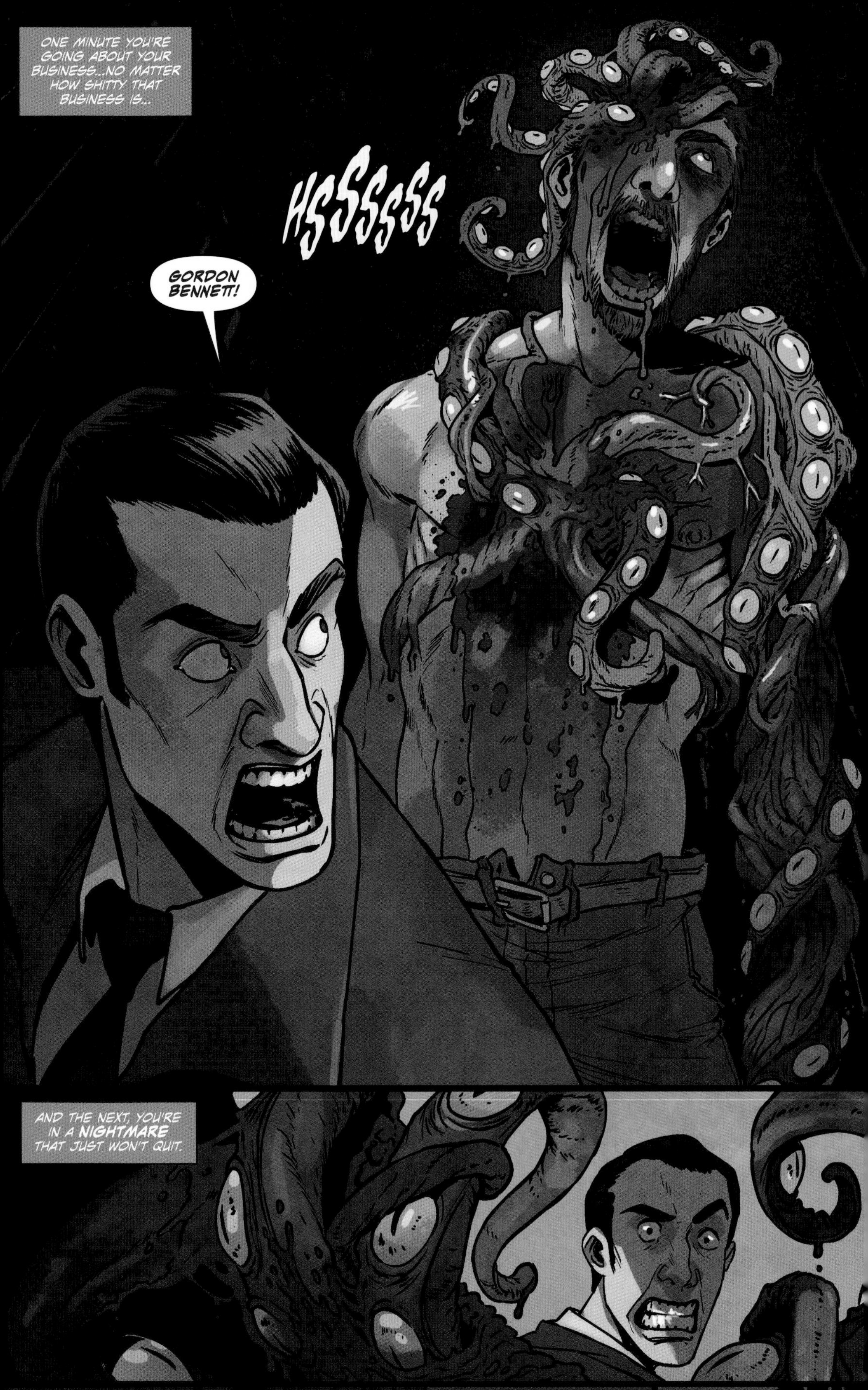
ONE MINUTE YOU'RE GOING ABOUT YOUR BUSINESS...NO MATTER HOW SHITTY THAT BUSINESS IS...
HSSSSSS
GORDON BENNETT!
AND THE NEXT, YOU'RE IN A NIGHTMARE THAT JUST WON'T QUIT.

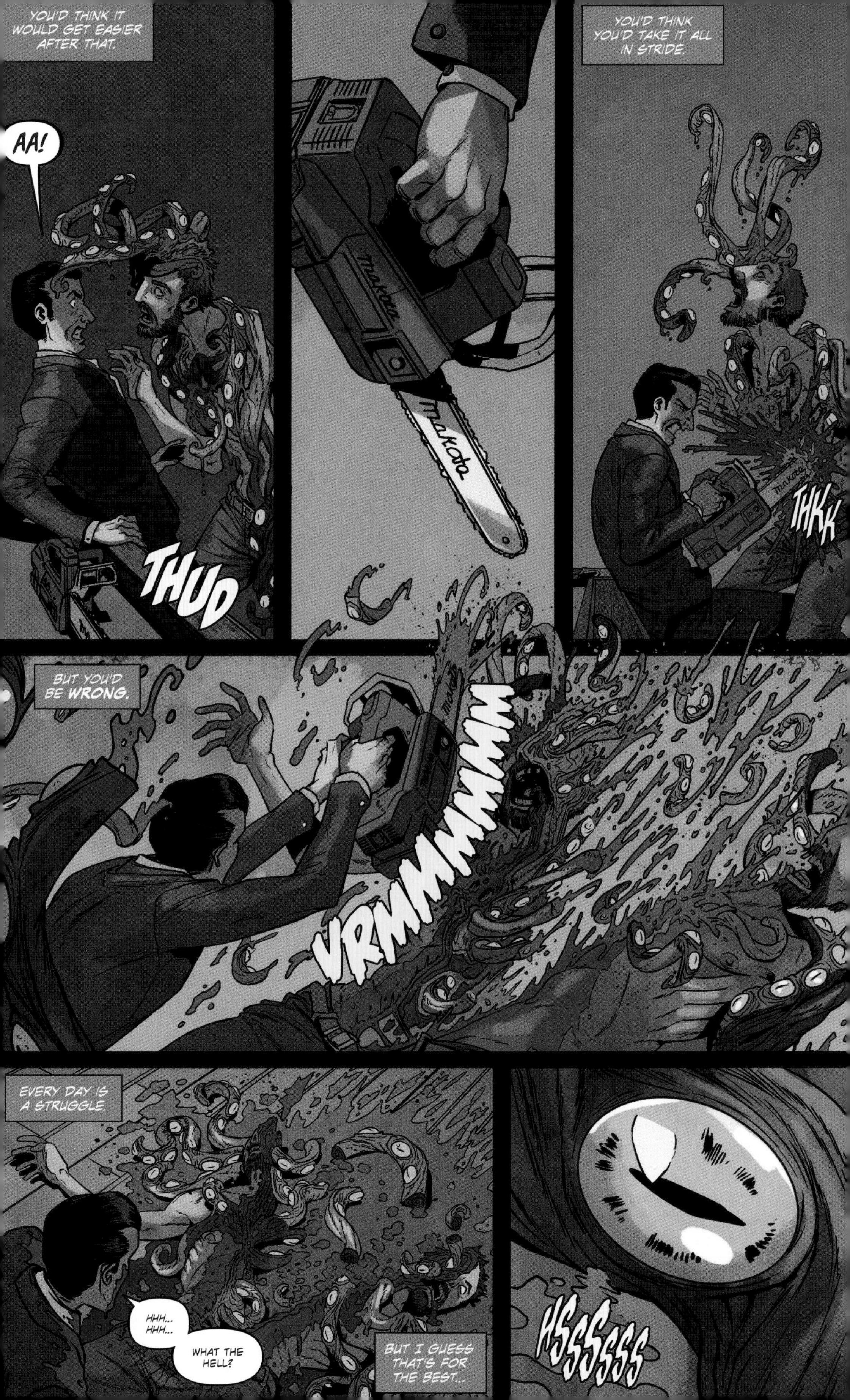
YOU'D THINK IT WOULD GET EASIER AFTER THAT.
AA!
THUD
makita
makita
YOU'D THINK YOU'D TAKE IT ALL IN STRIDE.
THKK
BUT YOU'D BE **WRONG**.
VRMMMMMMM
EVERY DAY IS A STRUGGLE.
HHH... HHH...
WHAT THE HELL?
BUT I GUESS THAT'S FOR THE BEST...
HSSSSSS

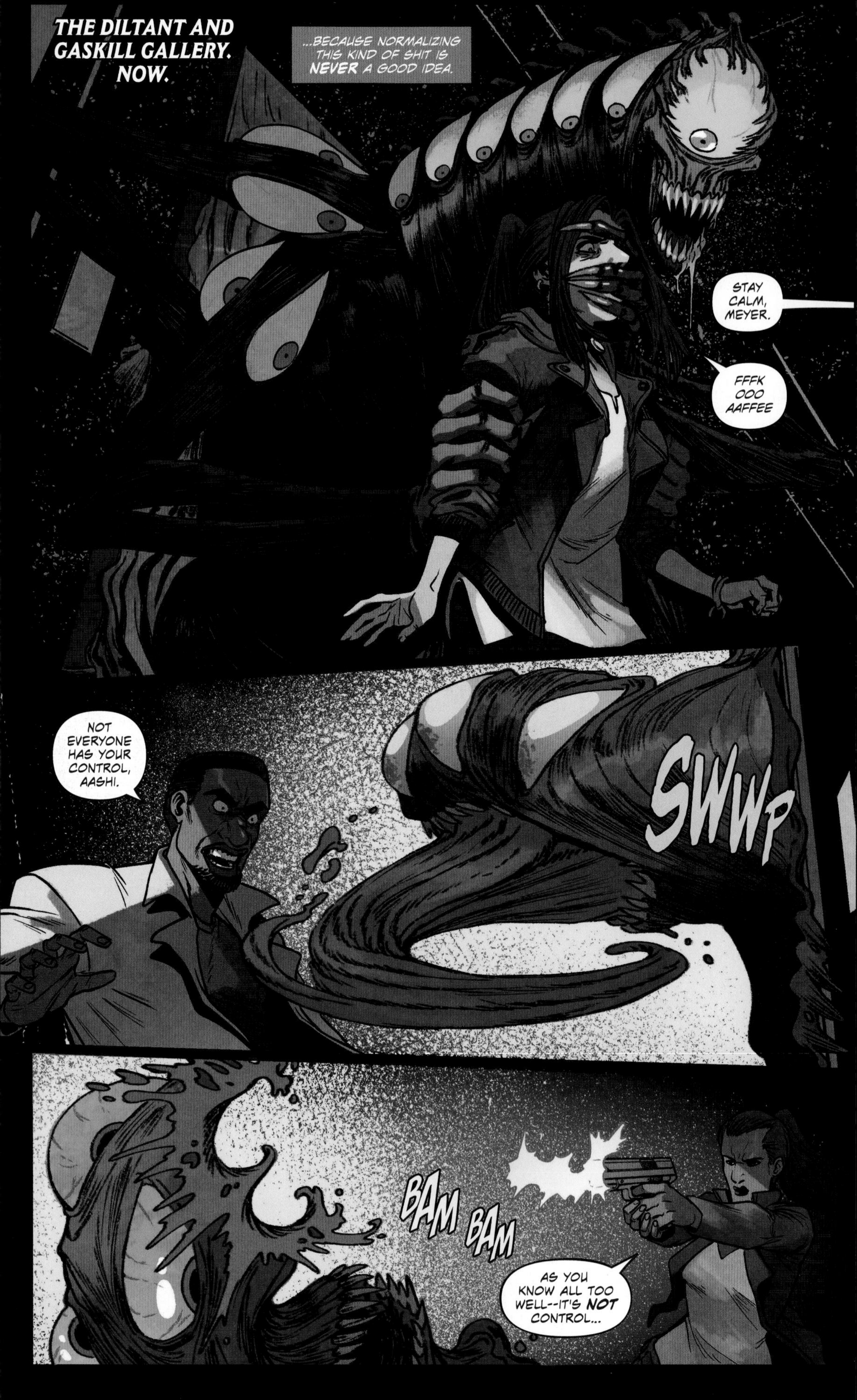
THE DILTANT AND GASKILL GALLERY. NOW.
...BECAUSE NORMALIZING THIS KIND OF SHIT IS NEVER A GOOD IDEA.
STAY CALM, MEYER.
FFFK OOO AAFFEE
NOT EVERYONE HAS YOUR CONTROL, AASHI.
SWWP
BAM BAM
AS YOU KNOW ALL TOO WELL--IT'S NOT CONTROL...

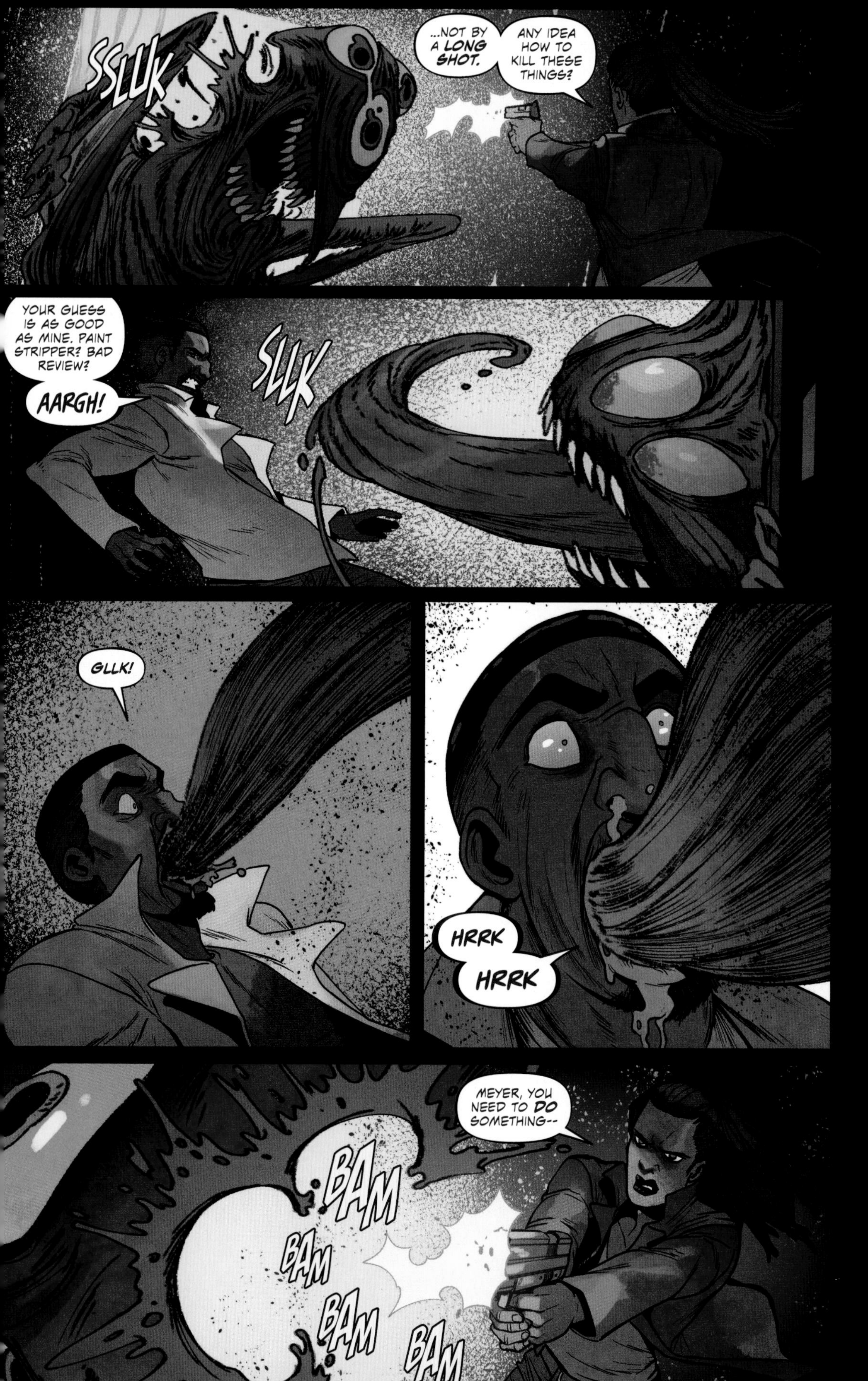
SSLUK
...NOT BY A LONG SHOT.
ANY IDEA HOW TO KILL THESE THINGS?
YOUR GUESS IS AS GOOD AS MINE. PAINT STRIPPER? BAD REVIEW?
AARGH!
SLLK
GLLK!
HRRK
HRRK
MEYER, YOU NEED TO DO SOMETHING--
BAM
BAM
BAM
BAM

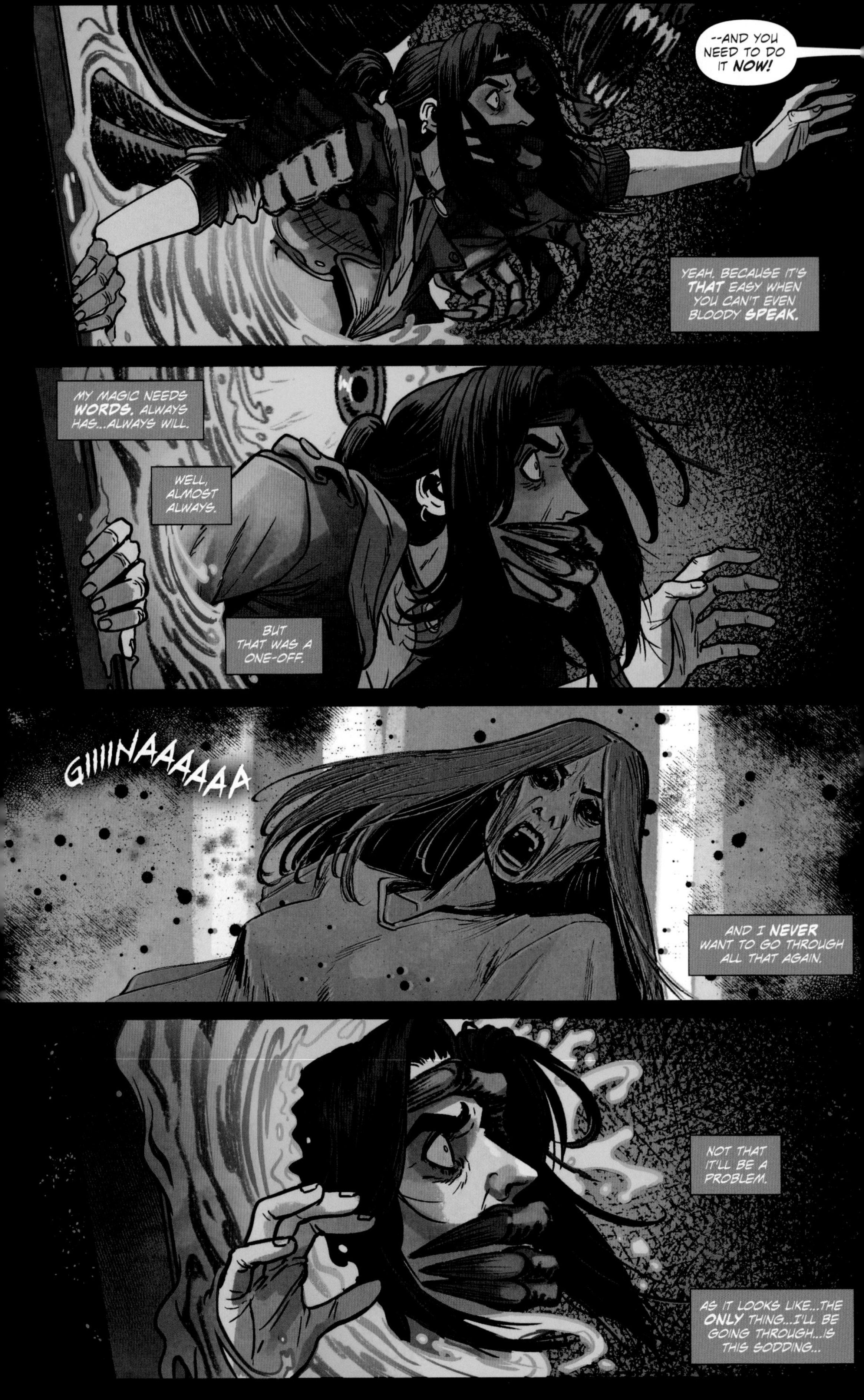
--AND YOU NEED TO DO IT NOW!
YEAH. BECAUSE IT'S THAT EASY WHEN YOU CAN'T EVEN BLOODY SPEAK.
MY MAGIC NEEDS WORDS. ALWAYS HAS...ALWAYS WILL.
WELL, ALMOST ALWAYS.
BUT THAT WAS A ONE-OFF.
GIIIINAAAAAA
AND I NEVER WANT TO GO THROUGH ALL THAT AGAIN.
NOT THAT IT'LL BE A PROBLEM.
AS IT LOOKS LIKE...THE ONLY THING...I'LL BE GOING THROUGH...IS THIS SODDING...

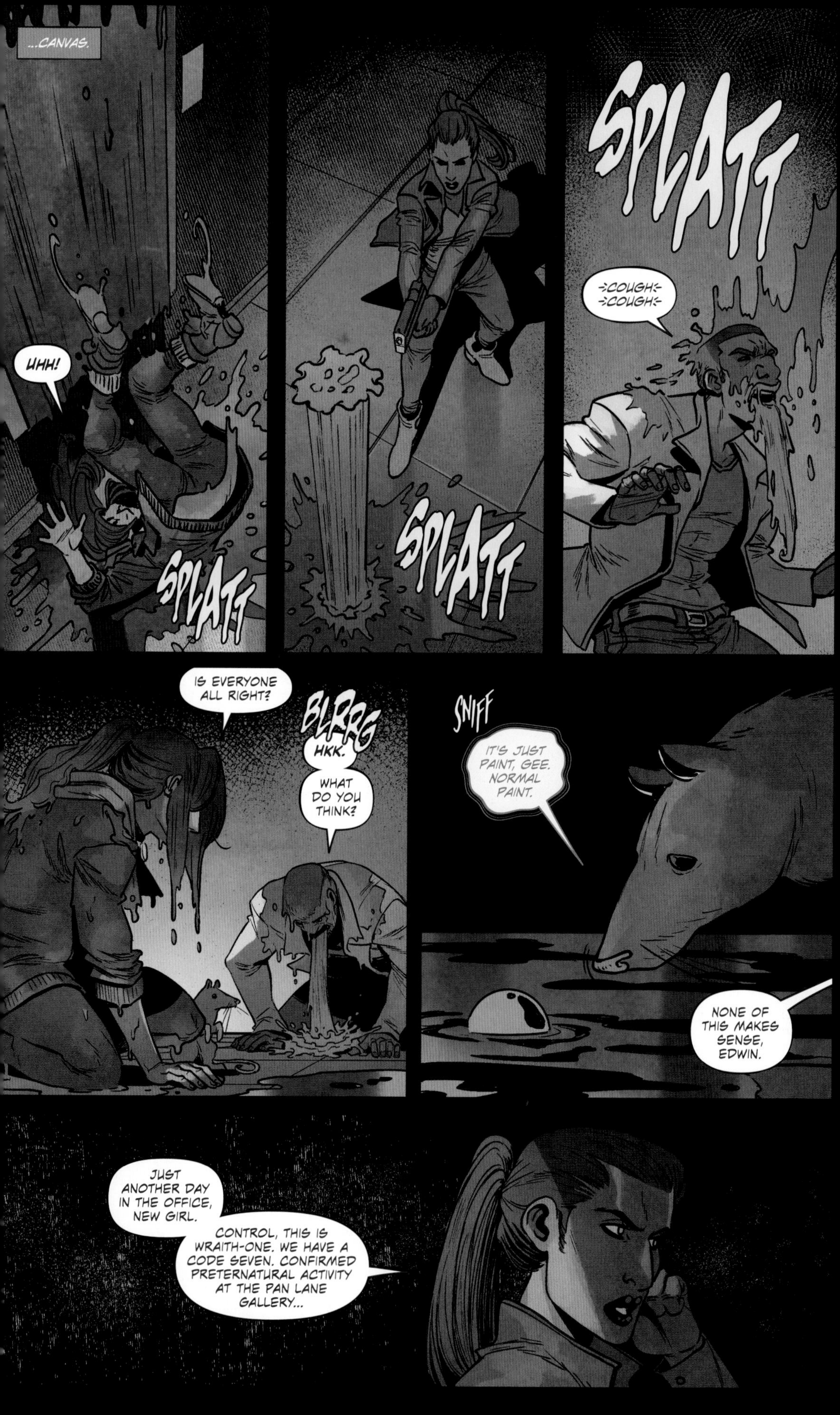
...CANVAS.
UHH!
SPLATT
SPLATT
SPLATT
COUGH COUGH
IS EVERYONE ALL RIGHT?
BLRRG
HKK.
WHAT DO YOU THINK?
SNIFF
IT'S JUST PAINT, GEE. NORMAL PAINT.
NONE OF THIS MAKES SENSE, EDWIN.
JUST ANOTHER DAY IN THE OFFICE, NEW GIRL.
CONTROL, THIS IS WRAITH-ONE. WE HAVE A CODE SEVEN. CONFIRMED PRETERNATURAL ACTIVITY AT THE PAN LANE GALLERY...

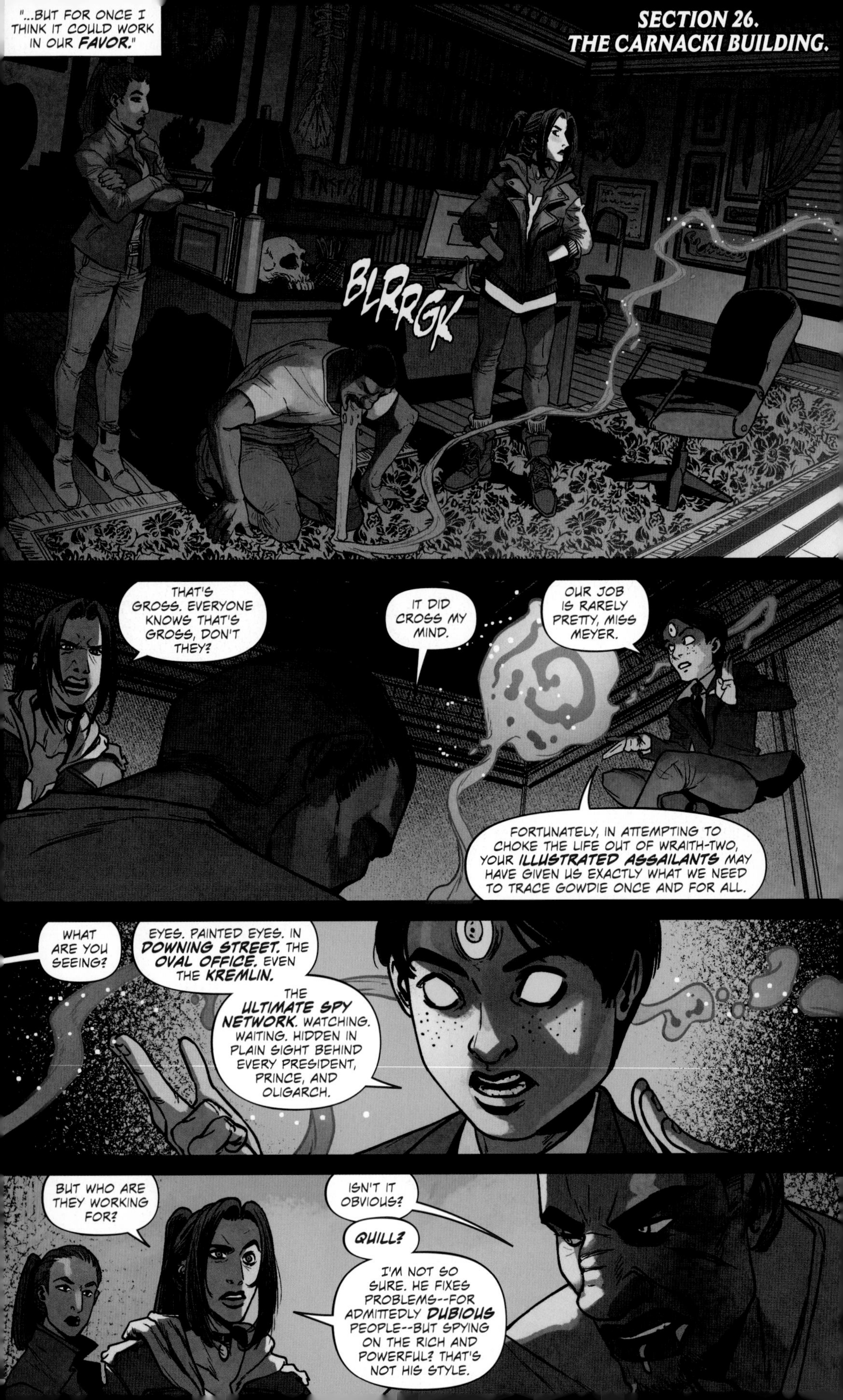

"...BUT FOR ONCE I THINK IT COULD WORK IN OUR FAVOR."
SECTION 26.
THE CARNACKI BUILDING.
BLRRGK
THAT'S GROSS. EVERYONE KNOWS THAT'S GROSS, DON'T THEY?
IT DID CROSS MY MIND.
OUR JOB IS RARELY PRETTY, MISS MEYER.
FORTUNATELY, IN ATTEMPTING TO CHOKE THE LIFE OUT OF WRAITH-TWO, YOUR ILLUSTRATED ASSAILANTS MAY HAVE GIVEN US EXACTLY WHAT WE NEED TO TRACE GOWDIE ONCE AND FOR ALL.
WHAT ARE YOU SEEING?
EYES. PAINTED EYES. IN DOWNING STREET. THE OVAL OFFICE. EVEN THE KREMLIN.
THE ULTIMATE SPY NETWORK. WATCHING. WAITING. HIDDEN IN PLAIN SIGHT BEHIND EVERY PRESIDENT, PRINCE, AND OLIGARCH.
BUT WHO ARE THEY WORKING FOR?
ISN'T IT OBVIOUS?
QUILL?
I'M NOT SO SURE. HE FIXES PROBLEMS--FOR ADMITTEDLY DUBIOUS PEOPLE--BUT SPYING ON THE RICH AND POWERFUL? THAT'S NOT HIS STYLE.

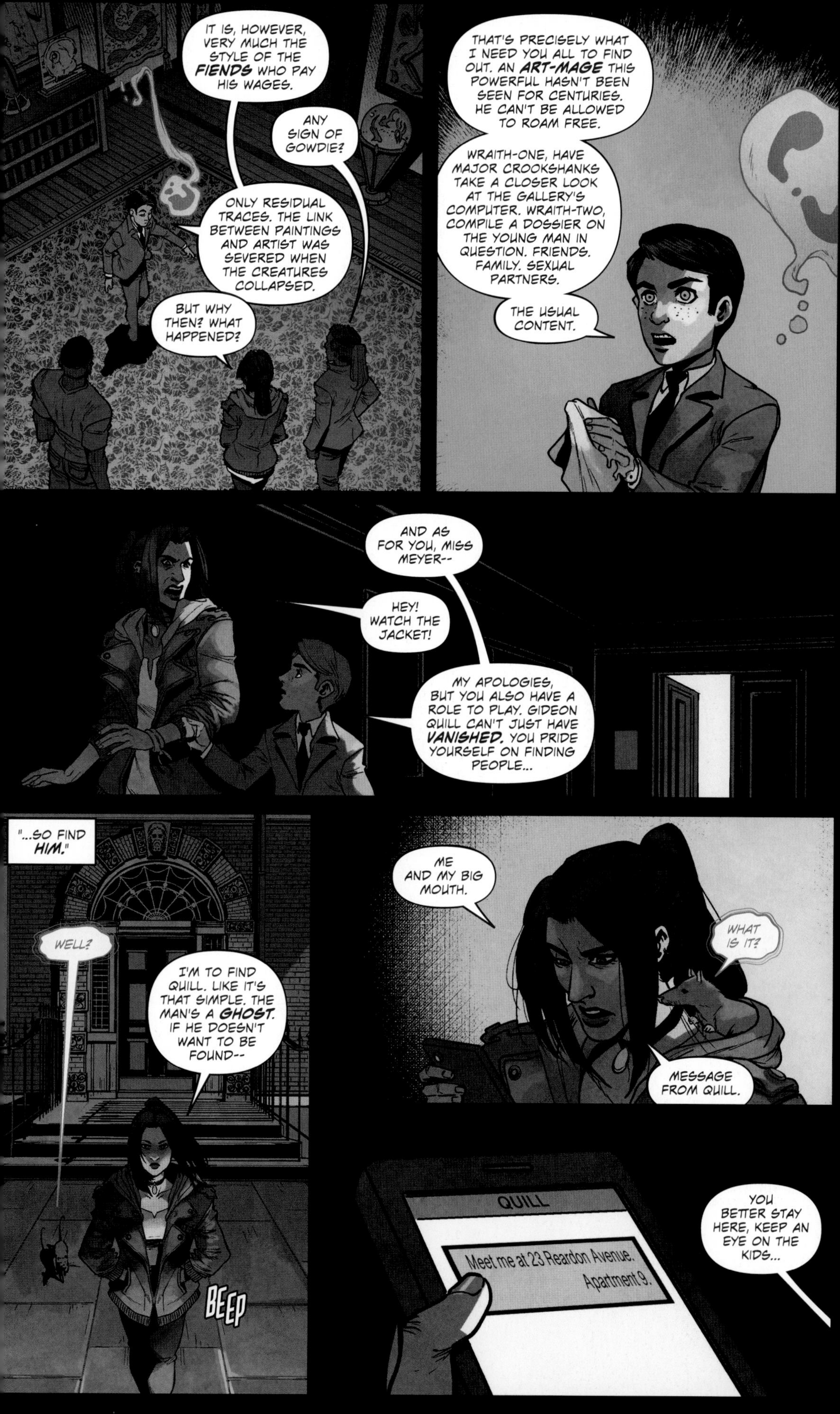
IT IS, HOWEVER, VERY MUCH THE STYLE OF THE FIENDS WHO PAY HIS WAGES.
ANY SIGN OF GOWDIE?
ONLY RESIDUAL TRACES. THE LINK BETWEEN PAINTINGS AND ARTIST WAS SEVERED WHEN THE CREATURES COLLAPSED.
BUT WHY THEN? WHAT HAPPENED?
THAT'S PRECISELY WHAT I NEED YOU ALL TO FIND OUT. AN ART-MAGE THIS POWERFUL HASN'T BEEN SEEN FOR CENTURIES. HE CAN'T BE ALLOWED TO ROAM FREE.
WRAITH-ONE, HAVE MAJOR CROOKSHANKS TAKE A CLOSER LOOK AT THE GALLERY'S COMPUTER. WRAITH-TWO, COMPILE A DOSSIER ON THE YOUNG MAN IN QUESTION. FRIENDS. FAMILY. SEXUAL PARTNERS.
THE USUAL CONTENT.
AND AS FOR YOU, MISS MEYER--
HEY! WATCH THE JACKET!
MY APOLOGIES, BUT YOU ALSO HAVE A ROLE TO PLAY. GIDEON QUILL CAN'T JUST HAVE VANISHED. YOU PRIDE YOURSELF ON FINDING PEOPLE...
"...SO FIND HIM."
WELL?
I'M TO FIND QUILL. LIKE IT'S THAT SIMPLE. THE MAN'S A GHOST. IF HE DOESN'T WANT TO BE FOUND--
BEEP
ME AND MY BIG MOUTH.
WHAT IS IT?
MESSAGE FROM QUILL.
QUILL
Meet me at 23 Reardon Avenue. Apartment 9.
YOU BETTER STAY HERE, KEEP AN EYE ON THE KIDS...

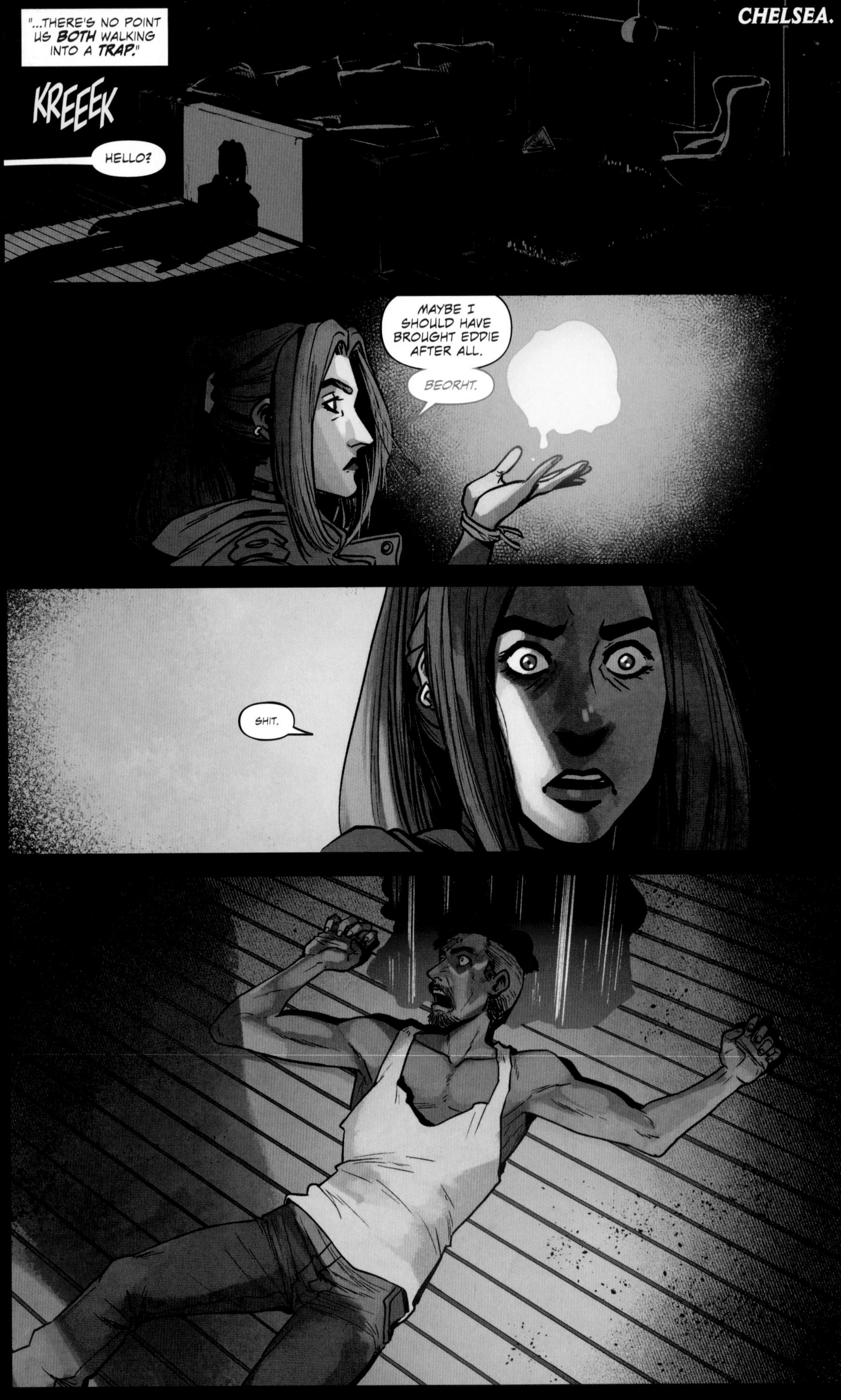
CHELSEA.
"...THERE'S NO POINT US BOTH WALKING INTO A TRAP."
KREEEK
HELLO?
MAYBE I SHOULD HAVE BROUGHT EDDIE AFTER ALL.
BEORHT.
SHIT.

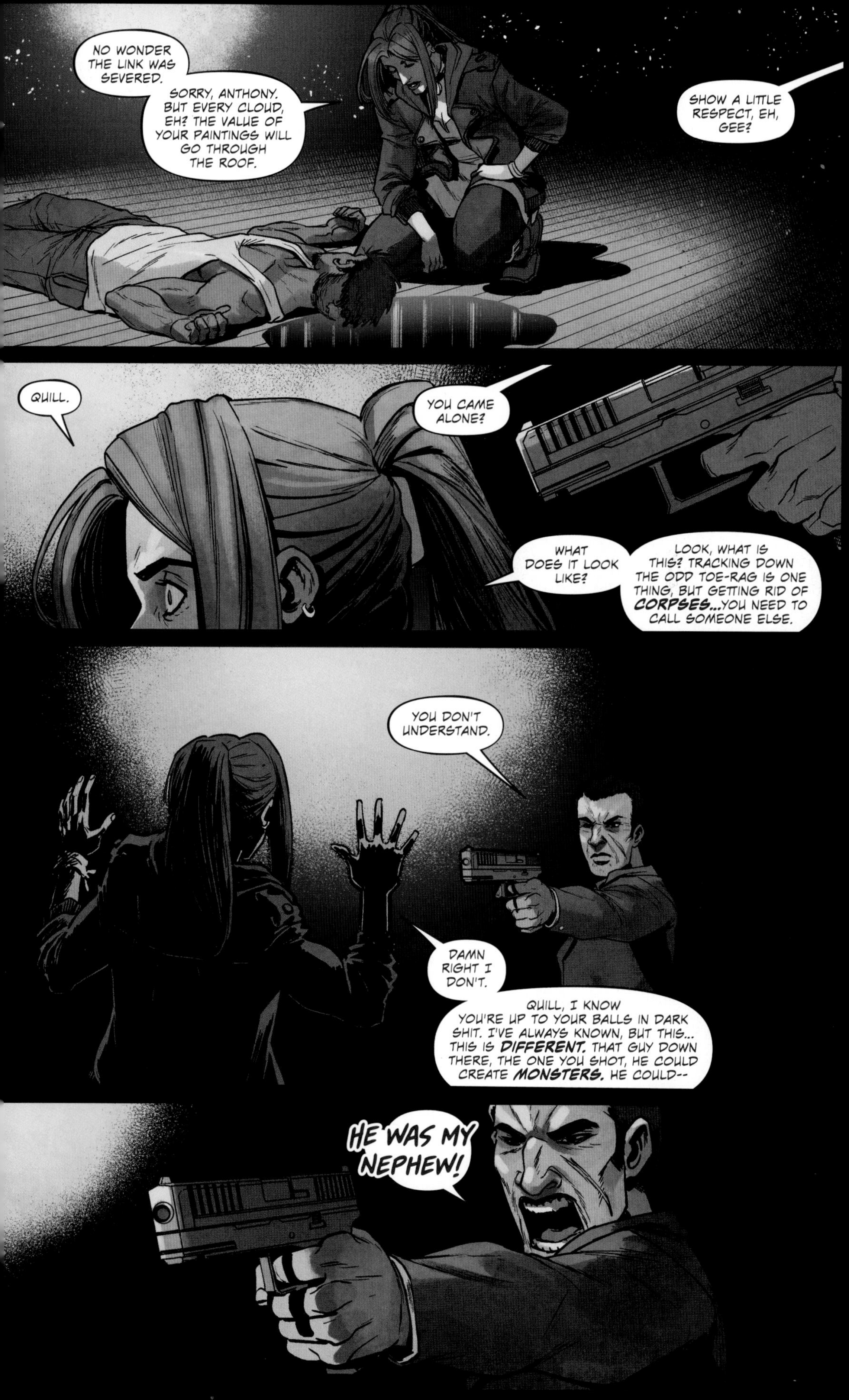

NO WONDER THE LINK WAS SEVERED.
SORRY, ANTHONY. BUT EVERY CLOUD, EH? THE VALUE OF YOUR PAINTINGS WILL GO THROUGH THE ROOF.
SHOW A LITTLE RESPECT, EH, GEE?
QUILL.
YOU CAME ALONE?
WHAT DOES IT LOOK LIKE?
LOOK, WHAT IS THIS? TRACKING DOWN THE ODD TOE-RAG IS ONE THING, BUT GETTING RID OF CORPSES...YOU NEED TO CALL SOMEONE ELSE.
YOU DON'T UNDERSTAND.
DAMN RIGHT I DON'T.
QUILL, I KNOW YOU'RE UP TO YOUR BALLS IN DARK SHIT. I'VE ALWAYS KNOWN, BUT THIS... THIS IS DIFFERENT. THAT GUY DOWN THERE, THE ONE YOU SHOT, HE COULD CREATE MONSTERS. HE COULD--
HE WAS MY NEPHEW!

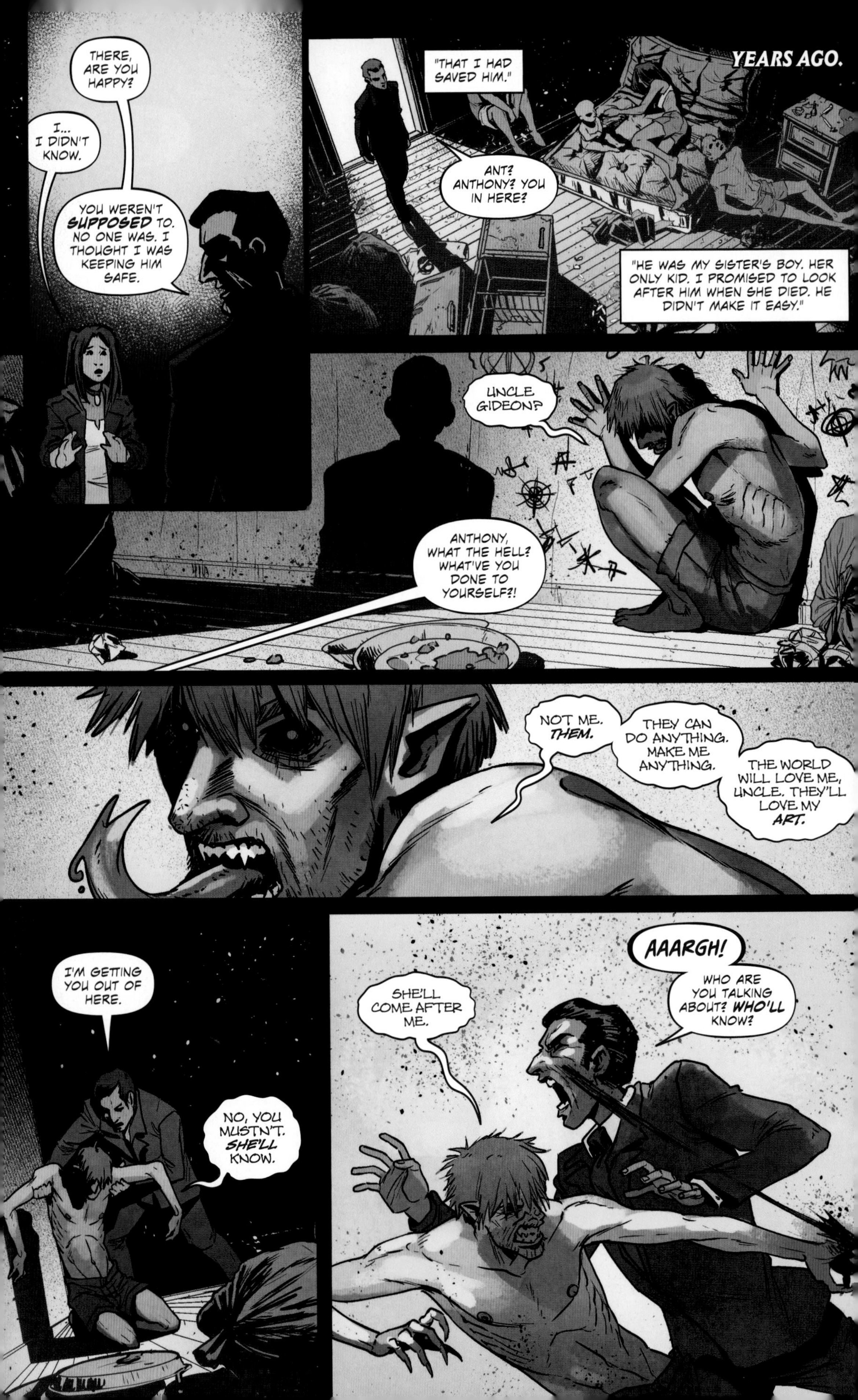
THERE, ARE YOU HAPPY?
I... I DIDN'T KNOW.
YOU WEREN'T SUPPOSED TO. NO ONE WAS. I THOUGHT I WAS KEEPING HIM SAFE.
YEARS AGO.
"THAT I HAD SAVED HIM."
ANT? ANTHONY? YOU IN HERE?
"HE WAS MY SISTER'S BOY. HER ONLY KID. I PROMISED TO LOOK AFTER HIM WHEN SHE DIED. HE DIDN'T MAKE IT EASY."
UNCLE GIDEON?
ANTHONY, WHAT THE HELL? WHAT'VE YOU DONE TO YOURSELF?!
NOT ME. THEM.
THEY CAN DO ANYTHING. MAKE ME ANYTHING.
THE WORLD WILL LOVE ME, UNCLE. THEY'LL LOVE MY ART.
I'M GETTING YOU OUT OF HERE.
NO, YOU MUSTN'T. SHE'LL KNOW.
SHE'LL COME AFTER ME.
AAARGH!
WHO ARE YOU TALKING ABOUT? WHO'LL KNOW?

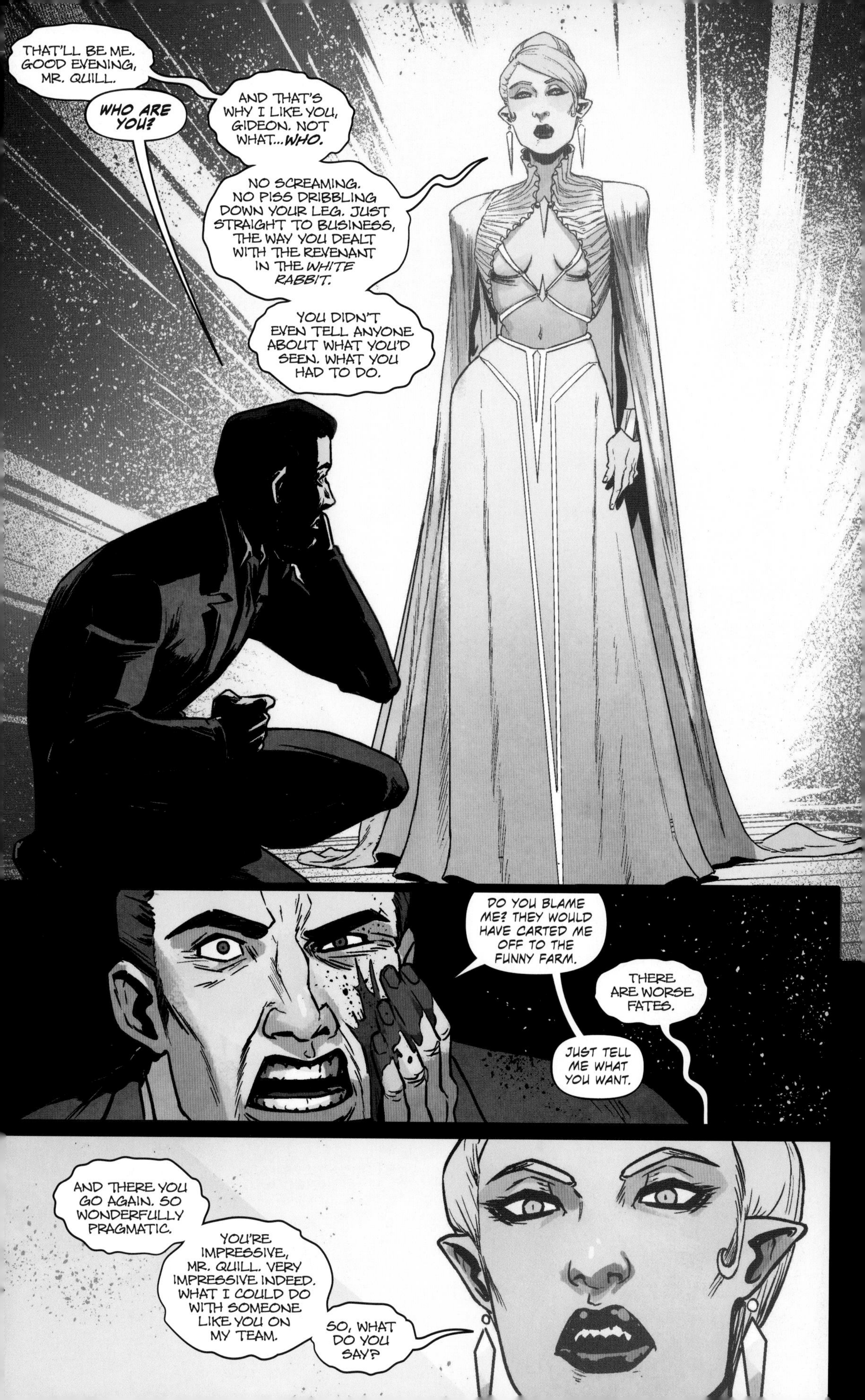
THAT'LL BE ME. GOOD EVENING, MR. QUILL.
WHO ARE YOU?
AND THAT'S WHY I LIKE YOU, GIDEON. NOT WHAT... WHO.
NO SCREAMING. NO PISS DRIBBLING DOWN YOUR LEG. JUST STRAIGHT TO BUSINESS, THE WAY YOU DEALT WITH THE REVENANT IN THE WHITE RABBIT.
YOU DIDN'T EVEN TELL ANYONE ABOUT WHAT YOU'D SEEN. WHAT YOU HAD TO DO.
DO YOU BLAME ME? THEY WOULD HAVE CARTED ME OFF TO THE FUNNY FARM.
THERE ARE WORSE FATES.
JUST TELL ME WHAT YOU WANT.
AND THERE YOU GO AGAIN. SO WONDERFULLY PRAGMATIC.
YOU'RE IMPRESSIVE, MR. QUILL. VERY IMPRESSIVE INDEED. WHAT I COULD DO WITH SOMEONE LIKE YOU ON MY TEAM.
SO, WHAT DO YOU SAY?

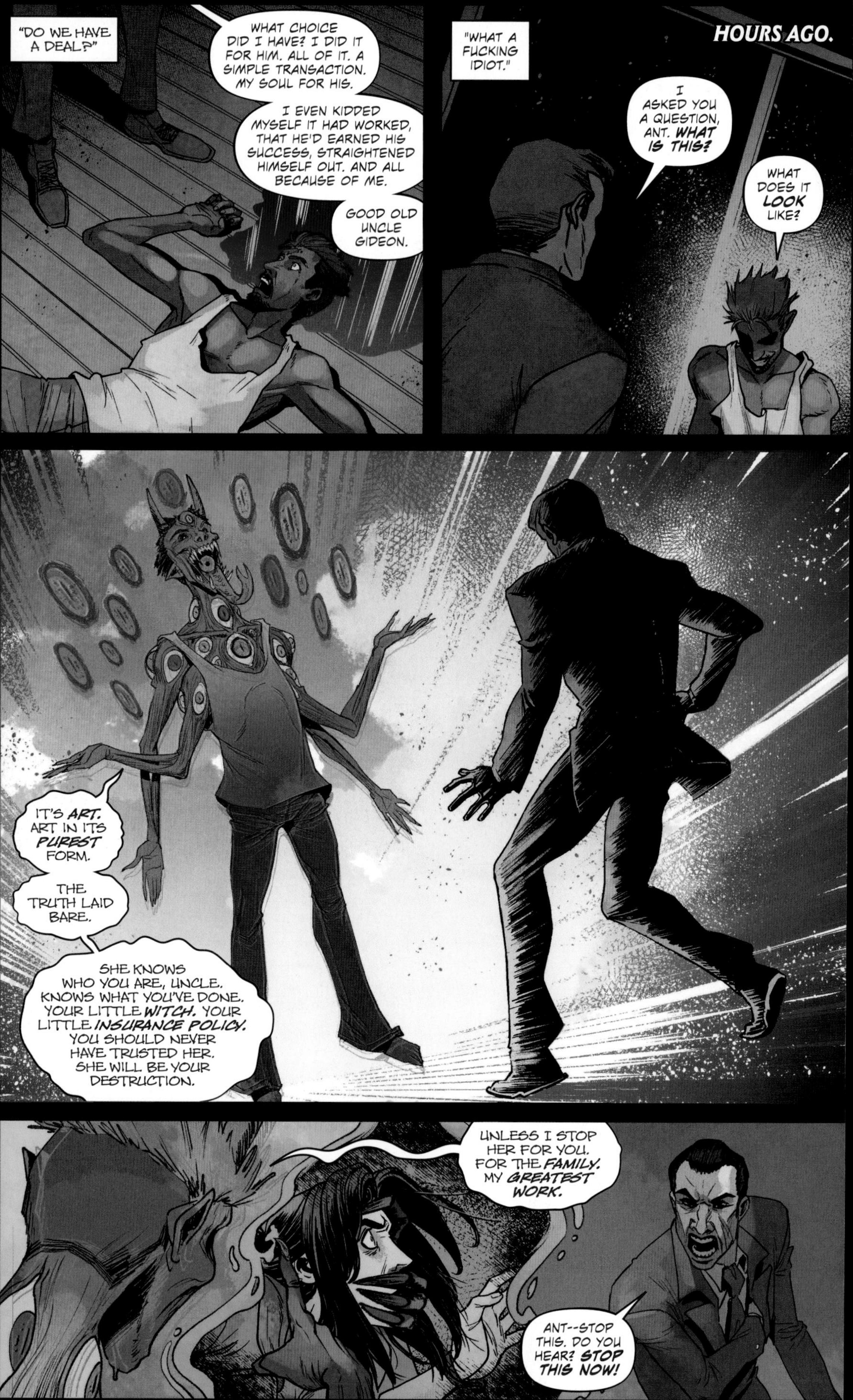

"DO WE HAVE A DEAL?"
WHAT CHOICE DID I HAVE? I DID IT FOR HIM. ALL OF IT. A SIMPLE TRANSACTION. MY SOUL FOR HIS.
I EVEN KIDDED MYSELF IT HAD WORKED, THAT HE'D EARNED HIS SUCCESS, STRAIGHTENED HIMSELF OUT. AND ALL BECAUSE OF ME.
GOOD OLD UNCLE GIDEON.
"WHAT A FUCKING IDIOT."
HOURS AGO.
I ASKED YOU A QUESTION, ANT. WHAT IS THIS?
WHAT DOES IT LOOK LIKE?
IT'S ART. ART IN ITS PUREST FORM.
THE TRUTH LAID BARE.
SHE KNOWS WHO YOU ARE, UNCLE. KNOWS WHAT YOU'VE DONE. YOUR LITTLE WITCH. YOUR LITTLE INSURANCE POLICY. YOU SHOULD NEVER HAVE TRUSTED HER. SHE WILL BE YOUR DESTRUCTION.
UNLESS I STOP HER FOR YOU. FOR THE FAMILY. MY GREATEST WORK.
ANT--STOP THIS. DO YOU HEAR? STOP THIS NOW!

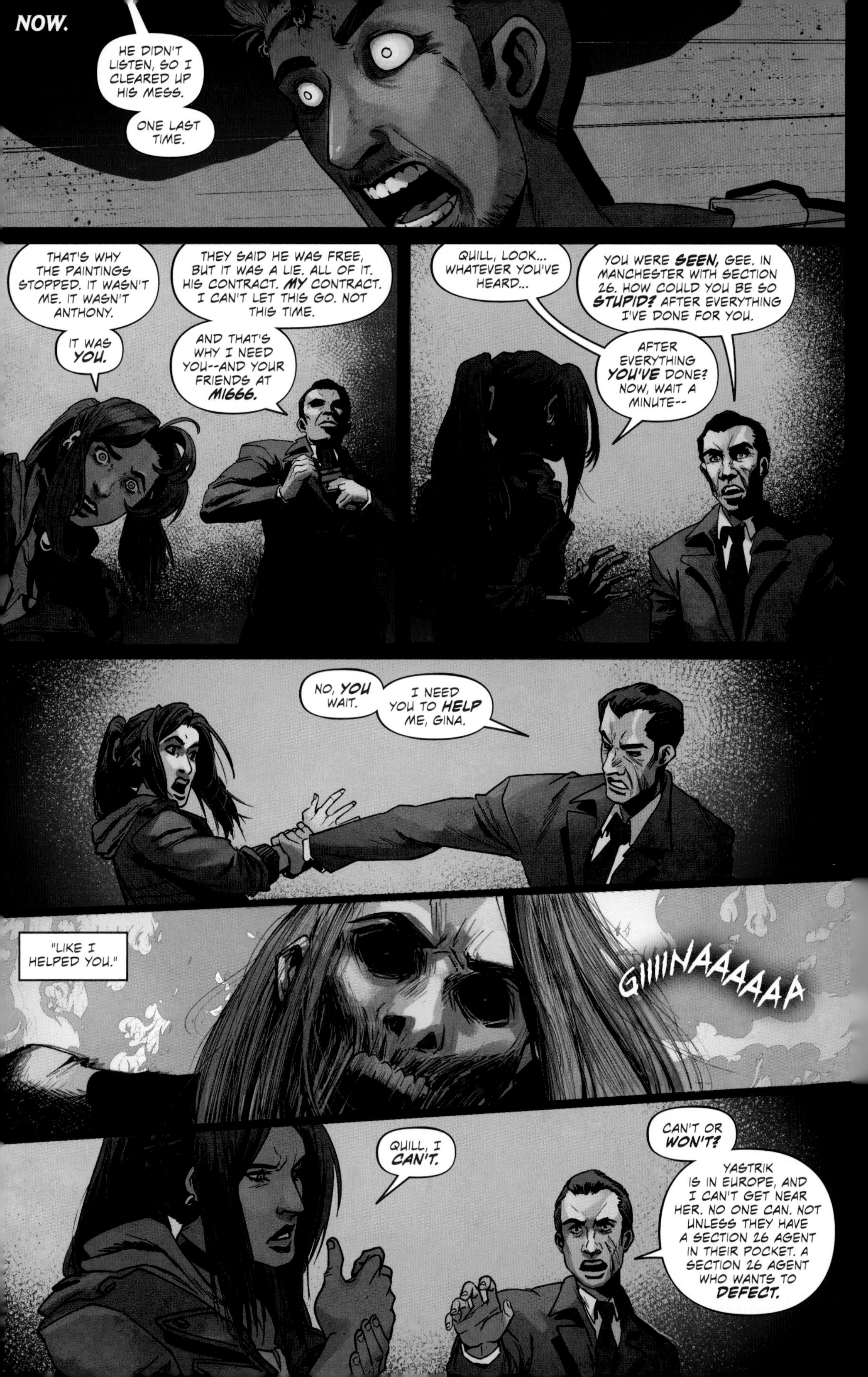
NOW.
HE DIDN'T LISTEN, SO I CLEARED UP HIS MESS.
ONE LAST TIME.
THAT'S WHY THE PAINTINGS STOPPED. IT WASN'T ME. IT WASN'T ANTHONY.
IT WAS YOU.
THEY SAID HE WAS FREE, BUT IT WAS A LIE. ALL OF IT. HIS CONTRACT. MY CONTRACT. I CAN'T LET THIS GO. NOT THIS TIME.
AND THAT'S WHY I NEED YOU--AND YOUR FRIENDS AT MI666.
QUILL, LOOK... WHATEVER YOU'VE HEARD...
YOU WERE SEEN, GEE. IN MANCHESTER WITH SECTION 26. HOW COULD YOU BE SO STUPID? AFTER EVERYTHING I'VE DONE FOR YOU.
AFTER EVERYTHING YOU'VE DONE? NOW, WAIT A MINUTE--
NO, YOU WAIT.
I NEED YOU TO HELP ME, GINA.
"LIKE I HELPED YOU."
GIIIINAAAAAA
QUILL, I CAN'T.
CAN'T OR WON'T?
YASTRIK IS IN EUROPE, AND I CAN'T GET NEAR HER. NO ONE CAN. NOT UNLESS THEY HAVE A SECTION 26 AGENT IN THEIR POCKET. A SECTION 26 AGENT WHO WANTS TO DEFECT.

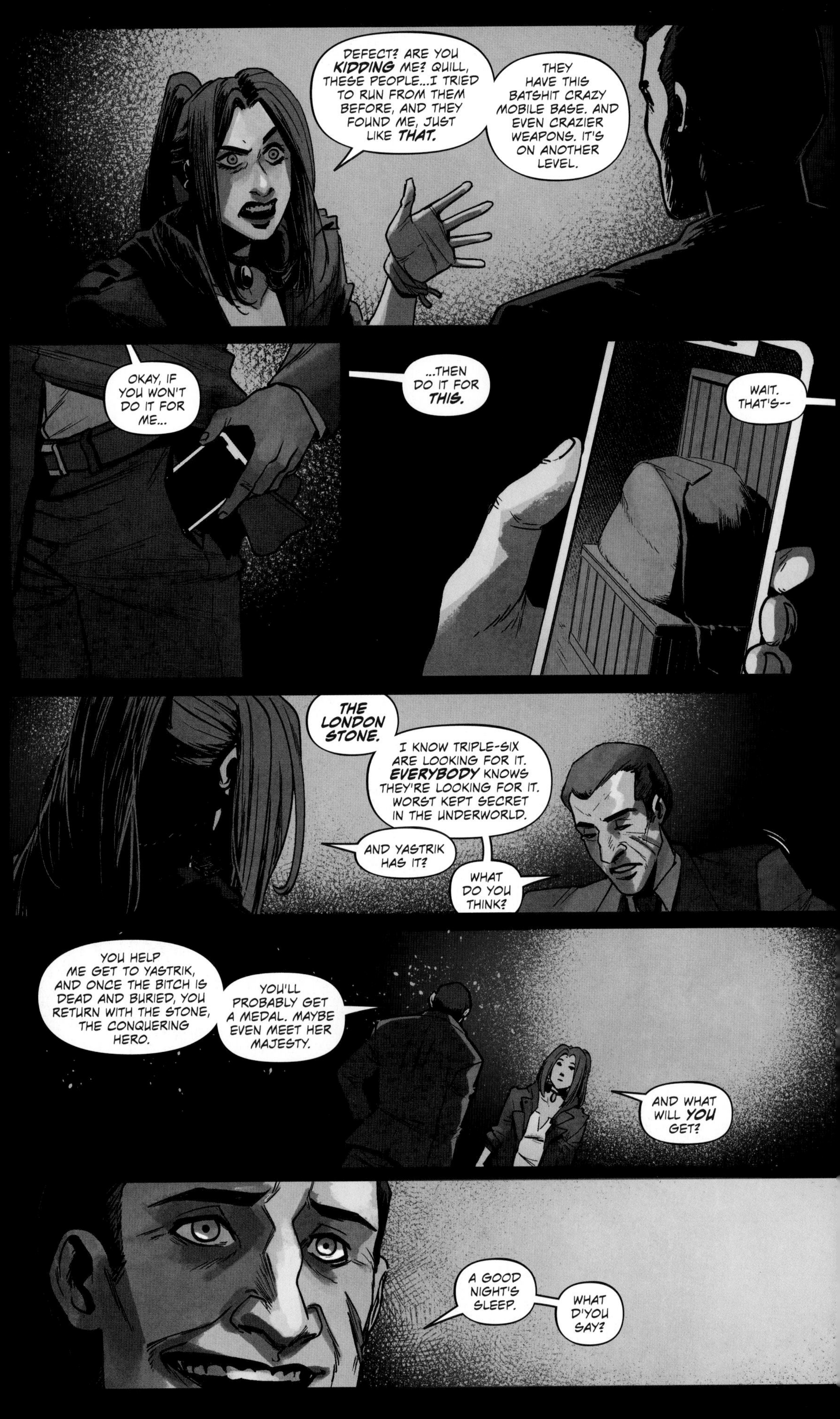
DEFECT? ARE YOU KIDDING ME? QUILL, THESE PEOPLE...I TRIED TO RUN FROM THEM BEFORE, AND THEY FOUND ME, JUST LIKE THAT.
THEY HAVE THIS BATSHIT CRAZY MOBILE BASE. AND EVEN CRAZIER WEAPONS. IT'S ON ANOTHER LEVEL.
OKAY, IF YOU WON'T DO IT FOR ME...
...THEN DO IT FOR THIS.
WAIT. THAT'S--
THE LONDON STONE.
I KNOW TRIPLE-SIX ARE LOOKING FOR IT. EVERYBODY KNOWS THEY'RE LOOKING FOR IT. WORST KEPT SECRET IN THE UNDERWORLD.
AND YASTRIK HAS IT?
WHAT DO YOU THINK?
YOU HELP ME GET TO YASTRIK, AND ONCE THE BITCH IS DEAD AND BURIED, YOU RETURN WITH THE STONE, THE CONQUERING HERO.
YOU'LL PROBABLY GET A MEDAL. MAYBE EVEN MEET HER MAJESTY.
AND WHAT WILL YOU GET?
A GOOD NIGHT'S SLEEP.
WHAT D'YOU SAY?

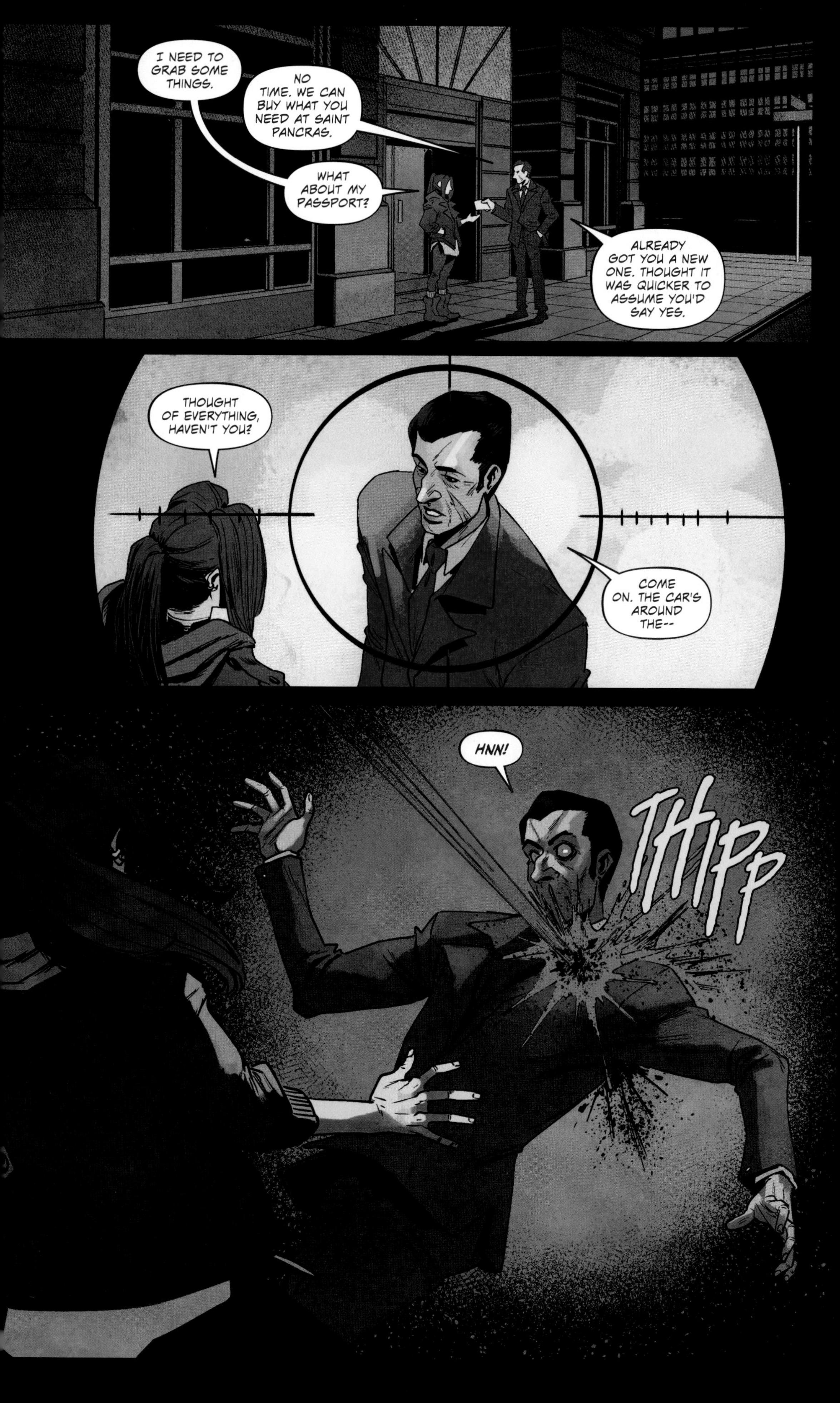
I NEED TO GRAB SOME THINGS.
NO TIME. WE CAN BUY WHAT YOU NEED AT SAINT PANCRAS.
WHAT ABOUT MY PASSPORT?
ALREADY GOT YOU A NEW ONE. THOUGHT IT WAS QUICKER TO ASSUME YOU'D SAY YES.
THOUGHT OF EVERYTHING, HAVEN'T YOU?
COME ON. THE CAR'S AROUND THE--
HNN!
THIPP

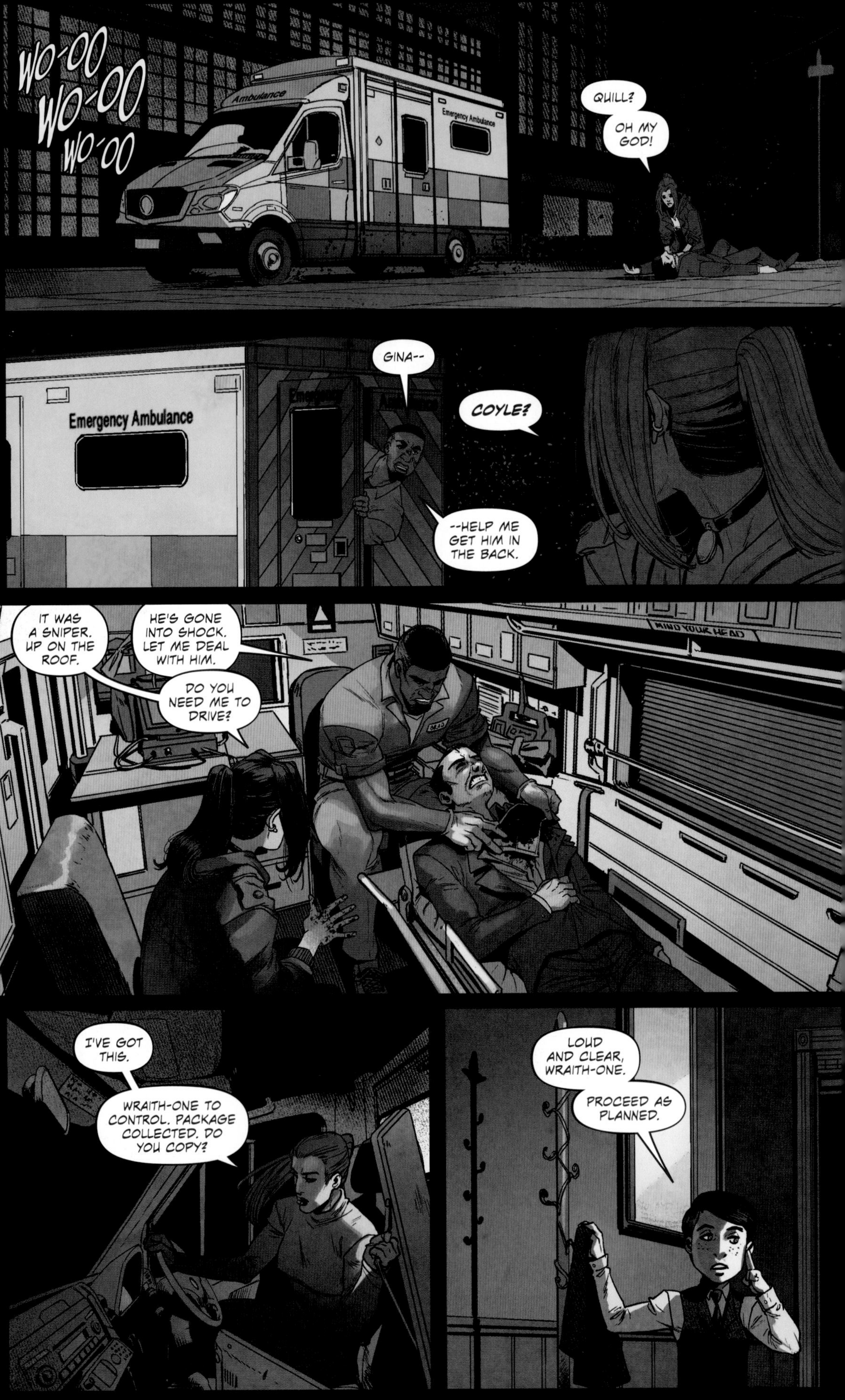
WO-OO
WO-OO
WO-OO
Ambulance
Emergency Ambulance
QUILL?
OH MY GOD!
Emergency Ambulance
GINA--
COYLE?
--HELP ME GET HIM IN THE BACK.
IT WAS A SNIPER. UP ON THE ROOF.
HE'S GONE INTO SHOCK. LET ME DEAL WITH HIM.
DO YOU NEED ME TO DRIVE?
MIND YOUR HEAD
I'VE GOT THIS.
WRAITH-ONE TO CONTROL. PACKAGE COLLECTED. DO YOU COPY?
LOUD AND CLEAR, WRAITH-ONE.
PROCEED AS PLANNED.

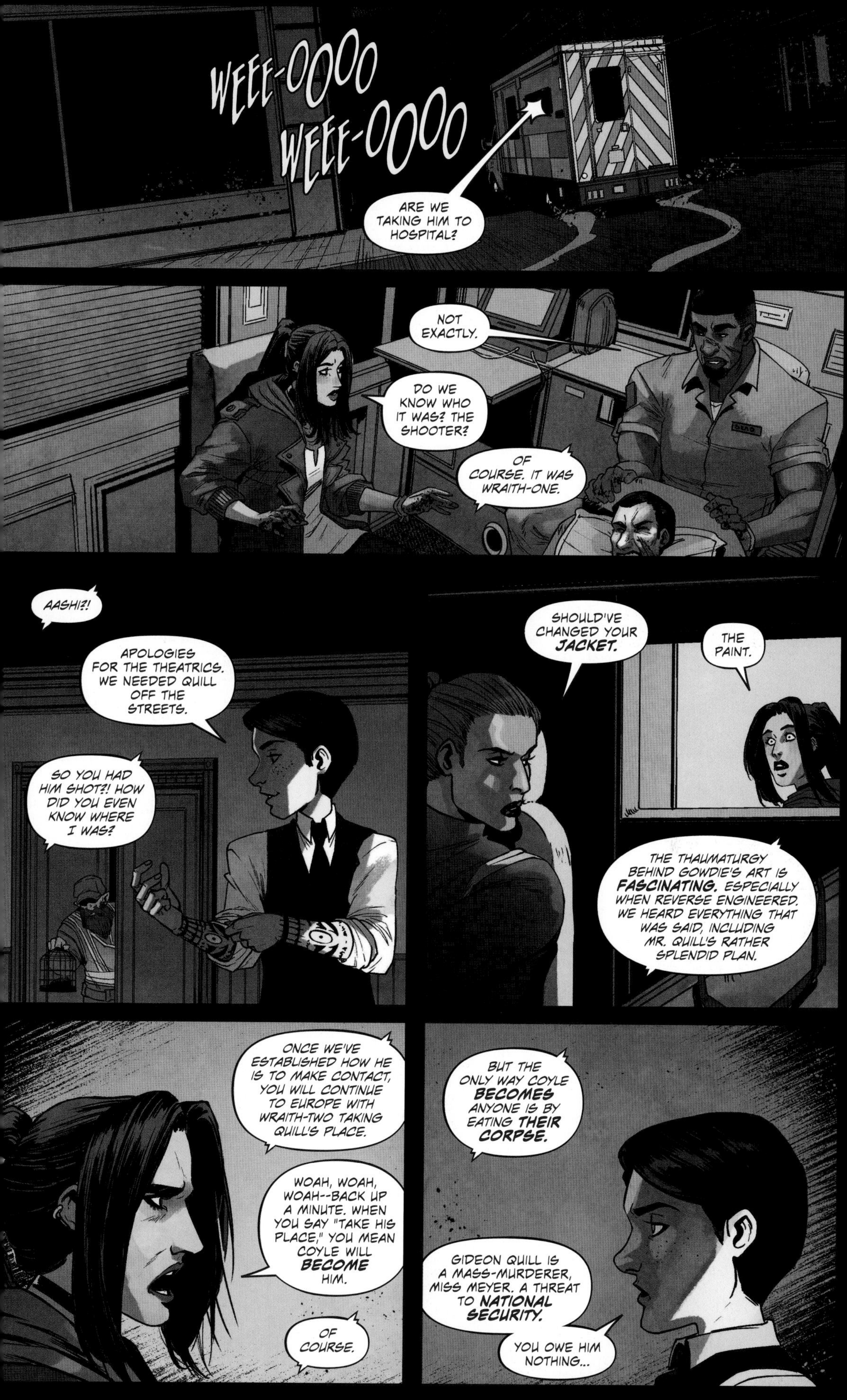
WEEE-OOOO
WEEE-OOOO
ARE WE TAKING HIM TO HOSPITAL?
NOT EXACTLY.
DO WE KNOW WHO IT WAS? THE SHOOTER?
OF COURSE. IT WAS WRAITH-ONE.
AASHI?!
APOLOGIES FOR THE THEATRICS. WE NEEDED QUILL OFF THE STREETS.
SO YOU HAD HIM SHOT?! HOW DID YOU EVEN KNOW WHERE I WAS?
SHOULD'VE CHANGED YOUR **JACKET.**
THE PAINT.
THE THAUMATURGY BEHIND GOWDIE'S ART IS **FASCINATING.** ESPECIALLY WHEN REVERSE ENGINEERED. WE HEARD EVERYTHING THAT WAS SAID, INCLUDING MR. QUILL'S RATHER SPLENDID PLAN.
ONCE WE'VE ESTABLISHED HOW HE IS TO MAKE CONTACT, YOU WILL CONTINUE TO EUROPE WITH WRAITH-TWO TAKING QUILL'S PLACE.
WOAH, WOAH, WOAH--BACK UP A MINUTE. WHEN YOU SAY "TAKE HIS PLACE," YOU MEAN COYLE WILL **BECOME** HIM.
OF COURSE.
BUT THE ONLY WAY COYLE **BECOMES** ANYONE IS BY EATING **THEIR CORPSE.**
GIDEON QUILL IS A MASS-MURDERER, MISS MEYER. A THREAT TO **NATIONAL SECURITY.**
YOU OWE HIM NOTHING...

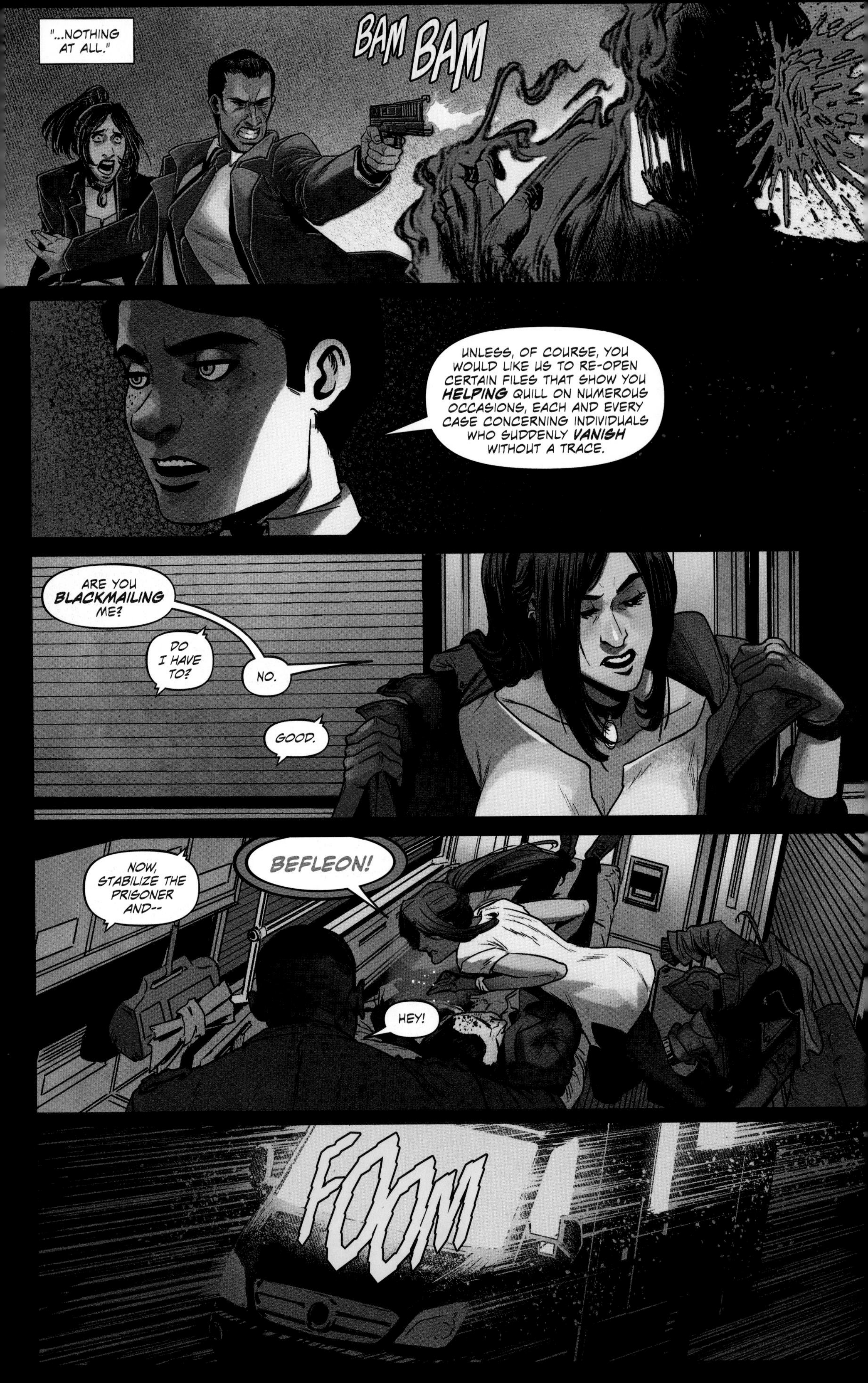
"...NOTHING AT ALL."
BAM BAM
UNLESS, OF COURSE, YOU WOULD LIKE US TO RE-OPEN CERTAIN FILES THAT SHOW YOU HELPING QUILL ON NUMEROUS OCCASIONS, EACH AND EVERY CASE CONCERNING INDIVIDUALS WHO SUDDENLY VANISH WITHOUT A TRACE.
ARE YOU BLACKMAILING ME?
NO.
DO I HAVE TO?
GOOD.
NOW, STABILIZE THE PRISONER AND--
BEFLEON!
HEY!
FOOM!

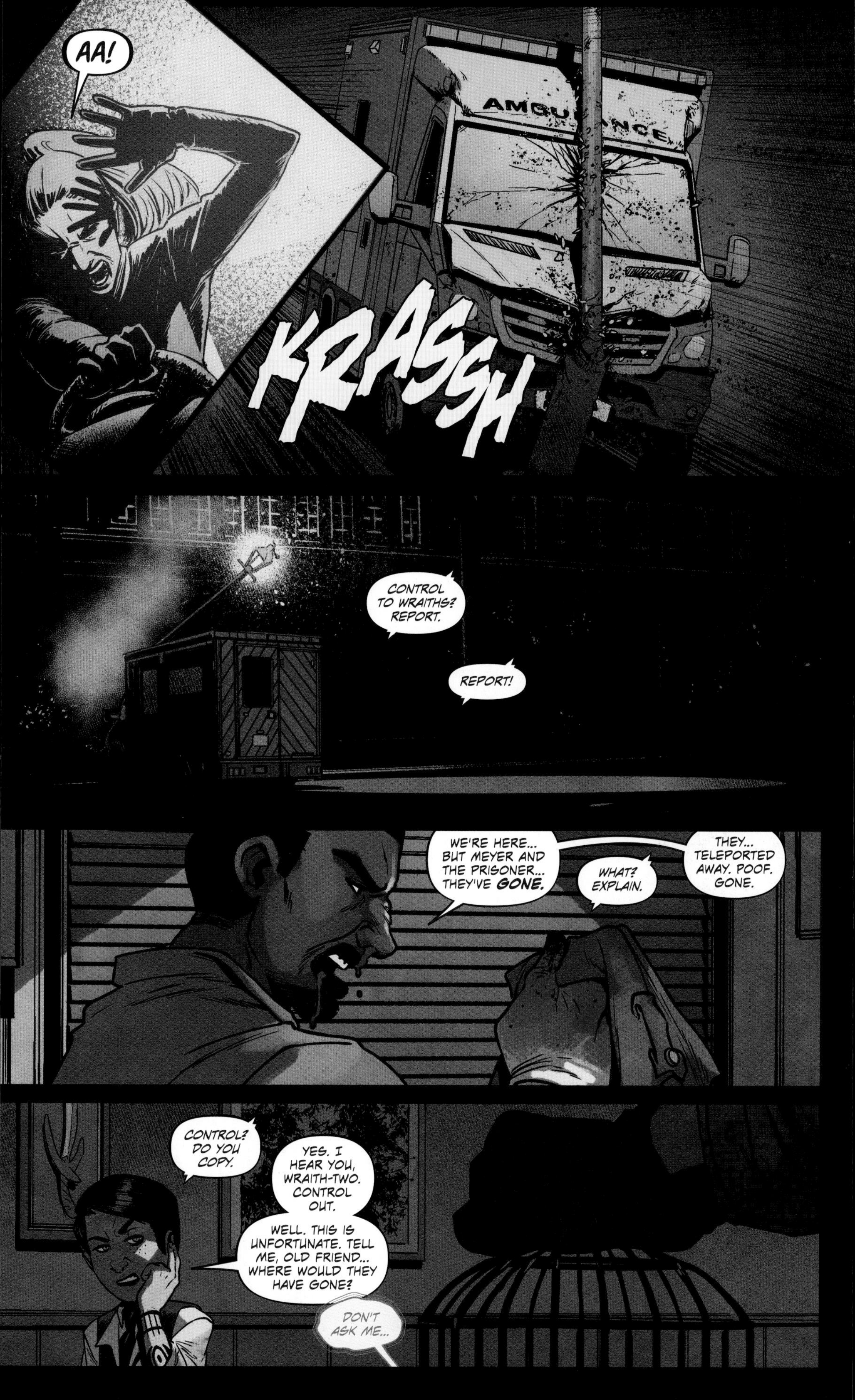
AA!
KRASSH
AMBULANCE
CONTROL TO WRAITHS? REPORT.
REPORT!
WE'RE HERE... BUT MEYER AND THE PRISONER... THEY'VE GONE.
WHAT? EXPLAIN.
THEY... TELEPORTED AWAY. POOF. GONE.
CONTROL? DO YOU COPY.
YES. I HEAR YOU, WRAITH-TWO. CONTROL OUT.
WELL. THIS IS UNFORTUNATE. TELL ME, OLD FRIEND... WHERE WOULD THEY HAVE GONE?
DON'T ASK ME...

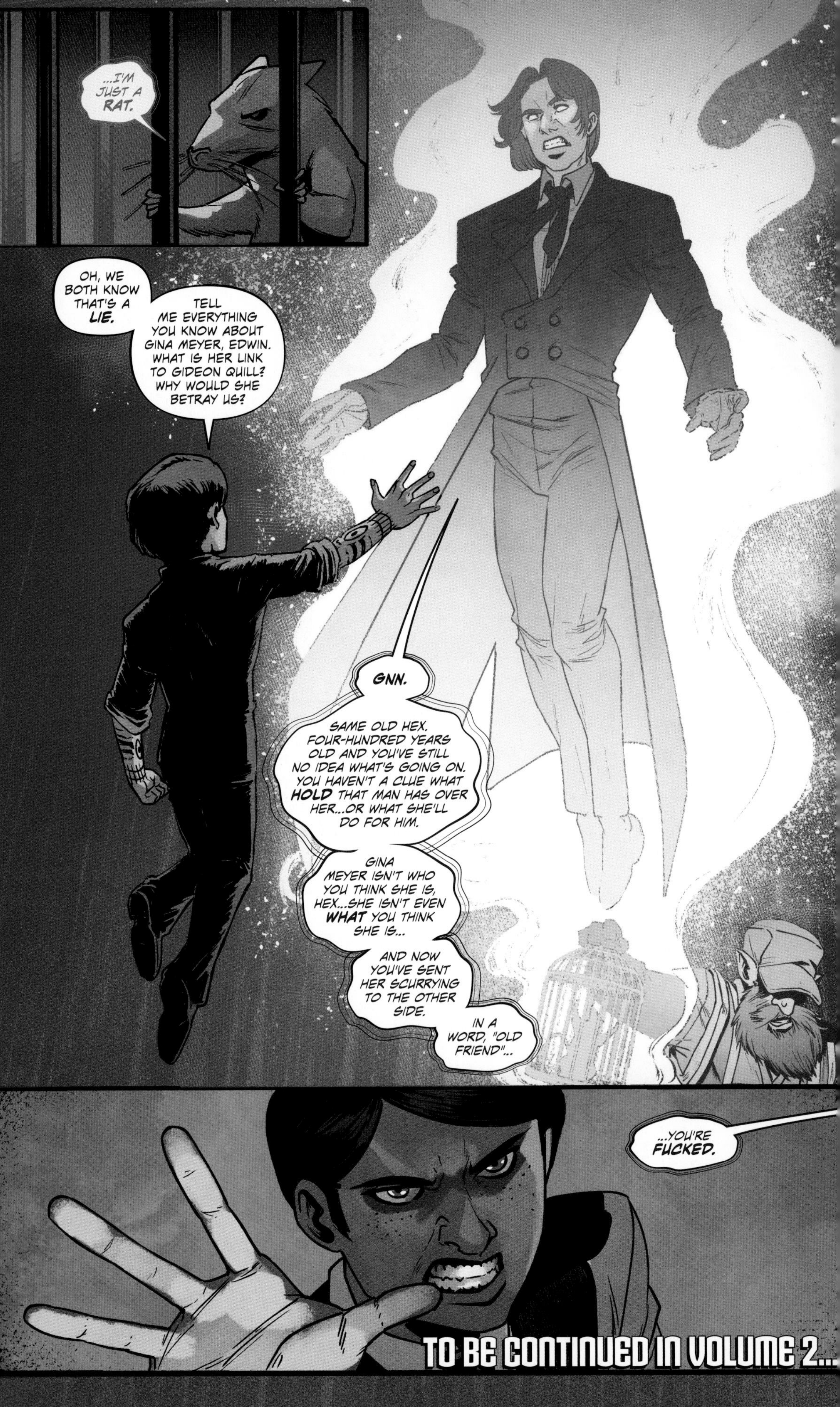
...I'M JUST A **RAT.**
OH, WE BOTH KNOW THAT'S A **LIE.**
TELL ME EVERYTHING YOU KNOW ABOUT GINA MEYER, EDWIN. WHAT IS HER LINK TO GIDEON QUILL? WHY WOULD SHE BETRAY US?
GNN.
SAME OLD HEX. FOUR-HUNDRED YEARS OLD AND YOU'VE STILL NO IDEA WHAT'S GOING ON. YOU HAVEN'T A CLUE WHAT **HOLD** THAT MAN HAS OVER HER...OR WHAT SHE'LL DO FOR HIM.
GINA MEYER ISN'T WHO YOU THINK SHE IS, HEX...SHE ISN'T EVEN **WHAT** YOU THINK SHE IS...
AND NOW YOU'VE SENT HER SCURRYING TO THE OTHER SIDE.
IN A WORD, "OLD FRIEND"...
...YOU'RE **FUCKED.**
TO BE CONTINUED IN VOLUME 2...

SHADOW SERVICE

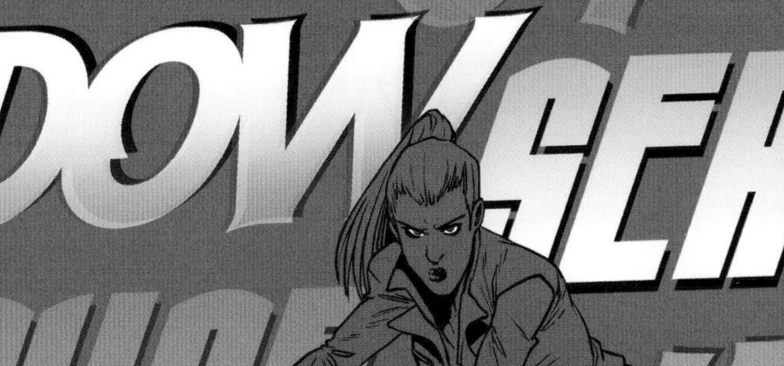

CORIN HOWELL
TRIONA FARRELL

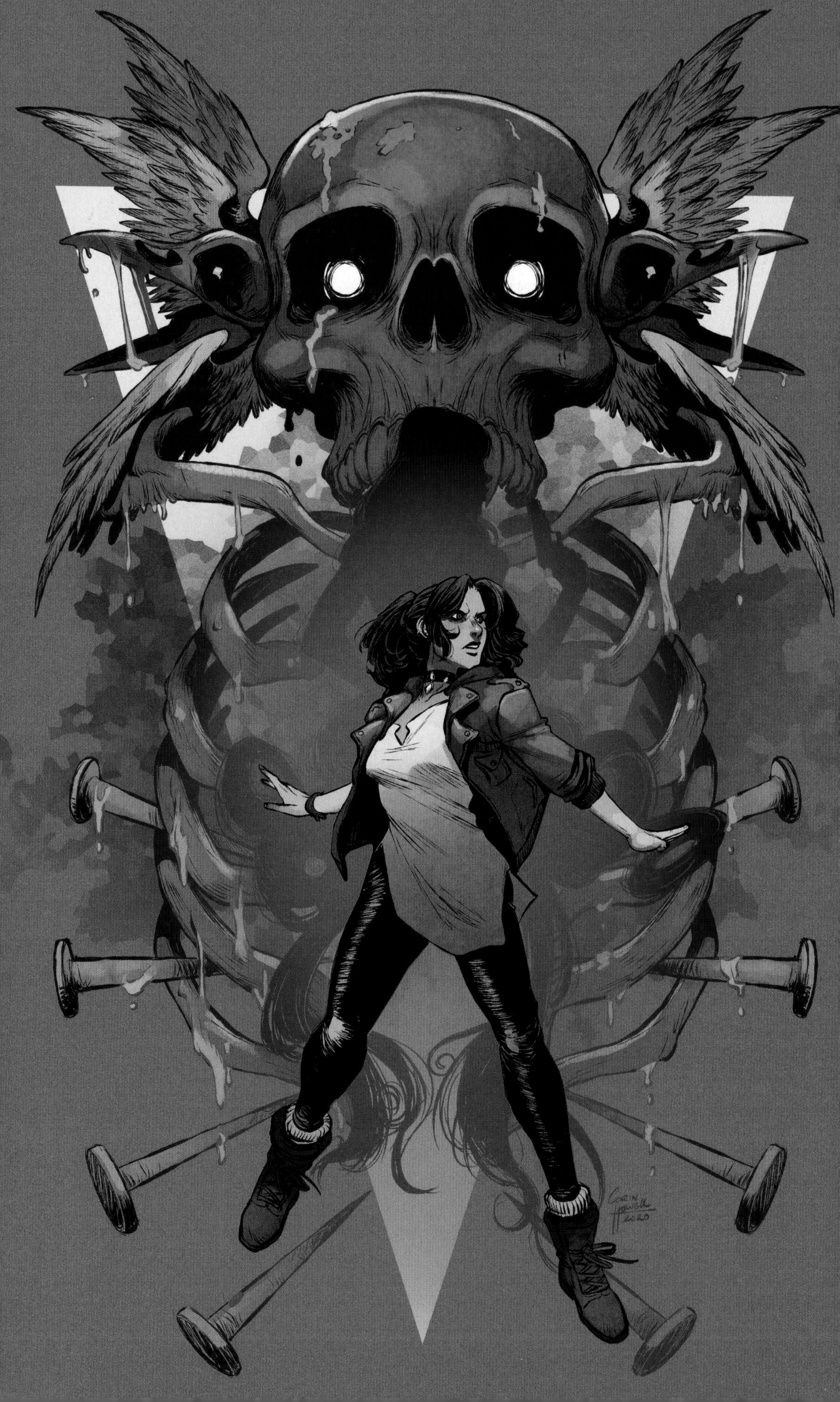

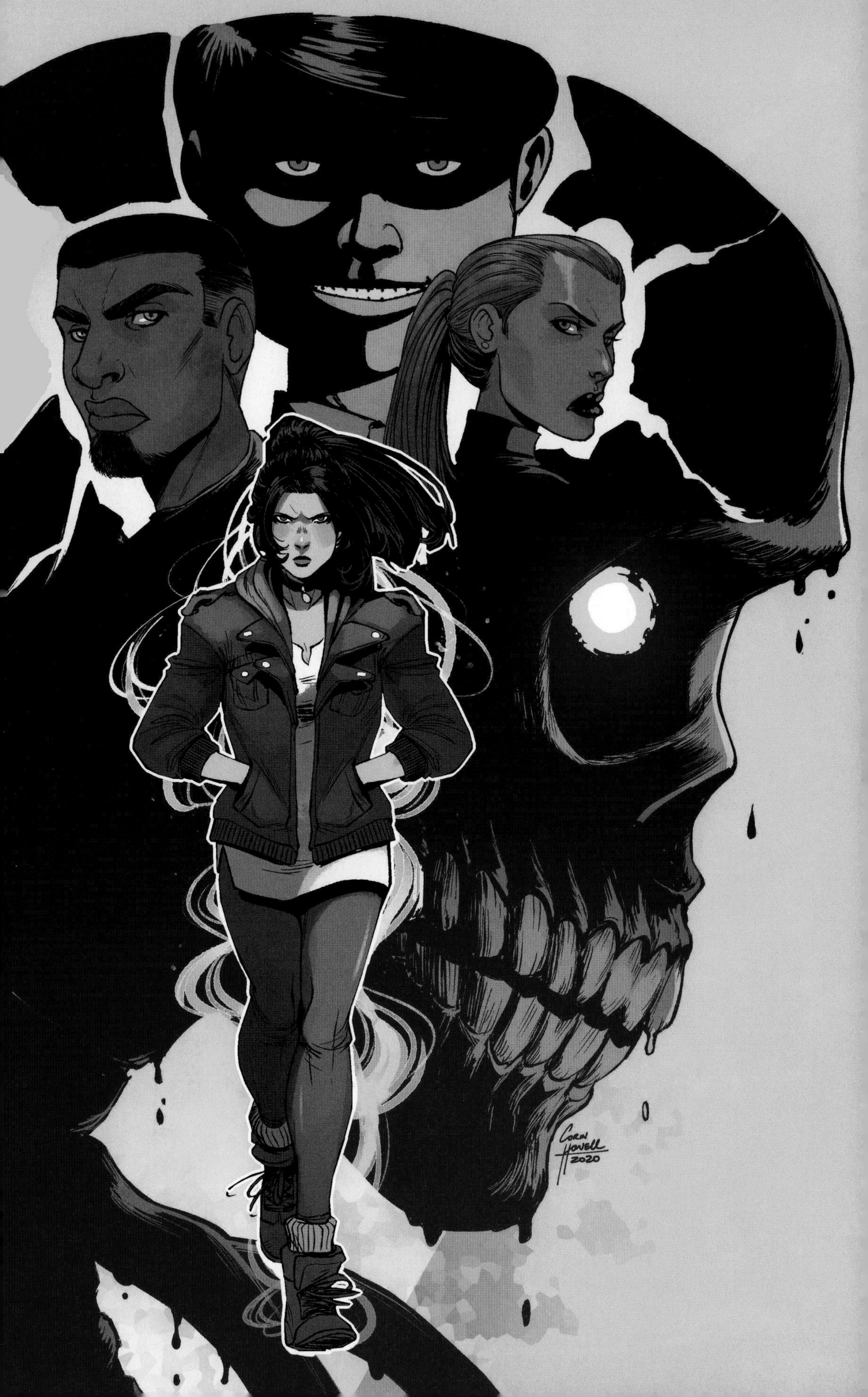
CORIN HOWELL 2020

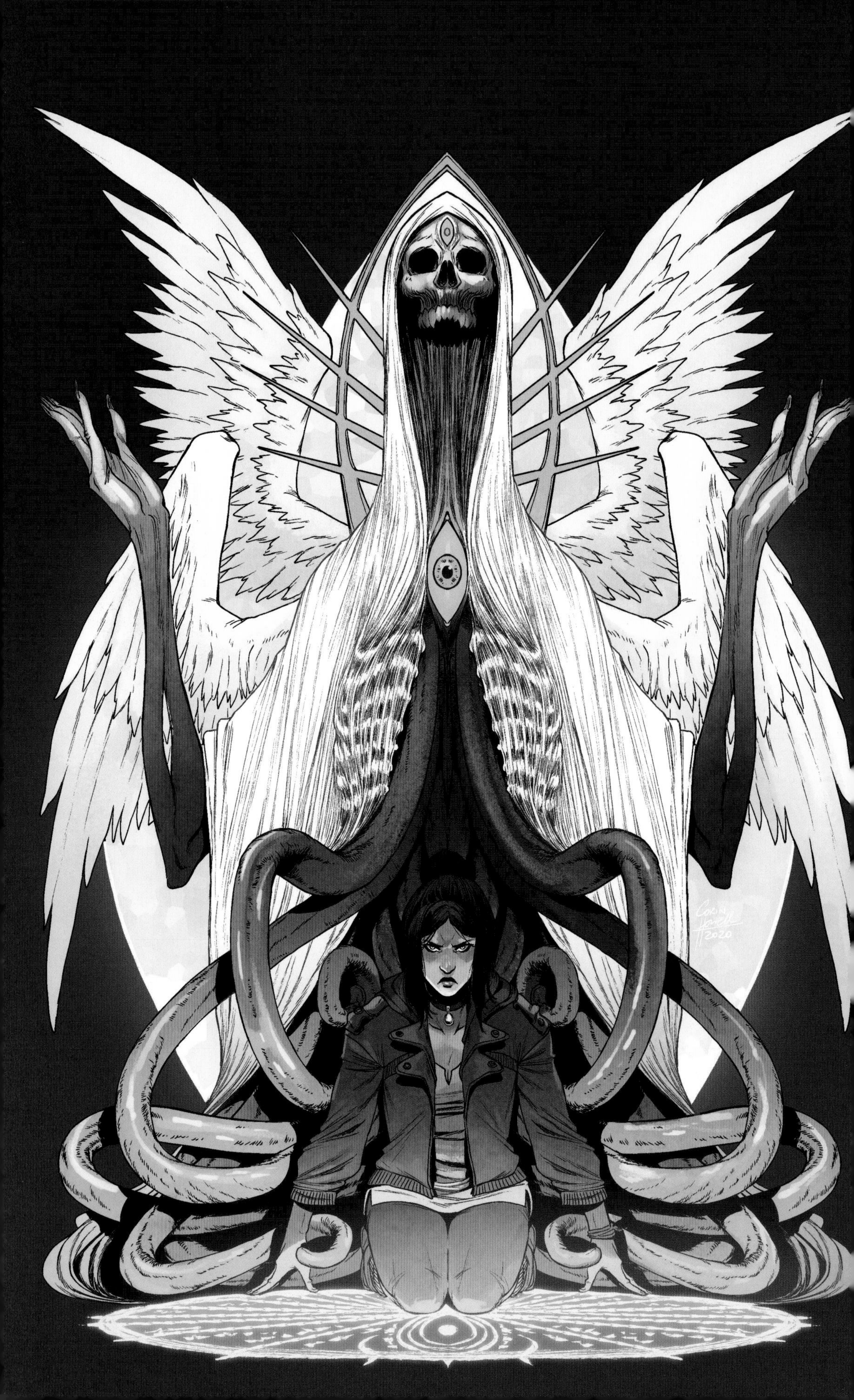

ISSUE 4-HOWELL & FARRELL

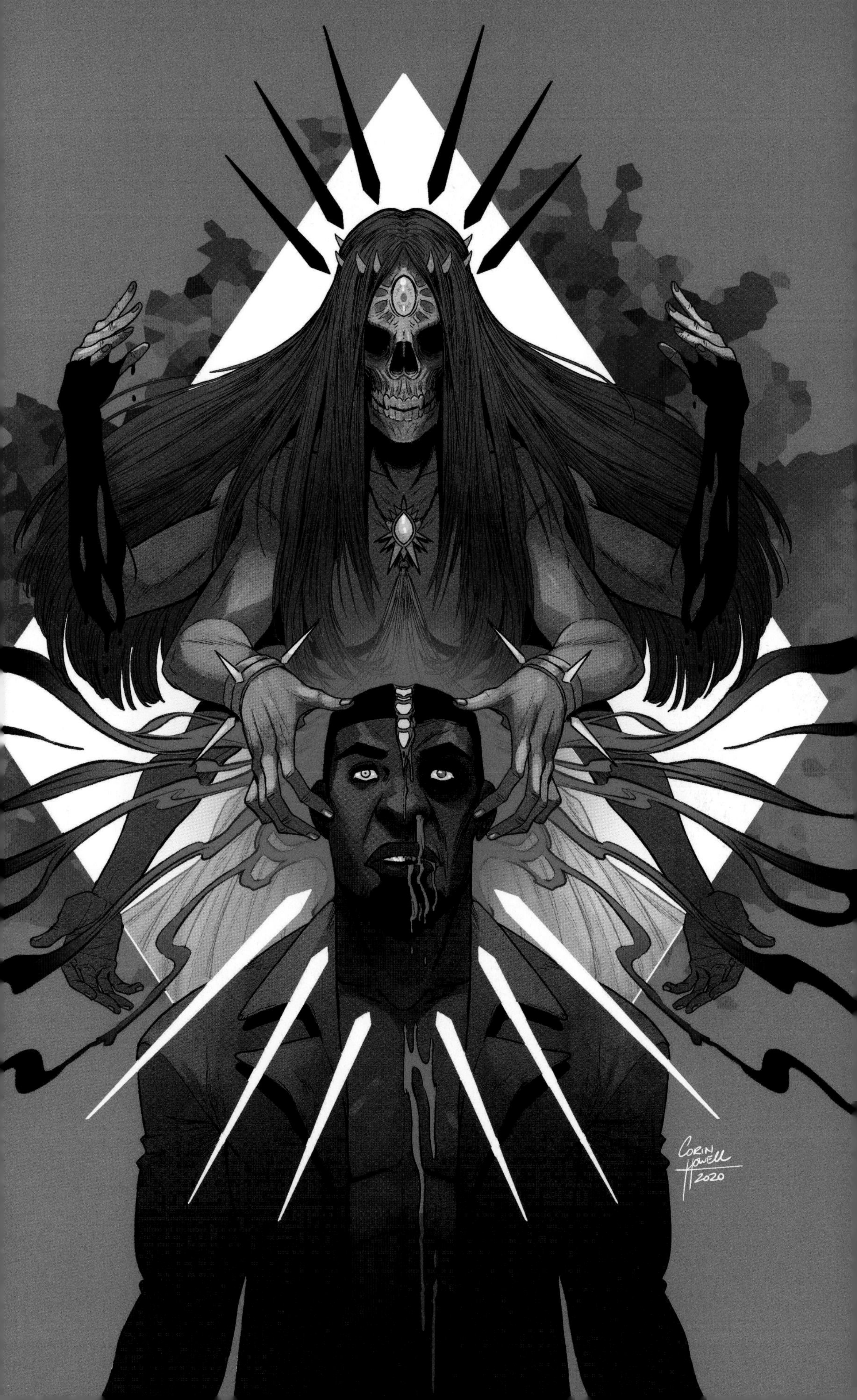
CORIN HOWELL 2020

ISSUE 5-HOWELL & FARRELL

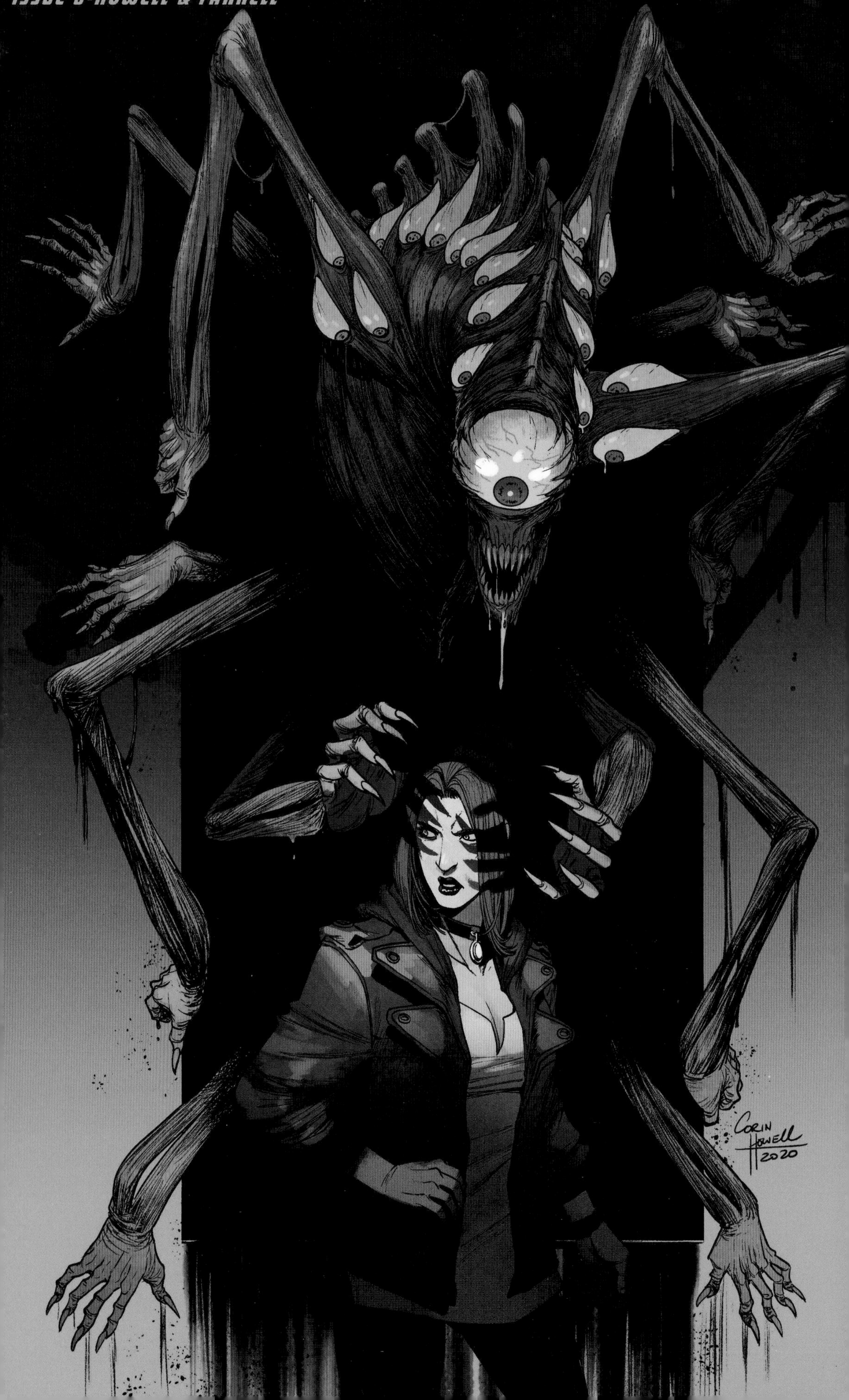
CORIN HOWELL 2020